The Communicative Constitution of Organizations

Foundations of Communication Theory

Series Editor

Marshall Scott Poole (University of Illinois, Champaign-Urbana)

The *Foundations of Communication Theory* series publishes innovative textbooks that summarize and integrate theory and research for advanced undergraduate and beginning graduate courses. In addition to offering state-of-the-art overviews in a broad array of subfields, authors are encouraged to make original contributions to advance the conversation within the discipline. Written by senior scholars and theorists, these books will provide unique insight and new perspectives on the core sub-disciplinary fields in communication scholarship and teaching today.

Published

Health Communication Theory by Teresa L. Thompson and Peter J. Schulz. *Organizational Change: Creating Change Through Strategic Communication, Second Edition* by Laurie K. Lewis.

Theorizing Crisis Communication, by Timothy L. Sellnow, Matthew W. Seeger.

Theorizing Crisis Communication, Second Edition by Timothy L. Sellnow and Matthew W. Seeger.

The Work and Workings of Human Communication by Robert E. Sanders.

The Communicative Constitution of Organizations: The Four Flows Model by Robert D. McPhee, Karen K. Myers, and Joel O. Iverson.

Robert D. McPhee
Arizona State University

Karen K. Myers
University of California Santa Barbara

Joel O. Iverson
University of Montana

The Communicative Constitution of Organizations

The Four Flows Model

WILEY Blackwell

Published by John Wiley & Sons, Inc., Hoboken, New Jersey.
Published simultaneously in Canada.

Library of Congress Cataloging-in-Publication Data Applied for:

Paperback ISBN: 9781119591924

Cover Design: Wiley
Cover Image: © Yuichiro Chino/Getty Images

Set 9.5/11.5pt Century by Straive, Pondicherry, India

Contents

Preface

This volume in the series Foundations of Communication Theory takes up an important or even crucial issue in organizational communication research, and organizational studies overall: How do organizations exist? What is involved in a human collectivity *being* an organization? That is, how is something—a group of people or associated set of people and material objects—*Constituted* as an organization? We think it is important to answer this question with special awareness of today's capitalist corporations, which stretch across the world in one way or another, governed by varied regimes of corporate laws. However, a discussion of this issue must recognize, no less governments with departments and military arms that are themselves organizations, and nonprofit organizations and organizations comprised by *definite*, *explicit* alliances and collaborations of these, like NATO or the American Federation of Labor in the United States. Many scholars have noted that organizations can possess immense, world-shaking power—indeed, the array of today's complex organizations can claim to rule the world. (We should admit that emergent forms—the older one of liberal democracy or the relatively new collectivities like the Internet—may be harbingers of new interactive arrangements with, potentially, equal or even greater power—if they are not themselves colonized by organizations.) If we use a group of people in a pick-up game of tag, or a nuclear family, or a pair of people in a conversation, as our prototype for understanding organizations, we may well be misled into emphasizing features that are inadequate to characterize the powerful organizations underlying practically all our everyday activity.

This volume puts forward our own view of organizational constitution, which, we will argue, is especially good for treating the issues mentioned above. We call it the Four Flows Model of the Communicative Constitution of Organizations (CCO). As we discuss later, it is surely a perspective, and might be a theory, depending on your definition of those terms. Obviously, we will be arguing that *communication* is what constitutes organizations—but only communication having certain features and interconnections. We will address merely in passing some equally basic and relevant issues, including those that Smith (1993), in a seminal paper for all of CCO, mentions as the questions of whether organizing, in a very broad sense, is the basic process underlying or constituting communication, and whether organizing and communicating are essentially equivalent. We address these, in passing, mainly in Chapters 3 and 4, by discussing what it means for communication to have constitutive force.

We think of our model as one among many organizational and communication theoretic positions, including many contributing to our own ideas and many more or less contrary to ours. This means that our discussion in this volume had to be multilayered and recursive, with later chapters reorienting as well as simply building on earlier ones. That being said, we propose in the remainder of this Preface to trace through the argument about CCO developed in these pages.

Our first introductory chapter sets the stage for our own argument and exposition, by recounting, in its first part, the array of fundamental positions in social and communication theory from the mid to late twentieth century, up to roughly today. These include empiricist or systems theories, critical theories, and interpretive theories. For very influential statements of this distinction, see Habermas (2015) and Burrell and Morgan (1979). Some later perspectives, perhaps even more distinct, were articulated as post-structuralism and post-modernism by authors such as Derrida (1976), Foucault (1977), Lyotard (1984), and LaTour (2007). Those revolts transformed, but also became incorporated in, the interpretive and especially the critical perspectives. This clash among perspectives led the way to the impressive synthesis achieved by the theorist to whom we owe the most gratitude, Anthony Giddens. Then, in the second half of the chapter, we identify some core issues that inspire developments from the triad of main earlier theories, concerning agency (the unique capacities of humans), materiality, and power. These also helped frame the development of structuration theory.

The second chapter articulates structuration theory, and organizational/communication research developing it, in some detail. One central structurational notion is the duality of structure: as humans interact, they draw on—use—the rules and resources of immediate context, language, and social order, while simultaneously reproducing—maintaining or transforming—those rules and resources for use in the very next act or episode, or more broadly as part of society. A second major notion is that of human agency—the sole type of *agency* in our perspective—for which Giddens' model elaborates the capacities agents need in order to interact meaningfully and effectively, and to produce/reproduce structural resources.

The third chapter elaborates our views of communicative constitution. Communication per se has constitutive power—it brings social realities into existence and makes them what they are. We develop several concepts to shed light on this process: Giddens' notion of *distanciation*—constitution as articulation of variance across time, space, and language; the *structurational hermeneutic*—the interplay between whole communication processes and their constituent parts; *perlocution*—the constitution of social realities through language, specifically in organized settings; and *transtructions*—the rules or relations that intertwine the meaningful, power-laden, normative, and constitutive dimensions of social interaction. These four facets of constitutive communication provide conceptual substance for our conception of communicative flow in the next chapter. We also discuss constitution of a sign or linguistic resource, and of a (human) agent, noting how those differ from constituting an organization, and discussing how all three are influenced by forces of social power and its distribution in interaction and society.

Based on these preliminaries, our fourth chapter explicates our idea of communication as flow. While *flow* has important differences from examples of communicative interaction, its positive analogies are strikingly useful in understanding organizational contexts. Like aquatic, electrical, or atmospheric flows, communication is dynamic: it moves temporally, but changes form and direction, and overflows preestablished channels. It is multidirectional and typically disseminates meanings and consequences. Its signs, whether written or nontextual, are material and accompany flows of other materials—people, fuel, and goods—while giving those larger flows meaning and significance. It can include currents with different speed, depth, and composition, and cross-cuts and roils itself in contradictions and paradoxes often enough that we find it appropriate to apply a flow label—contravention—to such strained social-interactive phenomena. Indeed, we find enough parallel and enlightening features and subtypes between physical and communicational flows to speak of flow as a model for communication in general. However, we end the fourth chapter with a more theoretic move, by articulating and justifying the distinction among the four flows of our 4F model, discussed in detail in the next four chapters, where richer accounts of their distinctiveness and relations can be found.

Our fifth chapter discusses our first flow: *membership negotiation*. Both these terms are important: *Membership* emphasizes that people's belonging, or connection as members, occurs as organizational agents become connected, through constitutive communication flows processes, into varying role-relational practices typically marked by varying activity expectations, hierarchic or power levels, and standard communicative ties (e.g., with bosses). *Negotiation* emphasizes that these connective processes—of search, actual hiring, and crossing the boundary onto the membership roster, then socialization into work roles, sharing narratives with other members to position themselves, actual work experience, and perhaps exit—are two- or multidirectional. In this communication, both members and organizational others negotiate, exercising agency based on power deriving from identity factors as well as past work and interactions. They negotiate tacit or explicitly, placidly, or turbulently to set or re-set the parameters of their role-relationships in processes through which the organization as a multi-member collectivity is constituted.

The sixth chapter concerns *organizational self-structuring*—a communication flow that is prototypically though not distinctly organizational—which influences members as they produce and reproduce overt or recognized resources, social-relational as well as material. Its influence typically structures the organization so that it can become a power vehicle or medium to serve the goals or interests of the collectivity—or, more narrowly, powerful members, groups, or even outsiders. Through three types of overt self-structuring flow—the formal (authoritative texts and orders), the informal (cultural patterns), and the technological (infotech networks)—other communication gets constituted in its direction, its sanctioned use of an official or cultural vocabulary, and its legitimacy as it proceeds in the other flows. Now, a member may, for example, find that covertly cooperating to disobey an order, or consulting an illegitimate advice-giver, or using a friend's log-in, all "work" in their role activities. However, those interactions are still (deviant) self-structuring, probably reducing the organization's internal control, reliability, and effectiveness—or, perhaps, yielding greater overall success!

The seventh chapter analyzed our third flow, activity coordination, which constitutes the activities of organizational members so that they mutually adapt and combine to serve goals legitimated in the organization. It accomplishes both on-the-spot informal adjustments among members as well as on-the-spot—usually routine, sometimes inventive, and even sometimes deviating—application of structural mandates to divide up labor and communicate only in sanctioned ways. It constitutes the organization as the flow in which organizational work gets collectively performed, thus practically connecting members (Flow 1) and outsiders (Flow 4), as well as putting into practice the self-structuring influences of Flow 2.

The eighth chapter elaborates on our fourth flow, *institutional positioning*. Engaged in this flow organizational members and collectivities constitute the organization through activities and interaction that cross (and thus constitute) organizational boundaries, engage and influence members and activities of other organizations and collectivities, and thus produce an organizational identity. Thus, corporate social responsibility efforts (as well, unfortunately, as environmental pollution) rest on organized members' communication and coordinated activities outside the structurated boundaries of a formally recognized organization. Efforts like social responsibility position the organization, through its members' responsible acts, in relation to (communicatively-constituted) institutions such as an industry, a sector such as education, an organized alliance such as the NBA, or even an organization so embedded and far-reaching as Meta or PBS. In this fourth flow, it is especially clear how the boundary-constituting force of each other flow, focused on in the earlier chapters, has impact on, and is even part of, Flow 4.

With the fifth through eighth chapters, we have set forth both the inner logic and the constitutive vitality of each communication flow in organizations, conceptualizing organizational constitution in a suitably variable and well-rounded way. Our final three chapters address some unavoidable issues facing a perspective like the Four Flows Model. First is the issue of confluence—the fact that a single interaction can be part of more than one flow, or even part of a single flow in more than one way. Indeed, that is commonly or even necessarily the case. Each chapter discusses this phenomenon in passing, but here, we focus on several key issues. One is the distinctive value of our model, compared to the numerous other category schemes for organizational communication. Another is the issue of strains and contradictions within and across communication episodes, a fact we seek to reconceptualize with the term contraventions. A structural preference for clear, consistent, productive communication can be found in many if not most other positions, we have striven to expose and essentially include the many instances where organizational communication is roiled. A third is the fact that complex organizations are comprised of systems within systems of flows, so we discuss the varied ways the flows work at varied hierarchical levels. Fourth is the issue of deep structures—the fact that communication flows, or enacts contextual change, at varied levels. Societal features such as identity politics, work life and the contraventions it exhibits, global inequities of wealth, prestige, and power—these change more, even much more slowly than interaction or jobs. Yet slow-changing deep currents and shallow rapids can at times, roiled by volcanoes or global warming, depart from our expectations.

Our tenth chapter concerns parallels and likely disputes between our perspective and others, and focuses on the two most fully developed alternative models or perspectives. With regard to the first major alternate, the Luhmannian School, we try to convey our great respect for their work on the importance and variegation of social systemic closure, while forging our own sense of social system boundaries produced and reproduced in the flows. With regard to the other main alternative, the Montreal School, we hope we have articulated our equally great respect for the insights they have generated into the nature of agency in communication, while ourselves still advocating a baseline notion of agency as the powers and constitutive force of interaction by humans.

Our final chapter gives a final summary of the main points for which we have argued, followed by a number of suggestions of ways practitioners can employ our general perspective or specific insights in everyday life and work. Our belief is that readers and researchers will find special utility in our approach to CCO.

Acknowledgments

We are naturally grateful to the past generations of scholars in social and communication theory who have done vital work forging intellectual foundations for understanding the communicative constitution of organizations and elaborating superb insights that have inspired us. In particular, we must mention our primary forebear Anthony Giddens, but also Talcott Parsons and Karl Weick in general social theory, and Stanley Deetz, James Taylor, Francois Cooren, and Linda Putnam in organizational communication studies specifically. We owe a special debt of thanks to Scott Poole for encouraging, facilitating publication, and providing valuable suggestions that helped give this volume its final shape.

Bob is monstrously indebted to Joel and Karen for their cooperation over years and decades working out the four-flows position and its articulation in this book, for their patience and good judgment, as well as to the first student who worked with him on it, Pam Zaug. He is beholden in very many ways to Scott, along with Dave Seibold, for their collaborative work with him, over the decades, formulating the structuration-theoretic study of communication, as well as the wave of other colleagues who have built on, or formulated rivals to, that work. He wants to acknowledge appreciation to many other colleagues and students at the University of Illinois, the University of Wisconsin-Milwaukee, and Arizona State University, and to several other specific individuals for support that contributed in inexplicable ways to this project. But he has been blessed above all by the encouragement, patience, and love of his wife Dale Kalika and of his son Karl.

Karen feels especially fortunate to have taken classes from and been an advisee of Bob during her doctoral program at Arizona State University. The classes he taught introduced her to structuration theory and the communicative constitution of organizations, both of which have shaped her research and the research of many of her own students and advisees. This book was an opportunity to honor and promote the enormously significant contributions that Bob's theorizing and writings have brought to the discipline, and to collaborate as well with an admired former ASU peer, Joel. Most especially, she is appreciative of her dear husband, Dave Seibold, who was supportive, and mostly patient, through the many years or work on this book.

Joel is grateful to Bob as a mentor, advisor, and colleague. His classes covering communication theory, organizational communication, and structuration provided rigor as well as humor while delivering a rich appreciation for academic work. This book is one way to extend our theorizing and continue the conversation regarding CCO theorizing with the community of scholars who engage in such work. He also thanks those who encouraged him to pursue theory such as his good friend, Pam Zaug, and many colleagues, including Karen. He especially appreciates the support and encouragement from his wife, Karen Iverson, and son, Ckhai Iverson.

1

Introduction

"The Communicative Constitution of Organizations" (CCO) has, since about 2000, been a focal point for considerable work by Communication, Organizational, and Social Theory scholars (Basque et al., 2022). From the beginning, several major theories have guided research and been the subject of much theoretical discussion. Schoeneborn et al. (2014) identified three of these, but some other alternative theories do exist, including—Weick's organizing theory and Kuhn's (2008) theorizing on materiality and communicative theory of the firm. One of these, "Four Flows" (4F) theory, is the focus of this book.

The 4F referred to are flows of communication; specifically, for any single organization, there are four "flows" of communication that constitute that organization—that make it what it is, an organization. There are four flows for organizations as well known as, for example, Apple Computers or Google or "the Mafia." At one extreme of size, we could point to the United States Federal Government, while at the other extreme, one would find social entities on the borderline of being organizations at all—maybe a local Thursday Night Book Club.

There are two important purposes for this book. One is to be a fundamental resource for work in disciplines that study organizations, like the subdiscipline of Organizational Communication, or Business or Sociology. We want to say, "This is how to conceive of and study organizations, or at least one way to do it." The second is to correct a common tendency in CCO theorizing, or at least advocate for a different flavor in that work, away from the question, "How do sociomaterial things, like an Apple Watch or the WWW, get constituted?" In a somewhat alternative direction, we emphasize that a major—we want to say **the** major—reason for studying organizations is that on the whole, they are social entities of a novel kind that rule the world. Companies like Google can span the world, own a major share

The Communicative Constitution of Organizations: The Four Flows Model, First Edition.
Robert D. McPhee, Karen K. Myers, and Joel O. Iverson.

of world resources, and reconstitute major institutions such as capitalism. The United States Government can set out to "spread democracy"—to fundamentally alter the contents of "politics." It is this kind of prototypical organization that we want to focus scholarly attention on (though, in varied ways, the focus is obviously already there). We urge CCO scholars to ask, "How are organizations communicatively constituted, such that they can (though obviously don't always) wield such power?"

Answering that question is the goal of 4F theorizing and concretely of our book. In the chapters to follow, we will articulate the grounding of our work in structuration theory (ST), explain what a *flow* means, explain what the four flows are, and articulate their significance for CCO scholarship. In the remainder of this chapter, we lay out the context of our theory and the key issues CCO theories like ours should address.

1.1 Theoretical Grounding

Neither 4F theory, nor its parent ST developed in a vacuum. To explain the 4F vision specifically, we need to lay out some larger contexts and histories within which it lies. The obvious context is *Organizational Communication*, itself a subdiscipline within larger intellectual contexts, especially *Communication* or *Communication Studies*, which are in turn inside a major category *Social Theory*, including allied disciplines such as anthropology and sociology.

Long ago, works in social theory gave birth to another important subdiscipline, organization studies, recognizing bureaucratic communication as an important feature of nascent forms of economic corporation as well as in long-established organizations such as governmental departments or the Catholic Church. Students of organizational communication, inspired by or coming from these disciplines, study not just one but many sorts of communication processes and phenomena that are relevant to organizations and organizing, drawing on ideas and methods from many scholars and conceptual schemes. Rather than try to organize on our own the welter we have today, we can employ an old, simplified, deceptively clear overarching distinction displaying the main currents of social/communication theory that ground the work of organizational communication scholars.

Organizational communication ideas themselves developed from three specific constellations of ideas, each with ancient ancestry and stultifying mutations. First is a set of conceptions of *general systems*, theories that actually elaborate ideas from hundreds of years Before Common Era (BCE). But modern ideas about systems developed, in novel insights and prominence, in the mid-twentieth century, as scholars and engineers tried to build on the analogy comparing complex machines, including military artillery, automobiles, electronic devices, and simple computers, to the human body. One key analogy they advocated involved the sources generating coordinated motion among system parts: in machines and electronics, coordination is achieved through electrical current flow and microwaves, while in the human body, the nervous system coordinates physiological processes. In this view, every person or group has their own role in the system and vaster ecology of systems, and action governed by the role is valid, right, because it sustains the whole.

All sorts of systems seem, to many systems scholars, to generate system needs and values, which can in themselves explain and validate member activities and organization attributes. Thus, a systems theorist would say that a company has a public relations department or a CEO describes company plans in an interview because the company needs good relations with publics, such as stockholders—it finds good PR to be necessary for its existence. (Contrariwise, 4F theory, to foreshadow our argument, will reject the idea that the organization is a giant agent tending to its needs. Instead, we will contend that the necessity of PR or any other function is the result of communication among individual agents that necessitates—communication that makes, e.g., PR *seem* necessary to powerful agents—that perhaps points out problems caused by inadequate PR, or advocates copying PR practices in other, successful firms—in arguments and decision processes that may or may not succeed in inculcating PR for the company, perhaps even leaving that company's constitution weaker.)

Systems theorists quickly ventured further, to argue that larger social units—relationships, groups, nations, and also in the mix, organizations—were also systems that could be studied using that analogy. Human communication in general could be construed as a series of signals/messages with measurable impact and often important feedback. Such interactive signals typically traced out a network of message interchange that integrated the overall system and helped it operate, just like the electronic signals that initiate and even power auto engines. (Such systems can, of course, also go haywire.) Just as for nonhuman systems, maintaining system performance is an overriding value, but social systems also involve cultures; cultures feature their own religious and moral value systems; all these values are system elements, functioning above all else to unify but stratify the systems. It is important to remember that, today and into the past and future, the metaphor of system, and of message flows integrating and coordinating it, is an enduring resource of communication, and especially organizational communication theory.

In a predictable dialectical swing, another group of scholars, today called critical theorists, argued that social systems theories, in their deepest notions, reflect and reinforce the worldview of currently empowered people, groups, or classes. System models insinuate that the current power distribution is simply there or unavoidable or optimally adjusted. Critical theorists instead argue that every element of social existence has an inner logic of development that generates external relations essentially opposing it, a contradiction that transforms their very essence. Thus, excellent and fulfilling work today conflicts with a simple fact: people work under conditions imposed by corporate powers that benefit from excellent work but still downplay the factor of workers' excellence to maximize profit. Some excellent employees can win promotion to higher-level work managing or "facilitating" others, subject to orders from above. Most of those "others," even ones equal in performance excellence, stay at unfulfilling lower-salary levels, to make the whole unit most profitable. A similar global process derogates some workers worldwide to be underpaid, constricted, stunted, deluded, and often have miserable roles, lives, and relationships. This occurs because work is monetarized, allowing its value to be controlled and expropriated to increase profits far beyond the return for management coordination and capital risk that is objectively their due. They also argued that monetarization leads to supposedly fair markets, but employees negotiating work and for organizational financial support can be manipulated using monopoly power, maximizing the inequality of distribution and control of work.

Critical theories today have evolved far past the Marxist economic-class focus and an emphasis on the multivariant consequences of economic inequity—the multiple, intersecting dimensions of injustice and bias (toward differences in race, ethnicity, sex, gender, and occasionally class or age) where violence and disgusting suppression efforts evince deep structural roots. Critical theory has been distinguished first by its strong emphasis on the workings and varieties of social power phenomena such as intermember relations, formations like social–practical knowledge, representation, and privilege/disadvantage, which then unclearly exhibit (or sometimes hide) biased and deeply rooted institutional/macrosociosystemic forces. The focus on power, and domination of individuals such as workers leads tendentially to a focus on the *limits* of human agency, with people as puppets at the mercy of power-bearing cultural and organizational forces. The second truly distinguishing feature of critical theory has been its fundamental value commitments. Critical scholars argue that all social/communication theory, like all human endeavors, is guided and lured by value judgments about features of today's situation and possibilities of change. However, research committed to the value of analyzing *what is*, whether the social system today or people's interpretive frames, inevitably slides toward acceptance of *what should not be*, and neglects reflective inquiry about the causes of absolutely foundational systemic bias.

We can best describe a third traditional variety of theory by noting its opposition to the first two variants. Interpretive social science opposes systems theory because of the willingness of the latter to invent variables based on outside theories or quick glances at the processes being examined. And they oppose critical theory's imposition of crucial concepts like class, ideology, and even Western notions of power. Interpretive theorists were inspired by philosophic schools, including idealism, phenomenology, existentialism, and pragmatism, along with some ideas and methods from anthropology, rhetorical studies, and literary criticism. They argue that meaning and significance do not derive in any simple way from the natural objects and processes we observe, nor from the definitions and syntax of languages we are taught. Rather, we develop, in collaboration with our conversational partners, a sense of language and event meanings that is grounded in context and the practices engaging us with the world, other people, and ourselves.

For interpretive scholars, organizations (and all social phenomena and processes) are communicative in their essence. It is no surprise that several interpretive concepts have been prominent on organizational communication research. The most well known of these is *organizational culture*. Several decades ago, the idea that organizations have unique cultures, including stories and keywords, was fresh, but soon was transformed by findings that organizations are in every way cultural themselves, with cultural elements that are vague, localized in distinct milieux, and internally conflicting with one another. A second prominent conception is *organizing* (and a correlate term *sensemaking*)—not the noun organization, but the verb. The parent of this conception, Weick (1979), argued that organization is a meaning-generating process starting from any initiating event or act (often by a manager), blossoming in a plethora of equivocal meanings. One or a few of these are selected to retrospectively interpret the initial act and give sense to inform/organize the consequent stream of acts/processes, and the relational forms characteristic of organizations. The sensemaking process thus inescapably generates a negotiated order (Clarke, 2021; Strauss et al., 1963), adjusting and intertwining the action and meaning threads of parties to the organizing. The focus of this school on meaning-making and its variability leads to a tendency to study communication processes in quite fine detail without seeking to generalize patterns that are discovered.

The three idea-clusters, systems, critical, and interpretive, have intertwined, clashed, and metamorphosed for decades or centuries, but remain easily detectible in organizational communication research and organize some of the intellectual clashes in organizational studies as well. In particular, the interpretive cluster of theorizing and research seems increasingly to recognize the power-ladenness and inescapable biases in the language, rhetorical figures and topoi, and communicative practices—biases articulated by critical as well as rhetorical scholars. Contrariwise, critical scholars have become evermore articulate about the amazing variations of the meaning of fundamental concepts like work and the individual worker (Mumby, 2019), but perhaps without fully critiquing the impacts of their own critiques or insights that might come from systems concepts.

ST was created by Anthony Giddens to transform the analysis of relations among these titanic intellectual conceptions. Giddens argued, as we shall see in detail in the next few chapters, that all action by individuals, and all institutional forms such as democracy and capitalism, answer the inquiries of all three groups of scholars because they involve three dimensions of social being, that we label meaning, power, and norms. Giddens argued that these dimensions have different importance, or loadings, for any act, communicative process, or social unit. As explained in Chapter 3, we emphasize the specific interweavings of these dimensions, called transtructions. This idea allows sensitive exploration of relations, for instance, between meanings/ interpretive schemes and power imbalances, just mentioned in broad strokes. We find it vital to add to the triad of dimensions by elucidating a fourth, independent dimension of social action and social orders, called *constitution*. This will let us reconceive the relation of communication to organizations. It grounds our theory of CCO. The *4F* are flows of communication (broadly construed, as we shall explain later) with varying constitutive significance, inevitably tangled by transtructions with the meaning, power, and value phenomena dividing past intellectual traditions. We cannot explore this issue in any depth in this first, introductory chapter, but even the discussion so far indicates how deeply 4F theory analyzes the communicative constitution of organizational phenomena.

1.1.1 Key Issues

The theorizing of the four flows approach has not emerged independently from other perspectives, but rather is developing as part of the dialogue about CCO and larger issues for organizational scholars. Specifically, we explain our theoretical developments through conversations regarding the other key schools of CCO thinking as well as important issues such as critical perspectives regarding organizing. Three of the key but inextricably overlapping issues that we address in this volume are the issues of:

- Agency, and *human centrality to human social systems*
- Materiality *and* sociomateriality of communication and organizations
- Power/domination in all its forms, as emphasized especially by the critical approaches to understanding organizations

We contend that ST, the 4F theory, and its underlying processes of conlocutions and transtructions (in subsequent text and in later chapters) offer a useful approach to advance the conversation regarding all of these issues, especially as they need to be part of any valid CCO thinking. We also contend that conlocutions and transtructions within the four flows provide a means to empower critical theorizing and explore issues of power, structure, and material history. While more details of these processes emerge through the book, a general description of the 4F position on each is useful.

1.2 Agency and Human Centrality to Human Social Systems

While agency has had many definitions across disciplines and approaches since the 1960s (Emirbayer & Mische, 1998), for us, agency is grounded in the capacity of involvement via social practices to not only make a difference, but also have the capacity to consider those differences as meaningful and value-relevant. While some approaches to agency in CCO theorizing remain grounded in explanations of firms through agency theory (Barnard, 1938; Coase, 1937 among others) working to explain the relationships of principals typically owners, to agents, or employees who act as agents of the principal (for a more complete explanation, see Brummans, 2018). We consider the *acting for* approach fundamentally tied to concepts of ownership and authority that do not work well with critical approaches seeking to decenter ownership nor with collectives that do not have clear ownership, such as nonprofit organizations and voluntary associations (Frumkin, 2002).

In informal discourse, the notion of agency rightly means the capacity to communicate or act so as to have an effect. Scholars discussing agency often argue that agents, deserving of full normal agency, instead are empowered only with partial agency, a complex notion that involves ideas reflecting some challenges constraining or slanting agency. These include material, social, and personal conditions. We provide a more detailed discussion in Chapter 2.

To mention cardinal concrete cases, people concerned about the environmental crisis or various dimensions or social injustice will recognize, with chagrin, the variety and impact of these limitations on agency that plague their own work as well as the others they seek to help. Communication—itself an action that is plagued by challenges—is still key in embodying, and dialectically in overcoming, these challenges, and thus in invigorating and transforming agency. In each case, analysis of such obstacles must be based on the model of the individual agent, to avoid muddling its relevance to people striving to act, and to avoid analysis at the level of social units (e.g., organizations) that are, inescapably, comprised of agents facing varied arrays of agency challenges in the organizational context. In addition, speaking of more or less agency is blatantly oversimplified when, as soon as one type of challenge to agency is overcome, another takes its place. All of the challenges are appropriate concerns of critical scholars, who have indeed devoted a good deal of study to them.

Twentieth-century social and communication theorists had somewhat different concerns about agency: whether unintended behaviors (unconscious, or issuing from distorted consciousness or an unintended result of an intended act) was truly action, by a valid agent. ST, as Giddens (1976a, 1976b, 1979, 1984) argues for it, responds to these challenges with a bedrock account of agency as based on "three overarching concepts: *the power to make a difference by appropriating structural resources (the capacity to act otherwise)*, *knowledgeability*, and *reflexive monitoring*, which includes rationalization of action" (Iverson et al., 2018, p. 44; emphasis in original). We elucidate this core conception in later chapters.

We distinguish our definition of agency from the actor–network notion of actants, which bunches together humans and groups with material objects, environmental system components, psychological phenomena such as attitudes, and other nonhuman entities. ST's conception reveals the error of lumping everything together under the ontological label of actants, especially if theorists must, in the next breath, declare as Cooren (in Schoeneborn et al., 2014, pp. 299–300) does,

> ... the human actor is an obligatory passage point in everything I have been talking about so far. If a logo communicates something in the name of an organization, it is not only because its designers might have meant it that way (sometimes, they can miss the point) but also because someone is able to make it say something when he or she sees it. ...The organizational world is...a world where humans play a key role, to

> the extent that they are the ones who mobilize or "ventriloquize" texts, values, and facts in their discourse. (We must note that he goes on to state: "...humans are not only ventriloquists, in that they make, for instance, policies say something in specific circumstances but also ventriloquized [by other actants], in that these policies lead them to say specific things and not other things. There is no absolute starting point....)

The materiality facet of this issue is explained later, but the key to agency is that it is grounded in *human* practices and the capacity of humans to articulate and change what are fundamentally human social systems. This approach focuses on the meanings of actions and the ability to process the meaningfulness of organizations from a communication perspective. That said, we argue that agency in relationship to organizing answers the question, "Is it an organization if humans are removed from the equation?" From a communication perspective, we would contend the answer is a resounding no. While systems certainly function in nature, in outer space, we contend that organizations are constituted from communication processes that fundamentally require human interaction as part of the process.

1.3 Materiality and Sociomateriality of Communication and Organizations

In short: The novel terms *materiality* and *sociomateriality* actually evoke ideas from systems communication science of the 1960s or before, of mathematically-analyzable information and communication as patterned matter-energy (Berlo, 1960; Shannon & Weaver, 1949). These were developed as alternatives to various schools of mainstream sociological and psychological theories of organizational, and indeed of all communication. The emphasis on these terms, especially sociomateriality, derives from the observation that mainstream theories often overlook the *things* relevant to communication, preferring to elaborate on the personality characteristics, attitudes, linguistic and interactive patterns, and relational types manifest in communication. Orlikowski, the originating scholar of the important theory-complex surrounding sociomateriality argues that we should not separate *the material* and *the social* as different essences, but instead should study contingent sociomaterial constitutive intertwinings of agencies. Our grounding in ST—one of the communication-theoretic wellsprings from which some sociomateriality scholars, including Orlikowski, LaTour, Cooren, and Kuhn draw leads us to several responses.

For one thing, we are not forced to use the label *material agency* because we have a long-lived and rich conceptual scheme available, organized around the term *causation*. It is commonplace, for instance, to say that using the instrument *hammer* causes a nail to pierce boards and cause them to stay in place, not that the hammer or nail has agency that leads to such effects. We need not ignore the causal powers of material phenomena like viruses, hurricanes, steering wheels, computers, or paintbrushes, nor the *statistical-interactive* impacts of genes and environment on personality, when we abstain from calling them agents; nor do we have to downplay or oversimplify their significance in our explanations of organizational phenomena. Many sociomateriality theorists advocate a well-defined sort of theory termed *practice theory*—but in fact, ST already is one! It is a sophisticated one, able to contain the dual ideas of strong human agency and decentering of agency in favor of practice (as we explain in later chapters).

We do seek, in concert with the theorists of sociomateriality, to avoid divisions of sociomaterial entities that reduce everything into humans vs. everything else. Noteworthy is that sociomaterial has embedded in it such a division, connoting the special status they often must give to human-interactive phenomena. That same observation runs through much of the sociomateriality literature: for instance, one of its central concepts, *affordance*, primordially means feature allowing manipulation or access by humans. A cardinal example involving affordance is a tool, manipulated to accomplish some further task, and about which humans can have tacit knowledge (Polanyi, 1966).

We think that a finer segmentation is preferable, into, say, simple objects vs. tools (with affordances) vs. self-reproducing entities like genes or viruses vs. automata like thermostats vs. informated entities (Zuboff, 1988) like computers, vs. insensate living beings (that cannot feel pain or frustration—arguably plants) vs. sensate beings vs. their specific subcategory humans, vs. social relations/collectivities including organizations, vs. more englobing conditions like modernity (Giddens, 1990) or weather/climate. Systems theorists strive to articulate lists like this, detailing levels of complexity entities can attain. However, for our money, the crucial list of social-material concepts is implicitly enunciated in standard ST. ST conceives agents with powers like reflexive self-understanding, rationalization, and discursive penetration, all of which enable them to engage in practices (explicated in later chapters). Then the crucial distinctions for theory focus on agents vs. practice vs. resources for action vs. constraints on action vs. contexts of action vs. conditions circumscribing action (McPhee & Iverson, 2009). Preserving the unique status of empowered human agents affirms the importance of ideas like meaning-in-context, value, significance, identity, and voice, for explanations of organizational (or any) communication (which thus is not equivalent to a causal chain of material signals or nonhuman agents).

However, we must add one final caveat about how ST relates to materiality/sociomateriality scholarship. Theory and research inspired by the interwoven-practice notion of materiality tend to underemphasize the historical-materialist insights of critical theory, especially the idea (Bleich, 2013) that language, and communication in practice, are both unequally available, unequally mastered, and in general help to create the whole range of obstacle to agency detailed just earlier. For instance, studies of affordances—mediating support for using—ICT generally ignore the fact that, for most of humanity, adequate ICT—and adequate living conditions of many sorts—are *unaffordable*—a fact that should roil the discourse of materialist social and communication scholars, as it does the insights of interpretive/deconstructive scholars.

1.4 Power/Domination

As well displayed in the accounts just earlier, critical scholarship has found fertile ground in the webs of ideas centered on the terms agency and materiality. Our overviews of those ideas, based in ST, already showed how structuration and 4F ideas might have unique value for critical, and all, organizational research. But our third key issue—power/domination—has a special affinity for that work. Like a city, an organization has "storage capacity (involving) time-space distanciation and the generation of power,... It is a special kind of container, a crucible for the generation of power" (Giddens, 1981, p. 95, 96) and 4F theory articulates the fact that power flows through organizations in more than one way.

To introduce the discussion elaborated in later chapters, Giddens' ideas regarding power are crucially tied to one of his most core ideas—resources, or structural resources. *Structural resources*, in his formulation, are comprised of two analytically separate and apparently distinct, subcategories, all of which are focal in critical theory. One is allocative resources—forms of transformative capacity—power to make a difference—generating command over objects, goods, or material phenomena. The other is authoritative resources—transformative capacities "generating command over persons and actors" (Giddens, 1984, p. 33). However, blatantly obviously, an allocative resource such as a meal from a famous chef often requires mediation by supportive personnel (subordinate chefs, waiters, etc.) via the agent's authoritative capacity. Equally obviously, those supportive personnel draw upon material resources like cookware and chopped onions. So to discuss: "command over...material phenomena" we must discuss not just raw supplies plus tools or other instrumental media, but the command over supportive personnel involved. Contrariwise, command over persons and actors is dicier. Take, for example, a manager of a work department. This *authoritative-resource* holder has to work, with variable success, to:

- induce the commitment of new, as well as old, subordinates and co-managers, plus even improve the quality of their efforts, plus induce persons of higher authority to provide support.
- maintain an acceptable and workable degree of goal clarity and system integrity (an impression of what their department does, of how they do it, of whether they do they do it right and legally, of how their department fits in, and of whether it achieves some level of good outcomes for everyone involved—but especially the bosses).
- achieve locally adapted, departmentally coordinated, and successful communicative and other work (not just an impression, but actually collaborate to deliver the goods).
- balance their identity (i.e., relatedness to their legitimate work organization) with their and their subordinates' attention to outside contributions and challenges.

Yes, these needs (overlapping, admittedly, the list of challenges to agency given in chapter two) intentionally correspond roughly to our 4F. But they, equally, reveal how agency is fundamentally linked to the critical-theoretic concepts that occupy the heart of ST, such as the power dialectic practice-based vs. merely utilitarian agency, and the discourse of self-identity, explained in later chapters.

Those basic issues will reappear throughout the book. But we now turn to explicate the central theory referenced in the discussion earlier—ST.

2

Communication and Structuration Theory

For decades, organizational researchers have treated organizations as relatively stable containers in which activity occurs (Kaufman, 1971; Negandhi, 1973). Most research framed by this perspective on organizations (for-profit, nonprofit, not-for-profit, etc.) were macro in nature and assumed an existing organization with most distinctions between organizations attributed to size or number of people involved (Hawes, 1973). From this view, activity occurred within the boundaries of the organization and communication as a focus was limited to predictable patterns in which members sent and received messages to one another (Haas & Drabeck, 1973). Little consideration was given to how the organization influenced and was influenced by changes in membership or society beyond responding to market changes. All perspectives "assume the independent existence of an organized organization within which other activities occur" (Hawes, 1973, p. 499). This container-like view simplified research and theorizing by limiting the focus to messages in bounded times and location, and gave little consideration to questions about human agency—how people, behaviors, and events associated with the social entity play out.

Weick (1979) offered an alternative view that slowly changed the way many scholars theorize and investigate organizations. He argued that organizations are not things or settings in which people perform activities. Instead, he proposed that organizations are organizing processes that establish, maintain, and dissolve social entities. To theorize and research organizations is to examine those processes which, by nature, are not static, but ever-evolving. However, like others, his writings reified the idea that these organizing processes occur within the boundaries of a given locale. Further, while communication is assumed in the organizing process, initially, communication was not an investigative focus of sense-making research.

The Communicative Constitution of Organizations: The Four Flows Model, First Edition.
Robert D. McPhee, Karen K. Myers, and Joel O. Iverson.

In the 1970s, sociologist Anthony Giddens introduced a meta-theory, structuration theory (ST), to explain the development and sustainability of social entities in society. In contrast to previous theorizing, ST accounts for social structures and also elaborates on the role of human actions (agency) in enacting social systems. Further, ST provides a means to explore the processes that connect human actions to structures as mutually influencing each other. Most importantly for the central focus of this book, ST provides an array of concepts to help answer the question: What are organizations? How are they created, modified, sustained, and dissolved?

2.1 Structuration Theory Tenets with Reference to Organizations

Sociologist Anthony Giddens is credited for developing ST, joining other scholars at the time who sought to explain human behavior in society through various *practice* theories. Years before, Berger and Luckmann (1967) argued for theories that would explain the reciprocal influence of society on individuals and individuals on society. They joined Popper (1962), who also argued that "all social phenomena, and especially the functioning of social institutions, should be understood as resulting from the decisions etc. of human individuals" (p. 98). In response, practice theories emerged in the 1970s and 1980s as scholars such as Bourdieu, Bhaskar, Foucault, and Giddens looked for ways to better explain relationships between material, knowledge, agency, and action.

Practice theories attempt to explain daily activities that form structures to influence everyday life beyond the popular *rationalist* theories that were widely used at the time. Practice theories define "practice or praxis" as "the whole of human action" and "practices" as a routinized type of behavior involving physical and mental activities, material understandings, skills, emotion, and knowledge (Reckwitz, 2002, p. 249). Structures become an important element because humans rely on structures in practice and their individual actions frequently have more enduring and broad implications in the production of praxis (practices that reproduce the regularities in systems; Bourdieu (1977)).

Based on the writings of these and many other scholars, Giddens proposed ST, which not only explicates individual behaviors, but very effectively explains the relationship between human agency and structures. Giddens articulates the production, reproduction, and transformation of systems and structures and allows for the examination of these phenomena at micro, meso, and macro levels. We briefly review key elements of ST, which is the basis of our model of the communicative constitution of organizations.

2.2 Structure: Rules and Resources

Even though they are generated by human action, *structures* can be described as external to action and understood as the foundation of civilized society constraining and directing behavior. All human activity is based on structures, which are themselves intertwined in social life into a larger fabric that can be referred to as structure. In fact, a primary fact about structure is that it is dual, both enacted or *produced* as it is drawn on to guide and constitute activity, and *reproduced* through activity. Thus, we do, for example, chess by following its rules; thereby, we maintain it as "the game of chess," though we can transform it by shifting into a variant like instructive chess (where a teacher discusses alternate moves and their disadvantages, allowing moves to be taken back, etc.), or one of the innumerable variants of chess (Wikipedia, List_of_chess_variants), or even creating our own variant. We discuss these ideas more in the section "Duality of Structure."

Giddens' idea of structure refers to phenomena at two distinct levels of generality, as we already indicated. One is the level of macro-scale institutions, such as the world economy, the system of nation-states, or a broadly used language. Structures at this level involve resources such as the inequality of wealth or the different vocabularies, belonging to specific languages, for expressing one group's ideas versus another's. Structural resources, as general as this, are relevant to people's lives mainly by corresponding to the rules and resources for common social interaction. We also will discuss the relation of macro to micro structures more in the section "Duality of Structure."

Second, structures at the level of social interaction can be described in two overlapping ways through rules and resources. First, they include *rules*, both formal and informal, that guide individuals to not engage in some behaviors, thereby restricting their activities. At the same time, they also guide them about what they should do and how to do it. Some rules permeate society such as rules to avoid killing or stealing, while others are contextual such as giving two weeks' notice before quitting a job, though that rule may be disappearing or have less power with quiet quitting (Johnson, 2023). Regulative rules are those that imply sanctions such as the rules (laws) that set speed limits. In this way, rules cause many to think of rules as constraining actions. However, rules also are constitutive. Rules of language, for example, enable individuals to intelligibly communicate, even though they many not adhere to all formal rules in a given interaction. Rules keep us from playing video games at work and direct us not to wear pajamas in the office. While rules tell us what we *cannot do*, at the same time, they tell us *what we can and should do*. Rules tell us, for example, that we should not engage in leisure-time activities while we are on the clock, but other rules tell us we should make some effort at wearing clothing that will not offend customers. Thus, rules tell workers they should limit their computer activities to work-related tasks while at work and wear ties and jackets (or similar) in the office. Some rules also operate at a macro system level such as those that tell organizations they should treat their workers humanely and not cheat their customers, while others can operate at the micro level such as rules that suggest that workers in a particular workgroup inform their supervisor before leaving for the day. Giddens (1984) argues that the difference between regulative and constituting rules is a difference that has no difference. Giddens (1984) describes *constitutive rules* as guiding principles that make the organization or practice what it is. *Regulative rules* are those that do not define the essence of an organization or practice. Instead, they apply to the particulars within the organization or practice. In NBA basketball, a constitutive rule is the team that earns the most points at the end of four quarters wins, but a regulatory rule is that players are removed from the game after committing six fouls. Despite that distinction, Giddens also notes all rules are constitutive; they constitute normative behaviors, and most assuredly, they tell us which activities we should avoid. Giddens borrows from Wittgenstein, who said, "To know a rule, is to 'know how to go on'" (Giddens, 1979, p. 67).

Resources, another form or way of describing structure, are assets that facilitate activity. For example, at a material level, a resource can be machinery or tools that enable individuals to construct the frame of a house or a set of instructions that guide people in assembling furniture that was delivered in a box. Resources can also be nonmaterial such as knowledge or skills that help a physician to diagnose her patient's illness or play the drums in a band. Similarly, structures are implicated by the conferring of a master's degree making it a resource in applying for a job as a social worker. Later, the knowledge the individual gained in graduate school is a resource enabling them to effectively work with and help clients.

In many ways, rules are a subset of resources with many overlapping functions. For example, mathematics contains sets of rules that enable individuals to solve mathematical equations. At the same time, knowledge of the rules of math is a resource that can be drawn upon enabling individuals such as architects to design a structurally sound building or engineers to calculate the necessary arc of a rocket.

2.3 Systems

Systems are an essential element of human life (nonhuman life, too, but that is another discussion). Systems are relationships and interdependent patterns of human activity. Systems at the micro, meso, and macro levels are interconnected. For example, at the micro level, individuals employed in an automotive manufacturing facility coordinate their work to put together the body of a car. A set of workgroups that coordinate their production outputs so the car's exterior fits and coordinates with the car's interior and all the other elements of the car is an example of a system at the meso level. At the macro level, car manufacturers must consider distribution channels, car dealerships, and the preferences of the general public as they make decisions about their products and operations. So, although each level can be considered separately, they are interdependent as part of the larger, layered system. For example, if individual members in the workgroup responsible for building the car engines do not effectively coordinate, the result can be a defective car that results in product recalls, affecting consumers, dealerships, and the car manufacturers' reputation and profitability. Various metaphors such as these from the automotive industry suggest an engine system or, more frequently, draw on our understanding of the human body, would have readers believe that parts of systems are coordinated rather automatically. Systems that involve humans who operate with at least some level of autonomy or volatility are much more complex and operate much less automatically.

2.4 Agency

In everyday language, *agency* might bring to mind an organization such as the Central Intelligence Agency, but in social and communication theory today, one major conception was formulated by Anthony Giddens, as influenced especially by English philosophy. For Giddens, agency refers to an individual's ability to act (or not act) and to understand the meanings associated with action. Agents (or actors—those who have agency) draw on structures to perform acts (Giddens, 1979). They have the power to make choices, as McPhee and Iverson (2011) describe, *the power to draw on structures to make a difference.* Their actions and ability to make a difference are part of a flow of communication and activities as individuals are part of larger social entities (Cohen, 1989; Iverson et al., 2018). Agents are limited by the resources available to them. In addition, they must have knowledge of various types of resources and understand the extent to which they can use their agency in meaningful ways.

As agents draw on their knowledge and act, they *reflexively monitor* their activities and outcomes allowing them to make adjustments to better attain desired results. Monitoring occurs at three levels. *Discursive consciousness* signals an awareness of knowledge and behaviors that can be described by the agent, and that agent also can describe how she performs these tasks. For example, an experienced sales representative can draw on discursive consciousness to describe to a new sales trainee how she prospects for new clients and how she describes their product to potential customers. She has full awareness of her choices and the procedures she uses. For *practical consciousness*, individuals are aware of their activity, but they would find it impossible to fully describe their awareness—or how they know something. For example, the experienced sales representative has the ability to know when the potential client has been persuaded and is ready to buy. She can easily determine this point in the interaction, but she finds it difficult to describe it to a new sales representative.

Giddens (1984) describes the third level, unconscious, as an "internal security system" (p. 41) that is vital to experience the self as a whole person that exists in time, or *ontological security.* Unconsciousness agency is so pervasive humans would find it overwhelming to actively exert mental energy attending to these processes. When humans avoid walking down dark alleys at night, for example, they may rely on *unconscious monitoring.* They may have never made a conscious choice to choose walkways that are better lit or even walk rather than crawl; instead, their internal monitoring system guides them to act in a way that better ensures their ontological security. Many experienced high-reliability workers (e.g., physicians, police officers, pilots, etc.) behave in ways that avoid dangerous situations, but claim no awareness of doing so, potentially an indication of unconscious monitoring.

(Giddens, 1984). To improve their chances for positive outcomes, agents are able to assess a given situation and interpret how they are being perceived and how their actions are contributing to their objectives in a process called *reflexive self-monitoring*. This interpretation allows them to shape their current and future actions with reflexivity and rationalization. Thus, individuals intermittently and within the context of their interaction find that some decisions and actions result in favorable outcomes, causing them to choose to continue with similar activities (Bhaskar, 2015). This maintains and strengthens the structures that contributed to the action. However, they might assess the outcomes negatively because they have not achieved their objectives or perhaps because they interpret the responses from others to be unsupportive of their actions. As a result, they make changes in how they respond to ongoing and similar situations. For example, a supervisor might reflexively monitor how she communicates with employees. She might believe she is being too harsh on more experienced workers and too lenient with newcomers. Reflexivity causes her to adjust her behaviors to be more mindful about the criticisms she offers to some, while extending more praise to others. However, her monitoring is not based purely on internal cognitive processing. Instead, reflexive monitoring and adjustments agents make are based on context—what fits within the culture of one workgroup and organization may not apply to another. This being the case, individuals adjust their monitoring from one situation to another. Giddens (1984) notes that while monitoring is an essential human process, agents are not continuous in their sustained reflection, but draw on discursive consciousness at critical moments to resolve problems.

Agents also must have the ability to provide accounts of their own and others' actions and to *rationalize* their conduct (Bhaskar, 2015; McPhee & Iverson, 2011). Within the flow of their actions, individuals frequently feel the need to explain or justify the choices they make to themselves or others. Individuals must have enough knowledge to rationalize actions, which can bring those actions known only in practical consciousness to the discursive consciousness level. In the workplace, a supervisor might offer an explanation to rationalize her firing of a worker who consistently made errors resulting in lost sales. The process of rationalizing extends the effect of her actions when others within the organization buy into her explanation—and even she herself uses her rationalization as sense-making for the action—increasing the potential effect of the structures. In the future, the supervisor and others in the organization will recognize that a pattern of making errors (a rule) is justification for termination (an action). In this way, the rule becomes a resource that she and other supervisors draw upon for guidance. Giddens (1993) argues that "[t]he rationalization of action is closely bound up with the moral evaluations of responsibility which actors make of each other's conduct, and hence with moral norms and the sanctions to which those who contravene them are subject" (p. 165). It also can make an action understandable (by describing it or stating its motive) with respect to an interpretive frame and reveal how the legitimacy of an action transforms into a basis for the power to act.

The nature of agency has been a hotly contested debate among social science researchers (see Brummans, 2018, for a recent example). Many have been critical of Giddens' and Bourdieu's focus on structures such as habitual and routinized practices and their role in human agency. Emirbayer and Mische (1998) argue that individuals' purpose, judgment, and intent are evident in their agency. They proffer an alternative perspective on agency that incorporates temporal-relational contexts into the constitution of human agency. Their perceptions of agency are instrumental—they evaluate and anticipate potential outcomes of action, and they are normative—because they also maintain the ability to act governed by self-legislating morality. They define agency as "the temporally constructed engagement by actors of different structural environments—the temporal relational contexts of action—which through the interplay of habitus, imagination, and judgement, both reproduces and transforms those structures in interactive response to the problems posed by changing historical situations" (p. 970). In many ways, Emirbayer and Mische's stance on agency does not differ greatly from ours. They argue that while humans are subject to habitus, current settings and situations cause them to envision and enact agency differently. Frequently, and especially in more mundane environments and situations, individuals engage in iteration, which constitutes and reinforces existing routines. And, similar to reflexive monitoring, they affirm that humans possess the ability to respond to contingencies that would cause them to change their behavior. They also explicate humans' abilities to project themselves into the future, reflecting their dreams, anxieties, or fears in making choices about action. Thus, their relational–temporal view of agency emphasizes that individuals' agency is premised on their relationships to contexts and their anticipation of outcomes associated with action. We do not disagree with these arguments.

However, as mentioned in our introductory chapter, we would reframe Emirbayer and Mische's formulation of the contextuality of agency. In light of current concern for the agency of women, racial minorities, etc., we would say that agency—the human power to make a difference—can be challenged—limited or even blocked—by a number of factors, each potentially demanding resistant, effortful, tenuous response to allow effective action to continue. Consider the following (incomplete) list of challenges:

1. understanding one's immediate situation—or long-term consequences;
2. making a difference at all, or one that matters;
3. getting noticed or gaining attention;
4. be understood; the challenge to be recognized (Honneth, 2003), respected, and have legitimate voice;
5. gathering and mobilizing the resources grounding action and communication—information, supporters and followers, striking social events to target;
6. establishing relationships in and through which agency can be exercised;
7. using the medium of communication that is itself crippled by biases and equivocality;
8. finding strategies to avoid or subvert opposed, organized agents with their own secrets and capable, but equally challenged agency;
9. finding a path of action leading to success; and

10. possessing a sufficiently powerful sense of self that articulates a goal, value, or ideal result, that avoids or controls contrary motives, that can be "successful," can motivate and guide, and gain fulfillment from one's activity.

One inference we can draw from this list is that the human agent is not an all-powerful figure or even a self-sufficient one. While ST may deserve to be called humanistic, it joins posthumanistic theoretic currents in seeing social interaction as a flow in which agents are carried. They act as agents when *they take a stand* in this flow, understanding where they are and how they mean to act or communicate—only to have acts or words carried along in varied directions in the flow.

Although scholars in the field of communication draw on Emirbayer and Mische's ideas of relationality, praising what they call "a turn toward relationality" (Ashcraft & Kuhn, 2018, p. 170). Cooren (2018) criticizes Emirbayer and Mische's stance and argues that animals and objects "do things, too, albeit differently" (p. 146). He nonetheless joins Ashcraft and Kuhn in advocating the relationality as a move away from more "structural" views of agency that privilege individuals, organizations, and objects' role in shaping interactions. According to a sociomaterial ontology, humans are not especially prototypical agents (Ashcraft & Kuhn, 2018). Instead, they argue for equal emphasis on material and hybrid agency. Additionally, they borrow a term coined by Callon (2007), *agencement* to describe how multiple influences, including humans and nonhumans combine and adjust to have effects, the "ongoing flow of sensory force that animates worlds" (Ashcraft & Kuhn, 2018, p. 177). Thus, they argue that agency is not a property exclusive to humans, but their version of agency emerges as a result of relations that create it. While we agree that nonhumans behave in organizational systems in significant ways, for organizations, which are human social systems, we see essential differences in the ability of materials and technologies to act and the agency of humans. Before detailing the distinctions in our position, another perspective must be considered.

Murray et al. (2021) offered a different perspective on agency and the agentic-like properties of technology. Their purpose was to theorize how various forms of technology possess agentic qualities that can alter organizational routines, they argued that both humans as well as technologies can produce outcomes for organizations. They borrow from Emirbayer and Mische's (1998) views of agency, which include an ability to reflect on the past, consider the present, and predict the future to act with intent. Newer technologies can be described as having "agentic" qualities because they possess "a temporally embedded capacity to intentionally constrain, complement, and substitute for humans in the practice of routines" (p. 553). When these technologies are linked to human processes, a form of *conjoined agency* results, which they define as "a shared capacity between humans and nonhumans to exercise intentionality" (p. 553).

Murray and colleagues identified four types of technology that hold different types of human-technology conjoined agency. First, *assisting technologies* do not have agency, but they help humans in their activities. An example they offer is a human creating a presentation using PowerPoint in which the software assists the process, but it makes no decisions for the human user. Second, *conjoined agency with arresting technologies* cannot develop performance protocols ("rules and customs"; Feldman, 2000, p. 611), but they can select actions that are not predetermined, giving them agentic properties. Humans lack the power to work around the technology's automatic authority to control routines. For example, blockchain systems work based on encoded controls that are locked in by the community to guard against an individual attempting to take control. The third type with agentic qualities is *conjoined agency with augmenting technologies*. Murray and colleagues describe this as a form that can develop protocols, but it cannot select actions. These algorithms complement humans' decision-making by sorting through data to provide predictions. Algorithms such as these are used by judges to help them make decisions about whether to offer parole to inmates by examining patterns and rates of recidivism. The last form Murray and colleagues present is *conjoined agency with automating technologies* that can develop protocols and select actions. This form of technology has the highest level of agentic qualities because it can analyze large amounts of data and learn over time about how to optimize their ability to make choices on behalf of humans. A well-known example is IBM's Deep Blue, the computer that defeated chess champion Garry Kasparov in a six-game match. Conjoined agency offers theorists and practitioners another way to consider and debate whether nonhumans can exercise agency. Certainly, this perspective has emphasized that action is not a solely human endeavor but intertwined with the materiality of the world as well as technologies of our own creation. We agree with the complexity. Nevertheless, for us, they do not meet the criteria for *agency* because the algorithms that guide their behaviors were developed and programmed into the systems by humans, which dictates the parameters of their actions; thus, the systems do not have the ability to go beyond their programming (acting otherwise) to be reflective about their choices nor the ability to consider the meaningfulness of the choices.

While the relationality, materiality, and conjoined agency arguments have generated fruitful discussion about the influence of nonhuman objects and animals on action, we maintain that the entities they describe are crucially different from human agency, especially for social systems that are communicatively constituted as meaningful such as organizations. Humans, unlike the wind, artificial intelligence or a pet, have the power to draw on organizational structures to act. Reflexive monitoring and the ability to contexalize are the crucial difference. Computer systems have the ability to consider large data sets, make choices, operate as automated processes within organizations, and even learn, in a sense. However, humans have the unique ability to contextualize the situation in a socially meaningful way. They can reflect on the meaning of a situation and potential choices and actions relative to their personal values and/or the values of their organization. They can also consider how their past actions have impacted their personal goals and the goals of others, given what they know from larger discourses. For example, a manager can consider whether the time is right to hire another software engineer. Before taking action, the manager evaluates many standard indicators that trigger hiring such as excessive workload for current software engineers and incoming project projections, both indicating that an additional employee is warranted. However, because the manager has the capacity to fully assess the situation, they also consider the company's larger goals to cut costs in preparation for potentially taking the company public in the coming year. At the same time, the manager reflects on a similar situation the company encountered several years ago and its effect on the morale of workers. Fearing those social implications, the manager makes a decision to delay hiring, but to start discussions with the team about the skill sets needed and about when the timing will be favorable. As this example demonstrates, humans can reflexively monitor their own activities but also can examine the opinions of others and use a more meaningful means of assessing the context than nonhumans. While AI systems can act according to rules they have learned and make adjustments based on feedback from system users, they cannot assess social context, meanings, or consider choices beyond existing rules as humans can (Iverson et al., 2018). For us, one of the central questions to ask is, "absent humans, do organizations exist?" If so, are they communicatively constituted? Are they different from other systems in nature? We can imagine some automated processes that keep producing goods, automated sales, and delivery that occurs through human-free delivery. Is that a system or an organization? A similar question can be asked about agency.

First, consider the automated system. Early organizational studies from the classical model considered organizations to be like machines that required people and treated people as machines. Soon, scholars discovered that humans have needs, thoughts, feelings, values, and other capabilities that go beyond machines (Mayo, 1933/1946; Roethlisberger & Dickson, 1939). Second, Corman (1997) developed a compelling argument about quasi-agents. Examining technology specifically, Corman stated that automated systems act like agents and we interact with them as if they are agents, but they do not possess the ability to move beyond their limitations and reflexively monitor unanticipated consequences or other factors of meaning for their actions. Finally, we see usefulness in considering the communicative constitution of organizations as a valid reason not to conflate nonhuman capabilities with the idea of human agency.

As agents act, they draw on structures—rules to guide their activities and resources to make their actions possible. It is important to note that these actions are not discrete activities disconnected from others and society. Activities occur within a flow of conduct that results in the constitution of structures that extend beyond one individual's communication and activities to the *flow* of activities within a social system (Bourdieu, 1977). These flows of activity are context dependent. Agents possess an awareness of social rules and their actions are based on the current situation, but also based on the past and guided by intentions for the future. Thus, as human agents maintain certain structures, and make adjustments in others, they transform structure. At other times, they may choose to break rules which, over time, can erode the power of a rule, or dissolve it entirely. Giddens (1984) also notes that while agents may be free to act, they can be constrained by other actors, material situations, or rules within various interconnected systems. These constraints have a similar effect of reproducing, transforming or eroding structures. And, as we have argued elsewhere (Iverson et al., 2018), these processes of agency are a uniquely human capacity. While animals and even artificial intelligence can display elements similar to agency, they are not equipped with the ability to reflexively interpret, reflexively self-monitor, rationalize, or make a difference in the same way humans can.

2.5 Duality of Structure

Perhaps *the* central element of ST is the principle of the *duality of structure*. Structures are created and shaped through structured practices, at the same time, structures cannot exist or continue without enactment. Structures are presumed in practice because individuals draw on structures, both rules and resources, to guide and assist practices. Much of agents' practice is routinized and obscure to themselves and potentially others, but is part of *habitus* that draws on structures of the given context (Bourdieu, 1977). Thus, whether wittingly or not, individuals' activities that are enabled and constrained by structures, reproduce and reinforce those very structures and practices. When a practice is changed either by the conscious decisions of an individual or by an unintended action such as a mistake, structures can similarly change. Even when new practices are introduced, structures remain foundational. In creating new practices, individuals borrow from existing practices and structures to guide them. For example, in developing a set of recruitment practices for a new company, human resource directors are likely to model practices they know to be useful from their previous work experiences. Thus, all human activity is recursive; as individuals act, they draw on structures within the system, but as they do so, they maintain, reproduce, or alter those very structures.

We note that both production and reproduction have a variety of senses, not explicitly described by Giddens. Production involves (a) drawing on resources available from the past to perform an activity now, as well as (b) acting via structure in a way that produces future results. We use our power to initiate new entrants to legitimate a statement like "you are now members," and our informed activity makes our statement have an impact on the newbies hearing it, as well as socializing talk that introduces new ideas for them. Similarly, *reproduce* involves (a) revivifying past resources by basing a current action on them as well as (b) keeping our acts available to ground upcoming actions. Using the well-known vocabulary term *member* in our statement keeps English alive in our employment talk, and using that term right now refreshes its significance for future talk about membership. Our use of *revivifying* may also be reproduction for some or it may introduce a new vocabulary term. Either way, we are reproducing it as an English vocabulary resource. One other important implication of *reproduce* is (c) by acting in localized situations, we maintain a society's structures (or transform them) even at the macro-institutional level. Thus, by using words of English, we keep their meanings alive for others, perhaps adapting or otherwise transforming the word-meanings in small ways. However, we also reproduce English word meanings by paying taxes to support schools with English literature classes. *Reproduce* is usually a result of a complex system—keeping a meaning alive in institution-level English isn't simply a scaled-up result of individuals using the word occasionally.

Giddens uses the paired terms *maintain/transform* to articulate the insight that any human activity, by reproducing structure, both brings past resources into present significance—no action or production is created out of nothing, and all human activity transforms structure, at the very least by recontextualizing and thus reinvigorating it. This account will become more nuanced in our later discussion of the presence-absence dialectic, but as is, it points to part of what *communicative constitution* will mean in this book: constitution partly involves interaction that accomplishes things by maintaining or transforming structural resources in the sweep from past to future.

2.6 Modalities

As individuals act in social settings by drawing on structures, they also articulate and depend on the dimensions, or modalities of structure that include *signification*, *legitimation*, and *domination*. These dimensions of structure are produced, reproduced, and transformed (Giddens, 1984). All structures exhibit these modalities which help to explain their influence. Consider, for example, a workgroup norm to respond to emails from coworkers within 24 hours. As workers continue the practice of responding to their coworkers by the end of the day, the significance of the rule is reproduced—workgroup members understand the expectation and make efforts to adhere. Because the practice is largely accepted by the members, not following the rules would be noticed. At the same time, the legitimation of the norm also is reproduced, workers who do not quickly return emails are made to feel guilty when asked by their coworker whether they received their initial email. Dominance of the rule is also reproduced when workers make extra efforts and potentially even stay at work late to follow the rule. Based on this example, it should be apparent that the rules and associated modalities are context specific. The rule about responding to emails in 24 hours is not present in all organizational cultures, and some individual members may have consistent patterns of not adhering to the norm because they have varying perceptions about its modalities.

Similarly, modalities can also influence how structures are prioritized. At an interpersonal level, two coworkers might extend their lunch hour because they are celebrating a birthday. Their meaning of the birthday lunch as a special occasion allows them to feel justified to break the rule to return to their desks on time. At an institutional level, the signification, legitimation, and dominance of rules can also be transformed. For example, years ago, air travel, even in coach class, included the service of a meal. In the late 1990s, airlines realized that although it was an expectation, they did not need to serve passengers a meal as part of their standard service. Instead, they could sell food to the flying public rather than offering meals for free. Soon, nearly all airlines changed course and stopped offering free meals to passengers on domestic flights. At first, passengers questioned the legitimacy of the airlines' decision to stop meal service, but the airlines' dominance over passengers' disapproval prevailed. Thus, once the legitimacy of the structure was diminished, the significance of the meal was transformed. Today, most coach-class passengers likely see the lack of meal service as insignificant.

Every action uses more or less various forms of power, like making a speech in the US Congress that is effective in persuading people to change their minds. Indeed, Giddens argues that *every* act, communicative or not, requires power enough to perform the physical activities necessary to manifest meaning to make the expression noticeable and intelligible for an audience. So, the *power* to articulate intentions, and to draw knowledgeable attention, underpin a Congressional speech or any other communicative process. In addition, to be an effective speech it obviously needs to be *meaningful*—delivered in a language shared by other members of Congress, on a topic that's overtly relevant to the Congressional session in a clear way, even if the speech is off the current topic. Similarly, a speech needs to be justified, legitimate, and appropriate to have the sort of impact that Congressional speeches are supposed to have. A representative who uses foul language on the floor of Congress, probably will distract his/her audience instead of attracting attention to the meaning of their speech. And as we already noted, this property is interrelated with legitimacy and domination, and the power to make a speech is itself constrained and dialectical—other members may try to halt the speech rather than listen to it.

The idea that any action or interaction has inherent dimensions of power, meaning, and norms lets ST give full emphasis to, and integrate, the notions of action implicit in past interpretive, critical, and systems approaches. Humans interpret the meanings, norms, and power in the situation to be reflective in making agentive choices affecting their behavior. It also, we should reiterate, supports Giddens' argument that the macro structures visible in theories about nation-states and economics link up essentially with their multidimensional nature of episodic action.

2.7 Distanciation

Many structures endure over time and span numerous contexts. Giddens (1984) defined this phenomenon as *time-space distanciation*: "the stretching of social systems across time-space" (p. 181). Although action is localized, praxis and their associated structures are reproduced at micro, meso, and macro levels in various places. In the localized setting, *social integration* occurs as reciprocity takes place between copresent actors. At a system level, *system integration* has the same reciprocity between actors and/or collectives as they extend across space. When structures and practices are enacted, they are reproduced and transformed, not only in the here and now, but with potential to endure across time and to extend their influence and relevance to other locations.

In particular, distanciation has power implications. In an integrated social system, agents can sometimes influence situations far from them in time-space. Thus, an executive, in deciding to discontinue a product line, can bring about the firing of thousands of employees. Such a decision might stimulate or justify decisions in other companies to similarly reduce their workforces. Further, the decision and resulting responses might increase unemployment to the point of creating a recession, throw thousands of households into poverty, or affect occupational choices by young workforce members.

Giddens (1984) also argued that both *between* and *within* society and social entities, individuals are positioned relative to time and space. Responding to critical comments about the notion that actions and objects are simply "there" at a static time/space instant and point (Derrida, 1976; Heidegger, 1967; Mead, 1932), Giddens (1979) emphasized that ST is devoted to revolutionizing that notion with a "presence/absence dialectic" characterizing time, space, and structural resources. "Social activity is always constituted in three intersecting moments of difference: temporally, paradigmatically (involving structure which is present only in its instantiation), and spatially. All social practices are situated activities in each of these senses" (1979, p. 54).

Thus in ST, an act, drawing on structural resources, *is* an act—is present—insofar as it connects and contrasts with a spectrum of absent alternatives in past, coresponds with constrained agentive design in solution in the present, and projects or is preinclined to a spectrum of future—in a way absent, not yet eventuated—possibilities. Thus, the context is not a surrounding environment at hand for the action, but is constituted as an emergent potential enacted into mutual significance. For instance, my office and the colleagues with whom I share it are not just there, but emerge, as fresh relational elements from the past, lived in the present, with possibilities imagined for the future—lived in my physical and primarily communicative interactions—in discursive practices among and about the context. But for us—previewing our stance developed in later chapters—the prototypical social activity is not the single unit act—not even the speech act, nor the practical doing involving tools in to-hand use. Nor is it even the utterance-cum-understanding (Luhmann), or Meadean (Mead, 1934) playful exchange of gestures, or 'adjacency pairs' (Sacks et al., 1978); rather, it is (to foreshadow) the *flow* of communication, of all action responsive to any focal act, however distanciated.

Giddens thus affirmed that roles could be better described as processual, or presence/absence dialectical, "position-practice relations" or *positions* (p. 83). The term positioning first appeared in marketing in 1972 when Trout and Ries suggested that product manufacturers attempt to differentiate, that is, *position* their products and services to differentiate those of their competitors in the minds of consumers (Harré & Van Langenhove, 1991). Similarly, individuals are socially positioned within social networks through dynamic interaction dispersed across time and space (Giddens, 1984). Through interaction, individuals place (or position) themselves and others in relevant categories that help structure ongoing interaction. These identities are not static but span within the *longue durée* of various institutions and one's life (Giddens, 1984). Bourdieu (1977) described the influences of the past on our actions and identities: "[I]n each of us, in varying proportions, there is part of yesterday's man; it is yesterday's man who inevitably predominates in us, since the present amounts to little compared with the long past in the course of which we were formed and from which we result" (p. 79). Thus, like with roles, one's position is frequently based on existing notions of the social identity and also includes certain obligations and agency, and are often based on the modalities of legitimation, signification and domination. Nevertheless, while rooted in the past, positioning occurs on a daily basis and reflects the current context (Giddens, 1984). In addition, positioning takes place in the social realm of three processes: conversations, institutional practices, and uses of societal rhetorics (Harré & Van Langenhove, 1991).

It is tempting to think of social interaction, even when it is unclear, disorganized, or conflict-filled, as behavior that, at least on its own terms, is coherent and internally consistent. Reading, or reciting, an important historical speech should make sense in a straightforward way, even if there are lots of hesitations and misstatements. But Giddens follows centuries of theory in holding that social interaction has uneven or even contorted consequences due to the contradictory character of its rules and resources. Even when we do not identify downright contradictions, we very frequently can find paradoxes and other interactive tensions in the foundations of interaction.

Giddens especially used the notion of contradiction at a macro-institutional level. He defined contradiction as "the opposition or disjuncture of structural principles of social systems, where those principles operate in terms of each other but at the same time contravene one another" (1979, p. 141). For instance, a contradiction might exist between individual freedoms and social well-being: individuals exercising freedoms can use them to harm or even undermine society—except that society's well-being *is* having individuals free to express themselves and contribute freely to the common good. Giddens argued that contradictions didn't automatically cause conflict, but embodied social strains that could ignite it.

However, communication scholars have used the idea of contradiction to illuminate fewer macro phenomena. For instance, Canary (2010a, 2010b; cf. Foot & Groleau, 2011) found several contradictory phenomena in research she did about the implementation of multilevel policy in a school system. As Putnam (2013, p. 625) summarizes her work, Canary "uncovered the intersection of four types of contradictions: (a) primary ones rooted [deeply in an education system], (b) secondary ones that arose when a new policy system could not be integrated into an existing one, (c) tertiary contradictions that occurred when a new motive was introduced to the system and altered how organizational members made sense of activity systems, and (d) quaternary contradictions that occurred when the central activities of one system interfered or blocked the accomplishment of another one." Canary found that contradictions could actually deepen member understanding about school policy issues, but also complicate the overall situation.

Overall, ST allows an exploration of the components and interconnected nature of systems to agency as enacted in practices. The duality of structure and modalities outline the relationship between structures and action. Distanciation allows for an understanding of the system across time and space. Taken together, this practice theory approach provides a framework for understanding organizations as enacted in practices, and more specifically, in communication.

2.8 Communication and System Structuring

ST is a useful theory for communication scholarship because of its focus on process and its ability to explain sustainability and changes in systems that occur over time and across situations. While Giddens does not specifically discuss the role of *communication*, he links the creation of structures and systems to *interaction* and practice. Premises outlined in ST guide toward an examination of how individuals and other social entities draw on habitus ("history turned into nature" Bourdieu, 1977, p. 78) and through communication create structures and practices. For organizational researchers, it explains the production, reproduction, and transformation of organizations and other social entities *through communication.*

ST, and in particular duality of structure, is a useful framework allowing researchers to easily (and often necessarily) move from level to level. It affords a close examination of how individual-level interactions and practices influence and are influenced by group- and organization-, and even societal-level interactions and practices (Giddens, 1984). At the same time, it allows researchers to investigate and describe the reverse—how societal-, organizational-, and workgroup levels shape individual actions and interaction (McPhee et al., 2014). This allows researchers to broaden the scope of research and examine issues and reverberating repercussions over time. This freedom to explore issues from the micro to the macro and back, is attractive to researchers who seek to more fully examine organizational phenomenon. However, a premise of the duality of structure is that action (including interaction) draws on and is dependent on structure (Poole & DeSanctis, 1992), but the structure is also created through action. Thus, action both produces and reproduces structures. An important implication is this—ST does not easily allow for causal explanations, which are best devoted to aspects of communication involving its constraint or even conditionality. Researchers commonly describe phenomena as *linked* or *associated* even though they might jointly influence each other. These characteristics have made ST most common in qualitative investigations.

ST has framed numerous organizational studies in communication including organizational climate (Bastien et al., 1995; Poole & McPhee, 1983), organizational culture (Witmer, 1997), workers' ability (or inability) to utilize family leave policies (Kirby & Krone, 2002), and ideology positioning (Gibson & Papa, 2000; Howard & Geist, 1995), Yates and Orlikowski (1992) described genres of organizational communication as a concept "that allows us to examine the production, reproduction, and modification of different types of organizational communication over time and under different circumstances" (p. 301). Examples include both substance (social motives, proposing projects, etc.) and forms (letters of recommendation, proposals, memos, etc.). Orlikowski and Yates (1994) extended this research by identifying genre repertoires. Their study described structuring email communication over two years that enabled a large technology community to collectively develop a common coding language. While not a study, Scott et al. (1998) used ST to link identity and identification with an organization. They argued that members' identities can be formed in part through discourse and action that draw upon structures of the organization, and their identity becomes the basis for their identification with their organization. When their identity is linked to their organizational membership, it becomes a structure for potentially shaping their alignment with the organization and enhancing their organizational identification.

In recent years, studies have usefully drawn on ST, for example, to examine how structures influence individual and group identities (Ault, 2018; Choi & Berhó, 2016), foster social structures that inhibit interaction between international teaching assistants and their American students (Li et al., 2011), develop a social network and practices creating problematic organizational relationships in NASA (Garner, 2006), manage tensions of differing goals by forging structures for collaboration (Kramer et al., 2017), examine the unintended consequences that occur as a result of organizational change (Guowei, 2007), and the mutually influencing relationships between organizational identification and technology use (Larson & Pepper, 2011). Several studies have focused on issues related to work-life balance. For example, Hoffman and Cowan (2010) analyzed employee requests for accommodation related to work-life issues. They identified six rules and three resources that were often used in such requests, and also how those rules and resources at times challenge but also reproduce existing systems. While we follow Giddens (1979) in resisting the urge to identify distinct rules or resources comprising structure, these authors do elucidate their topic through structurational analysis. To demonstrate how long-standing rules about workplace flexibility, Nordbäck et al., (2017) compared two Finnish organizations' perceived agency toward teleworking. While one organization embraced teleworking, long-standing practices and negative discourses constrained workers in the other organization, cocreating different policies, expectations, and workplace relationships between employees and management.

ST is particularly useful to acknowledge the role of social structures relative to individuals' agency. The theory accounts for some level of determinism, while also acknowledging the role that humans have in their own awareness, making choices, and altering their own behavior. In doing so, it demonstrates how individual action ultimately contributes to praxis, and ultimately structures and systems

(Reckwitz, 2002). At the same time, ST does not attempt to simplify that which is complex and also offers researchers an ability to tackle the micro versus macro issue by considering and examining phenomena at several levels (McPhee et al., 2014a, 2014b). Rules and resources include structural principles that operate at various levels, including individuals, organizations, and social systems, and with mutual potential production and reproduction. Organizational researchers can explore how individuals and workgroups draw on structures at micro, meso, and macro levels such as rules in onboarding and training newcomers, negotiating positions, coordinating activities, and development of group culture. ST requires that they examine the other side of the coin—how activity at various levels shapes those very structures. For example, want-to-be firefighters must spend time in fire stations to learn about fire station culture and demonstrate commitment to join. These streams of communication are not isolated to the workgroup (fire crew), but because individuals and workgroups become accustomed to and expect the practice, over time, this proactive socialization becomes an element of organizational processes. Organizational selection interviews are conducted with the expectation that candidates embrace this norm (Myers, 2005). At the organizational level, ST provides a lens to examine several organizational phenomena that are shaped over time by the interaction and practices of individuals, workgroups, and organizational and even societal influences. In Kirby and Krone's (2002) study, male workers felt pressure to not use work-life policies because society (and coworkers) were less accepting of men taking family leave. These studies blur the boundaries of the organization, thereby collapsing the organizational container.

Several specific organizational communication theories rooted in ST extend their usefulness. First, *adaptive structuration theory* has been used to explain the mutual influence of organizational systems and members' interaction with and their use of technologies (DeSanctis & Poole, 1994). Barley's (1986) field study on the introduction of CT scanners in two hospitals demonstrated the social structures of the relationship between radiologists—physicians trained to read scans and diagnose aliments—and imaging technologists—those whose job it was to operate the CT scanners—influenced how the technology was used. Similarly, Poole and DeSanctis (1992) and Contractor and Seibold (1993) demonstrated how social systems could shape, and at times, transform uses for technology and how that technology interfaces with human practices such as group decision support systems.

Second, *structurating activity theory* was proposed to explain the shared development of policy knowledge between concerned groups (Canary, 2010a, 2010b). As already described, she found contradictory structural resources drawn on for communication regarding policies such as employee rights, healthcare delivery and education, and their interrelated activity systems. Each of these stakeholders and groups includes its own resources and practices that center on the attainment of diverse goals over time. Their activities are constrained by larger social structures such as common practices, material artifacts, symbolic resources, and the individuals involved that influence how policies are communicatively constructed, interpreted, and transformed. Often interactions, interpretations, and practices result in contradictions that may foster transformation of policies and their use.

Third, Haslett (2013) develops a detailed analysis of structuration and Goffman's work. Specifically, Haslett analyzes multiple levels of frames. *Metaframes* represent globalized knowledge and meaning structures while *frame systems* are narrower with shared themes. Finally, individual *frames* occur in interaction as shared meaning in practice. Each level, from metaframes to frames, is an interconnected structure of meaning at varying levels of abstraction.

Finally, Nicotera and Clinkscales (2010) and Nicotera and Mahon (2013) developed structurational divergence theory as a means of examining the conflict between structural features that sit in opposition to one another, creating negative communication cycles (Nicotera et al., 2015) and making the position of individuals untenable. When those incompatible structures collide, a structurational divergence *nexus* is created that is enacted through iterations of communication (structurational divergence *cycle*). Nicotera and colleagues have examined the inherent conflicts in healthcare, with particular emphasis on nursing (2010, 2013), providing useful insights into the way communication constitutes inherently contradictory organizational outcomes.

Structurational studies and theories capitalize on the interconnections of structure and agency as a system enacted in practices and impacting organizations. As a result, these works capture the dynamic processes of communication. We extend that work by further examining the processes of the communicative constitution of organizations. Our goal is to not only explore the four flows approach based on ST but also to develop a deeper understanding of the *ways* communication constitutes organizations. In the next chapter, we discuss what is meant by *constitution* and introduce our theory about *how* organizations are communicatively constituted.

3

Communicative Constitution

While many organizational scholars have agreed that communication goes well beyond an information transfer role and has a constitutive role in organizations, the deeper process and means of constituting require further exploration. For us, a primary resource for understanding the constitution of sociocultural systems is based on the structuration theory (ST) framework of Chapter 2. How ST relates to the deeper processes of constitution requires elaboration through interconnected sets of ideas.

In this chapter, we explore the innate nature of social systems as they are (re) constituted across space and time. Our exposition is recursive and interwoven—that is, it is unfortunately complicated. A rough roadmap is: first, we elaborate statements about constitution in the prior chapter by analyzing some more relevant conclusions by Giddens. In our analysis, we augment the range of his ideas of the virtual and the presence/absence dialectic. Second, we review and transform two past ST-relevant concepts, the hermeneutic circle and the speech act, for use in our reconception of communicative constitution. Third, we depict the (communicative) constitution of organizations in contrast to the constitution of signs and of agents, partly to emphasize how organizations are different, in their very constitution, from names in a newspaper account or from human-like agencies. Fourth, we articulate our conception of the communicative and constitutive process by focusing our analysis on a crucial array of concepts, the modalities or dimensions of action, and institutions in ST. We explain how the modalities exist and relate in compounds we call *transtructions*, describable in *transtructive rules*, and reiterate our argument for the importance of the dimensions and combinations for understanding organizational, and in general social-system, constitution. Simultaneously, we explicate the view, implicit

The Communicative Constitution of Organizations: The Four Flows Model, First Edition.
Robert D. McPhee, Karen K. Myers, and Joel O. Iverson.

throughout this chapter and earlier, that the three modalities can and must be augmented by a fourth dimension, the best-called *constitution.* What we are offering here is our reconceptualization of our account of communication, which we think is a considerable revision of the ones being offered in other versions of CCO.

3.1 Structuration Theory and the Constitution of Organizing

Giddens' (1979) writings about ST, expounded in our second chapter, do include some important idea-clusters, as well as fragmentary comments, focused on *constitution* and the *constitution of society*. See, for instance, the quotation on p. 14 in our prior chapter, or

> ...the differences which constitute social systems reflect a dialectic of presences and absences in space and time. But these are only brought into being and reproduced via the virtual order of differences of structures, expressed in the duality of structure. The differences that constitute structures, and are constituted structurally, relate "part" to "whole" in the sense in which the utterance of a grammatical sentence presupposes the absent corpus of syntactical rules that constitutes the language as a totality (p. 71).

In other words, any one sentence implicates the whole system of language because it stands in contrast to the many possible word meanings and sentence structures—ones that could have been chosen but were not as well as actual or conceivable repetitions and conversations using the sentence, in past memory or future possibility. Thus, the constitution of a language system happens in the choices of language that is used and not used. And the system Giddens references could be a nation-state (Giddens' supreme focus), organization, or conversation. For a system to be constituted, it must exhibit time-space distanciation, or endure across space and time—for example, across worksites, offices, and markets, and with a past and future. It is a stretch of interrelatedness that exists only because human agents draw on structural resources to achieve it. Note that the entire system does not *exist* in each moment of communication, but across time and in various locations, its use is part of the process that constitutes the system and its structures.

Giddens (1979) further contextualizes this account by noting that more than the existence of the words written or spoken is required for systems to be constituted:

> (structure) implies recognizing the existence of: (a) knowledge...of "how things are to be done" (said, written), on the part of social actors; (b) social practices organized through the recursive mobilization of that knowledge; (c) capabilities that the production of those practices presupposes (p. 64).

This statement contains deeply embedded but crucial traces of three elements that we will elaborate and extend in this chapter. Structure, enabling and constraining social-systemic action, involves agentive *power* (capabilities, practices getting things done), *meaning* (knowledge and its recursive application to understand), and *normative* orientation (how things are to be done properly or legitimately). Connecting back, the distanciation constituting social systems is a stretching of power-laden, meaning-laden, and norm-laden resources from past to future and from present to absent).

This makes it clear that a communication process perspective requires a compound elaboration of the presence–absence dialectic characterizing interaction. Yes, as Giddens elucidates, linguistic theory correctly presents language (or the significatory system broadly construed) as an enabling/constraining structural array of language instantiation choices, such as choosing to label a person a *client* instead of a guest or friend. An identical point about *absent* and *present* corpus of options can be made for the ideas of power and norms. The implications of any act also reflect its choice compared to alternative chains of actions, consequences, and outcomes (power potentials) and to alternate judgments/sanctions, and frames for judging the good and the right (normative potentials). If we hire a job candidate, the implications of that hire are related to how that candidate (vs. others) fits into the organization's role-meaning system, but also vs. the others, we could have hired instead. It also relates to the worth and legitimacy of that hire vs. others. Additionally, we can already elaborate: hiring the candidate involves, or even presupposes, the candidate actually being in a position as hirable, with a relation to the organization that, indeed and in part, *constitutes* the organization in relation to the virtual structure of other ways hiring could have gone and the other past and current and potential future members, or parts, of the organization-system. Social interaction, that is, communication, has constitutive force because it projects a virtual structure of alternately possible and spatio-temporally separate constitutive acts. Hiring person X now is constitutive as an interactive process with respect to all other separate and possible hires.

Another example might make this point clearer. A referee signaling a foul in a US pro basketball game has significance because (a) it has a technical meaning, opposed to signaling, for example, a double-dribble; (b) it is something the referee is empowered to do, as opposed to a player or coach claiming a foul occurred; (c) it can be done correctly and legitimately, opposed to, for example, being overridden by another referee or corrected on replay; and (d) it can be a constitutive part of the actual flow of the game and contextualized in the 48 min constituting "the game," including earlier and later fouls, as well as the two or more hours the game actually consumes. Calling the foul is part of the constitution of the system, just as letting the play continue by not calling the foul (presence/absence) would have constituted the system along a different trajectory. Further, the *meaning* of the foul, the *power* to make the call, and the way it fits the expectations (*norms*) within the game and across the league are all instantiated at the moment.

The ideas in the quotations from Giddens, together with the elaboration we just suggested, provide us with a foundation for the understanding of organizational communication as the constitution of organizations and human practices fundamental to them. We believe that two additional concepts aid us in refocusing organizational theory on communication: the structurational hermeneutic, and conlocutions.

3.2 The Structurational Hermeneutic

As mentioned earlier, one prevalent source of insights for ST is hermeneutic philosophy (Bleicher, 1980; Palmer, 1969). Hermeneutics is broadly linked to interpretation. For instance, the earliest notions of hermeneutics involved the quest to interpret Biblical texts as a method to uncover deeper layers of scriptural meaning and implications. But a variety of scholars turned to the practice of Biblical interpretation as a model for the study of all sorts of meaningful material, not just texts. They hoped to find a method for human and social studies with the sort of power that quantitative scientific methods have for the natural sciences.

The most important hermeneutics scholar of the twentieth century, Gadamer (1975), slammed the door in hopes that hermeneutics could be a social-scientific method. Rather, he argued that humans and social relations are interpretive in their essence. Whenever we speak or hear, we do so in an interpretive context that is based in our social world to that point in space and time, and social researchers who may be studying those people in conversations also do so from their own different interpretive context.

Giddens, and structuration theory, exhibit deep influence from Gadamer's philosophy. Following our previous analysis (McPhee & Iverson, 2009), we can articulate the main ideas that have flowed from Gadamer's theorizing into ST. First, human topics of inquiry, such as culture and linguistic patterns, have a different ontological status than physical objects or instruments or methods. We live with objects and instruments but, we "live within" our human cultural and linguistic systems. Human life engulfs and gives sustenance to phenomena such as decisions, interaction, and social relations; as a crucial aspect of this, social interaction gives pragmatic as well as semantic meaning and relevance to material tools and work-objects, as resources, constraints, or conditions.

Second, Gadamer is especially famous for arguing that all discourse occurs from within a tradition which *prejudices* (meaning it preorients our anticipative understanding in usage) our comprehension of the discourse, and our understanding progresses through the mutual mediation of old and new reference frames. An understanding of what a *real job* means has certainly evolved from Clair's (1996) research, which showed that to young adults, a real job was stable, required an education, and entailed working a regular 8-5 schedule. Now, most people's definitions could now include remote and even gig work.

Third, this mutual mediation proceeds as a hermeneutic circle. Starting with some part of discourse—a word, a statement—we work to understand it in the light of our expectation and standpoint about the whole discourse—book or ongoing conversation; then our sense of the part to recast our understanding of the whole discourse, and our earlier standpoint, in the light of the part confronting us, in a process of bimodal reflection and linguistic/cultural articulation. This process is not a method, but an aspect of human life; it is always potentially contextually adaptive, creative, mutually transformative, and judgment-based, even though it typically takes advantage of available routine patterns (see Giddens, 1976a, 1976b).

As a result, social researchers should not be troubled by the fact that many or all of their findings are context-relative. Rather, they should treat context as an essential feature of their research and as a stimulus directing their study efforts toward a rich elucidation of any topic they focus on. Thus, Iverson's work on communication in *Communities of Practice* (CoP; Iverson, 2010b) opened up the study of a CoP's communicative failings, such as the L'Aquila communication crisis, where earthquake forecasters were charged with manslaughter for providing probability statements—statements that had one meaning in their CoP, but took on another meeting in the larger society. This led to their organization changing its community and communication approach to become a better organization.

We think ST makes possible a restatement of the central ideas of hermeneutics. Specifically, we claim it is richer to replace the idea of an interpretive circle from part to whole with a structurational circle built on the duality of structuration. When we interpret a sentence, we are producing an interpretation, but that act necessarily dually reproduces the structural resources (including the pre-interpreted whole text and *its* context) at that moment. Similarly, when we turn to the whole text, from the standpoint of the interpreted part, we are immediately, inescapably producing its resultant sense by drawing on, as a resource, the insight from the part—reproducing its unity with the whole, but also therein reproducing both as resources for future interpretation.

The idea of a whole, or even a part, possessing presence, or unity of meaning is challenged by poststructuralists, a challenge that we think is averted by ST's conception of the presence/absence dialectic and virtuality.

One aspect of interpretation, as involved in the hermeneutic circle recast by ST, is that a text or social act being interpreted is not just a literal part of a *whole* text. As social activity, it is the text-in-use produced, enacted, formulated, or performed as meaningful in an ongoing system of cooperative, or conflictive or chaotic, communicative and physical transactions and events. Equally, it draws on, and is understandable through, its connection, interwoven, in a virtual web of syntactic, semantic, pragmatic, and contextually related differences, and power-laden and norm-oriented, and is the absent structure implicit for, and thereby giving, a present act constitutive force. But any action is not just produced as part of these webs of relations. It reproduces them as well—makes the pre-given webs of signification and significance relevant in the present as an aspect of their very nature. In fact, a suggestive conception of social action or communication is a transformation from one structure, involving significatory, potency, and evaluation dimensions, into another—from the past into the new. Calling a foul in basketball, for instance, transforms the situation from a flowing game with its own structure, to a liminal time-space with its own rules, wherein players can mill around randomly until one lines up and is empowered to shoot free-throws while others interact to orient themselves to fight for rebounds.

The hermeneutic circle is an ongoing process of interpretation. That circle is not always a consistent process. Interpretive construction of a whole text, practice, situation, or interaction system may flow easily, or issue in routine conflicts, or it may be roiled by incongruencies or tensions (Putnam et al., 2016) or multiple layers that can contradict one another (Foot & Groleau, 2011). The structurational hermeneutic carries with it a basic paradox: every interpretation involves a constraint (X cannot mean Y), but every constraint is entangled with an enablement. Paid family leave seemed like a new option, but instead, "I'm trapped between taking leave and satisfying my family but violating my work culture, or not taking it, with opposite results."

The structurational hermeneutic-transformative circle makes possible, and inevitable, the mostly tacit bearing of the past on the present and the equally tacit anticipation of the future. The circle of past-present and present-future, of reproduction and production in Giddens' duality of structuration, is the richest possible departure, and the most productive orientation we can derive, from the idea that hermeneutics, or anything else, is primarily a method that can be used to lay bare the essence of communication for authoritative study.

In sum, and as expounded earlier, ST has formulated the idea that the constitution of society involves the presence/absence dialectic regarding both the latent, absent semantic web and the ongoing interactive social system with episodes distanciated in space and time. The structurational hermeneutic elucidates some aspects of societal constitution. But another added concept with special importance for understanding the communicative constitution of organizations is *conlocution*.

3.3 Conlocutions

The concept of *conlocution* uses and transforms some notions from speech act theory (especially Austin, 1975; Searle, 1969, 1975) and its conceptual scheme, broadly recognized as explicitly relevant to the constitution of social reality and thus of organizations. Briefly, the concept of conlocutions affords us a clear prototype to illustrate how organizational communication, in particular, is constitutive, representing "categories of accomplishments" (McPhee & Iverson, 2002, p. 7).[1] Conlocutions provides a means to identify and name the constitutive process in communicative acts.

[1] McPhee and Iverson (2002) offer a full description of conlocutions which includes a comparison of conlocutions in two organizations; McPhee and Iverson (2009a, 2009b, 2009c) provide an applied example of conlocutions.

To illustrate Speech Act Theory and conlocutions, an order such as "make some coffee," taken as an individual act (an *illocution* Speech Act Theory) can be complied with, as an individual choice by the hearer (*perlocution* or action in response to the illocution). The alternative might be a simple refusal, perhaps signaling disrespect, or a disagreement that can evolve into a discussion of the best course of action. Or it might provoke, from a child (or professor), a temper tantrum or adolescent insolence. All of these are possible *perlocutions*. However, more than speech acts are happening within the context of a social system such as an organization. The organization is being constituted in that moment as well, analytically we consider these *conlocutions*. In many organizations, following a legitimate order is part of the nature of the organization, an expected routine that is part of a larger framework of self-structuring, planning, and designed coactivity. Refusal of an order may not just be disrespect or insolence: it is insubordination or even mutiny, and is serious in a very different way from a temper tantrum—as was revealed, for instance, when executive after executive refused to follow orders of President Nixon in 1973, leading to a succession of, essentially, firings of undeserving executives and eventually to the impeachment of the President. Thus, responding to an order, an illocutionary act, typically results not just in a perlocutionary result but in a conlocution that, by its essential link to a mandated subordinate response (through yielding or resisting), constitutes a power/knowledge complex—the organization.

Another example is the initiation of new members, which is more than a ceremony, including the repetition of words. The illocutionary act of expressing the words of initiation does not merely result in others possibly reacting to people as new members (a perlocutionary act—the response of listeners), but also constitutes the organization as it accomplishes both membership and the organization (McPhee & Iverson, 2009). The accomplishment lies between the illocutionary act (discursive acts) and perlocutionary act (reaction by others), but it is useful to point toward the accomplishment. The organization, as accomplishment, is communicatively constituted in the process of communication.

Conlocutions accomplish changes in the organizational fabric that are constitutively interwoven. They are a specifically relevant case of words having consequences—not just linguistic-pragmatic or varied social consequences, but the injection of specifically organizational power—through meaning-imbued organizational discourse—into ongoing social interactivity. As such, they are a good example of what we will call transtructive rules in the following text.

3.4 Constitution

We have, in earlier work (McPhee & Iverson, 2009), chosen three foci for discussion: the constitution of signs, of agents, and of organizations. Other approaches have looked at signs and agents, treating them as equivalent to organizations. However, those perspectives ignore key differences. A sign or agent is not an organization. Next, we describe each type and discuss their interconnection.

3.4.1 Constitution of Signs

A sign is any sort of recognizable thing whose meaning stands for something else such as written words or emojis. Famously, signs have a two-part, or three-part, structure: the sign or signifier *per se*; the object or signified for which it stands; and perhaps an interpretant—a grounding (Peirce, 1955; de Saussure, 2011). Our common mental images of signs are written (Suassure), but most chicken-tracks in the dirt are not signs. Signs have meaning (they are constituted) insofar as they have a place in and are incorporated in, the symbolic/systemic web of language that exists across time and space (web of distantiation discussed earlier). For a new sign to emerge, a social process of expressing, sharing, and understanding the sign has to emerge as a place in the web. Communication and signs associated with that communication also are *situated*, that is, spatially and temporally located, whereas language is *virtual and outside of time (in a sense recognizing its rootedness in social practice)*. Communication presupposes an acting subject, *whereas language is specifically subject-less*. In addition, communication presupposes sign-meaning oriented, in the first instance, to other subjects, whereas the signage systems of language are virtually paradigmatic, but over the range of possible *conversations*, in ways analyzed by Mead (1934) and Bakhtin (1976)—intrinsically and practically "oriented toward another" (p. 118; Giddens, 1979, 46–48, 54, 68–71). Established phrases have a known place in the mesh through discursive as well as tacit understandings. Use or experience of the sign, of course, reproduces the web as a foundational and contextual phenomenon that it has already drawn on for meaning and significance.

Giddens does suggest supplementing the notion of the web of symbols with that of Wittgenstein's *language game*. We can use an example of an order, extrapolated from Taylor and Van Every (2000), to explicate the notion and relevance of the language game, which is a sort of interaction sequence in which participants need not have any sense of purpose or semantic meaning, just a pragmatic notion of what to say to keep going in the game. If a manager said, "Turn out the lights," and a subordinate flipped the switch, the language game would be constituted purely by the sequence of acts, which could be reiterated, ordering then obeying then ordering. Moreover, the order "Turn out the lights" is constituted by being foci in distinction from other word sequences, other English-language meanings, in a domain of practical uses of comparable sequences. *Microsoft* is a sign since it has a place in webs of names, of referents, and of company-name usage—but it is not the same as the process of webs that *is* Microsoft—on the contrary.

But, of course, the question of "how and why does this sequence get enacted?" arises, leading us to shift focus to the enmeshed understanding of the agents, then more broadly to the factors of *meaning* of the enactment, *power* to speak and obey, and *legitimate* accountability of each act in the game. When these facts about the mesh contextualizing language games are recognized, the model of a language game becomes a simple model of practice. For example, doctors performing an operation "know how to go on" after each contextually meaningful word ("scalpel!") or act, and their surgical team has complementary understandings of what happens, or can happen, next.

Following this chain of reasoning led Giddens to deny the primacy of the model of textual meaning open to interpretation by what Ricoeur (1981a, 1981b) calls *distanciation*, where, as a text is fixed, normally in words inscribed on a page, its meaning is opened to interpretation as an autonomous whole—even a sort of world. Giddens points out that texts are utterly dependent on practices, which may alter the conditions of their interpretation—even the "fixated" words themselves. Textual discourse is not elevated into, for example, special organizational significance by Ricoeur's distanciation, but rather is subordinate to the flow of ways it is treated in communicative practice. However, when we recognize the way practice vitally contributes to the constitution of signs, we are at or past the border separating this account from that of the constitution of organizations.

3.4.2 Constitution of Agents

We have discussed the specific concept of agency in structuration theory. An agent is typically a living, conscious human being who can act, and whose actions are meaningful and significant, as we discussed in detail in our prior chapter, as well as in the introductory chapter. In line with an earlier discussion (McPhee & Iverson, 2009), several points are important to reiterate.

As noted earlier, we find immense theoretic value in Giddens' (1984) well-known *stratification model of the agent*, which includes (a) discursive knowledgeability, (b) practical consciousness, powers of (c) reflexive monitoring, and (d) rationalization. These describe overt characteristics of socially empowered activity, embedded in tacit cognitive webs, that ground such public demonstrations of agency as purposeful conduct, accounts, judgment, anxiety management, and competent interaction. All require and develop human mental powers: if you try to treat oysters, computers, and committees like newborns, in the usual situation of nurturing, your efforts will all fail.

However, decades of social/communicative theorizing convinces us that the mental powers and the meaningful contexts supporting and maintained by them are largely social in origin—development and education, acquisition of contextual knowledge and practice of social skills, all transpiring through social involvement. However, *ability* to make a difference is by no means assured: challenges to agency for the subaltern or anyone else—themselves knots in the social fabric—are features of the web's circumscribing continuity and strength. Certain US residents are constrained from effective democratic voting, or being promoted to responsible corporate positions, by all sorts of deterrents. However, their action barriers are crucially unlike those facing low-status members of societies like medieval England, where enfranchisement would be not so much blocked as inconceivable and evidence of madness. Though, we should acknowledge, history is marked by figures—Joan of Arc, Elizabeth I—who achieved feats readily described as inconceivable and mad.

Opposed to this view that agency amounts to human powers in a meaningful social context, varied theorists have considered the notion that social collectivities are, equally, agents—that they might play agentive roles in the social/symbolic/pragmatic mesh. As US Supreme Court Chief Justice John Marshall noted, "The great object of an incorporation is to bestow the character and properties of individuality on a collective and changing body of men" (Providence Bank vs. Billings, 29 U.S. 514, 1830). In political theory, Allison (1971) argued for the ubiquity and utility of what he called the *rational actor* model of governments [or organizations], which described them as making human-like decisions in response to goals and manifest options. However, he immediately described two complementary, superior models: the *organizational-process model*, which explained the decisions as results of crafting as people follow specific organizational structures and routines, and the *government-politics model*, pointing to bargaining and decision-mangling that supplements the process model to lead to decisions attributed to the organizations as *actors*. In fact, both of these sources imply that some trouble is required to get to the agent image assigned to the collectivity, whether the legal machination of incorporation procedures or the social outcome from varied interpersonal processes. Koschmann et al. (2012) make this type of claim when they say a cross-sector partnership (XSP) is "a single organizational entity that has the capacity to act, to exhibit agency, or to otherwise 'make a difference' for the participants involved, their member organizations, and the broader communities and problem domains in which XSPs exist" (p. 333).

Our rationale for giving primacy to individual humans is rooted in the structurational model of agentive powers, which enables us to theoretically account for the appeal of this view that organizations can act, possess values and views, communicate, and even own property at the same time avoiding several basic conceptual dangers of that approach. First, saying the organization itself "does something" legitimizes the oversimplification of its members' capacities, interactions, and coordination processes, which really accomplish the "something." Second, the view that organizations "do things" falls into a tempting metaphysical thought pattern deriving from ancient times, and especially from romantic (i.e., the Romantic Age in the 1800s) mindsets, of depicting organizations, or other groups, as possessing a mind and needs, embodied in a leader, an authority—*"l'etat, c'est moi"*—so that the organization *needs* (a term we are tempted to read as wants or craves) clear authority in order to function (Meindl et al., 1985; Taylor & Van Every, 2014). Third, saying the organization itself "acted" or "communicated" implies that the whole organization favored the action, whereas usually it mainly served an elite group's viewpoint interest, masking power imbalances or conflict among members. Viewing organizations as agents is based on an ideology, in a sense we will cover shortly. Presenting the organization as the doer is as memorable as saying the giant head of the Wizard of Oz is really an agent speaking, no matter how much we protest that we, as students of organizational communication, really are also taking care to look behind the curtain.

3.4.3 Constitution of Organizations

Interestingly, we concur with the view that by *saying* organizations are powerful, willful, fallible entities, we do help constitute them—but not as agents in the sense common in social theories of agency, rather simply as the sort of social collectivity that can organize themselves to give, in certain situations, those reflexive impressions. When members [or outsiders] say "we, the army, triumphed" or "The Fed reacted," their speech positions them in relation to other members and events, and draws on and reproduces a system of discourse and practice that (in the specific confluences we describe later) indeed has constitutive power for the organization. However, that leaves out an awful lot. In a nutshell: Organizations must be constituted, at least in part, by the activity, especially communication, of their members.

We have discussed the constitution of signs and agents with the specific intent to distinguish them from the constitution of organizations. As discussed earlier, signs are constituted in systems that are primarily semiotic; though the powers and history involved in practice are sources of meaning, the system of signification itself is virtual, composed of differences/relations of a sign with all its practical possibilities; organizations are systems of meaningful communication and practice. Organizations (and, obviously, communication) *carry* and *accomplish* semiosis, partly by making effective history and therein enacting distanciation, a presence/absence dialectic of a sort very distinct from, though dependent on, the virtual system of signification [and of power-resources, and of normative sanction-structures], in that it has positive elements. An order from a manager, in organizational communication, is different in space and time, and different from all other possible linguistic forms the manager might use. However, the order does occur here and now, mobilizing managerial power to comprise an obligation, a threat—or even a helpful suggestion, but it is real, not primarily virtual, and has all sorts of future implications—results of those words being uttered. Even common sense will tell us that organizations, as well as various other sorts of social systems, differ from signs or (human) agents in ways that are not merely differences of features—organizations are made organizational insofar as they go beyond the sign that names them, and beyond the humans whose practices they organize, in the virtuality of distanciation. Now, equally, the constitution of organizations is codependent with that of sign systems, since, as noted in Giddens' comments at the beginning of this chapter, the presence/absence differences making up sign systems are perversely congruent with the complex of spatial/temporal/semiotic presence/absences constituting an organization, or other social system. (Refer to our discussion under "Constitution of Signs" earlier in this chapter.) Plus, *communicative relations* among agents, especially among the subclass of agents who are its members, are enacted and patterned in ways that precisely make an organization what it is. We should remember this idea—the constitution of organizations, and for that matter of social interaction of all sorts, rests on the idea of agency though is irreducible to agency.

A second aspect of the constitution of organizations is the dimension of power.

Giddens, at several points, blatantly emphasizes the importance of power and its centralization in his analysis of cities, but his tenets hold equally well for organizations. We can bring together several of Giddens' (1981) statements:

> [Like a city, an organization has] storage capacity [implicated in] time-space distanciation and the generation of power,... It is a special kind of container, a crucible for the generation of power. ...We may distinguish two forms of storage: [first,] storage of material or allocative resources, [which involves] a range of time-space control [like a bank account that can be drawn on almost anywhere. But that is] less significant than [second,] the storage of authoritative resources...[which] involves above all the retention and control of information or knowledge. But for relational and informational as well as physical resources, storage...involves not simply the physical containment of [resources] (which is its least interesting form.) The term should rather be understood as implying a range of time-space control. Power is generated by the transformation/mediation relations inherent in the allocative and authoritative resources comprised in structures of domination. [The organization is a] generator of effective space [for the exercise of power], or what I have called...a storage container, that permits a... unique level of...time-space distanciation, [by serving as the] locus of transformation/mediation relations.... (p. 144, 92, 94–95, 96).

Thus, if we start from the model of a simple but meaning-drenched practice—a socially contextualized language game as previously described—we need several added ideas to get to the constitution of an organization. First, a practice (especially an organizational one) cannot be merely simple, never self-sufficient, or even closed in the long run. Every private conversation or meeting already draws past interactions and practices in, and will spill out into others. Giddens phrases this idea as interactions shading off into the larger social fabric, and structurating spatio-tempero-paradigmatic distantiation. Boden (1994) and Taylor and Van Every (2000) phrase it as *lamination*. To foreshadow, we will phrase this idea with the more dynamic, less predictable terms *flow* or *confluence*. Another way practices are open regards power: agents must have the power to engage in them, avoiding the many challenges to agency noted earlier. *Spilling out* and *shading off* describe the way power flows or is distanciated across a social system.

Second, as practices spill over, if a complex organization continues to exist, it still requires a recognizable tendency toward unification (though processes of disorganization may overwhelm any such tendency). Not necessarily toward rational unity—not one ring to bind them—but a complex of bounding, coagulating, and orienting processes, usually driven, at least in part, by powerful agents. Giddens extended a discussion of processes like this as *social integration*. (He noted that, correspondingly, societal institutions can exhibit 'system integration.) Typically, for a complex organization, social integration processes are patterned enough to rise to a level that allows reflexive self-identification—and organization-identification—by members and others. In general, they can say, in a meaningful though ideology-plagued way, "We, my army, battled that other army to a standstill!" Tendencies like this accomplish distanciation, too, but by reducing or compressing distance. That can happen in varied ways, through varied media. Giddens stresses centralized records, first of material transactions and events, then of personnel surveillance, as concentrating power in ways that constrain and direct other social integration processes. I, the record-keeper, can constrain and orient your activity simply by overtly observing you, but even more by mobilizing my knowledge of your activity to reward or punish you. Similarly, an organization's administrative staff can be centralized to plan, adapt, and make future-oriented decisions; power-collecting processes like these constitute the distinctive systems that are complex organizations.

Third, as frequently reiterated earlier, somewhat definite processes of communication and action constitute the organization. We delineate four such processes in upcoming chapters. But we do need to turn, as part of our discussion of "constitution," to address in more depth a topic already emphatically exposed as crucial for and focused on by organizational communication scholars: the phenomena of power, meaning, and normative legitimation.

3.5 The Modalities—An Augmented Formulation

As we have reiterated multiple times, action and structure inextricably involve the modalities meaning, norms, and power, "integral elements of interaction" (Giddens, 1981, p. 123). Giddens introduced this trinary distinction in 1976 at the latest: "Structures of signification can be analyzed as systems of *semantic rules*, those of domination as systems of *resources*, those of legitimation as systems of *moral rules*. In any concrete situation of interaction, members draw on these…as an integrated set rather than three discrete components" (1976, p. 123–124). We use Giddens' term *modalities* to refer to the three elements or dimensions just as Giddens does: "the mediation of interaction and structure in processes of social reproduction" via "dimensions that are *combined* in differing ways in social practices" (1976 p. 122; 1979, p. 81). He gives some fairly specific illustrations of such combinations:

> language use is itself [normatively] sanctioned by the very nature of its *public* character. The very identification of acts or of aspects of interaction—their accurate description, as grounded hermeneutically in the capability [power] of an observer to go on in a form of life—implies the interlacing of meaning, normative elements, and power (1984, p. 28–29).

More specifically:

> [Argument in a conversation] is characteristically imbalanced in relation to the possession of ...resources or facilities which participants bring to and mobilize [i.e., articulate] as elements of its production, thus directing its course. These thus include the skills whereby the interaction is constituted as *meaningful*, but also...to control the conduct of others who are parties to that interaction, including the possession [of] superior linguistic or dialectical skills of one person in conversation with another, the possession of relevant types of *technical knowledge*, the mobilization of authority or force, etc. (p. 112–113).

And:

> Since the sanctions which follow the transgression of moral claims do not operate with...mechanical inevitability, but involve the reactions of others, there is typically some free space for the transgressor...to negotiate the character of the sanction which is to follow. This is one way in which the production of a normative order exists in close relation with the production of meaning [as well as power]. [Labeling of conduct] affects sanctions...[as is] familiar, and formalized in courts of law.... (p. 109).

Relations like these exhibit the grounding of each of these crucial social/communicative phenomena—meaning, power, norms—in the other two. This grounding goes beyond the fact that all three dimensions are crucial to our theorizing: based on the traditions of scholarship described in Chapter 1, the foundational importance of each of these phenomena is already well argued, in systems, interpretive, and critical theories. Moreover, ST posits that these three phenomena are all always present in social interaction, with different emphasis possible in different explanatory accounts. These are reflected in different everyday accounts, too: "here's how I saw the situation," or "I did it to achieve the following goals," or "it was the right thing to do." And, as we've noted earlier, Giddens notes important, even essential relations among the modalities.

While Giddens uses examples like this of relations among the modalities, he does not place special emphasis on the range of specific combinations that might be more characteristic of everyday interaction. Indeed, he announced early (1976a, 1976b) that he would avoid listings of relations like this, based on his argument that analysis of particular rules really required their study as used in combination with other contextualizing rules in strategic interaction [or as patterns in long-term institutions]. It made sense, as well, since his primary orientation was toward power/domination analysis. The other two dimensions or elements are regularly approached as depending on, providing, and patterning societal power.

However, we take a few steps beyond this juncture in ST theorizing. First, we argue that the set of three analytically separable modalities is not sufficient to explain the constitution of, for example, an organization. We therefore introduce a new modality, constitution, and argue later that, by the very nature of social action, we must explicate its transtructive relations with the other modalities.

Second, we provide a further analysis of relations among the modalities that will prove valuable for organizational communication. We rename such relationships *transtructions* or *transtructional* rules. The ones mentioned earlier are illuminating examples, and we cover several more later. However, we mostly explicate them in Chapters 5–8 of this book and illustrate them in Figure 3.1.

We find it valuable to distinguish the term *Constitute, meaning* "amount to" or "make it what it is," from a specific use of *constitute, as a necessary dimension implicit in social interaction.* The Constitutive force of communication is rooted in the duality of structure, since production (doing or saying something, making a move] and reproduction [reflexively grounding what's done/said in the past [and virtual future] that orient it, and equally, though tacitly, reiterating the already done in what's being done now) are both processes of Constitution. However, interaction—production/reproduction—enacts, and maintains/transforms, and constitutes the organization and its intertwined power/meaning/normative resources.

It may seem paradoxical to have constitution be a single dimension or part of overall social processes that are themselves Constitutive. However, a main principle of our analysis is that communication, itself, has constitutive force. So, labeling an object *spoon* indicates the object's meaning—what kind of object it is, within what class [kitchen utensils], and with what likely function. But, including

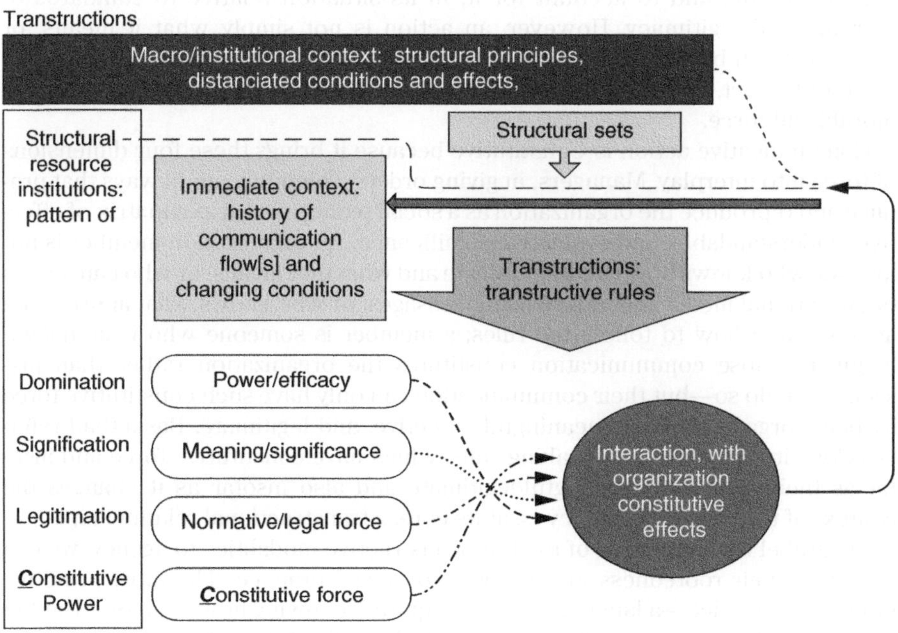

Figure 3.1 Transtructions.

and beyond those, labeling's constitutive force lies in its incorporation of the object into the human stream of discourse and practice.

As we just indicated, the specific examples cited from Giddens' writing are prima facie good examples of transtructive rules. They cover cases where the results of one action are dependent on the context involving other actions. The example of conversational argument, given earlier, is a good illustration of how the force of the arguer's meaningful words [in this case quite literally sanctioned by the power arrangement involving the speakers] is sanctioning based on the power-endowed context behind the statement. For instance, a manager starting their response to a subordinate's reasoning by saying, "Are you crazy?" serves to cast doubt on the sheer sensible-ness of the subordinate's communicative intent. However, a subordinate saying that to a manager may be tantamount to rebellion (dependent on the power and norms implicit in the context—in a loose hierarchic arrangement, it may be a form of kidding). Or saying to the manager, "Oh, you're sooo wrong," is easily heard as sarcastic implication of acceptance of the manager's correctness—and therein supportive of, reproducing the manager's power. It implicates the subordinate in the contextual power arrangement.

Correlatively, the deepest archetypes of transtructive rule can be found in the concepts of agency and social practice. We have discussed agency at some length: it is, at once, the capacity to make a difference—power; the capacity to give meaningful, knowledgeable rationalizations of acts; and the power to reflexively monitor action, and to account for it, in its situation relative to standards of morality and legitimacy. However, an action is not simply what it means, or whether it can be done, or should be done—it is what *is* done, the constitutive force of the act, distinct though in relation to its effective and interpretive and moral/legal force.

Communicative action is Constitutive because it brings these four dimensions of force into interplay. Managers, in giving orders, communicate in ways that produce and reproduce the organization as a social reality as well as a matrix of effective, understandable, and evaluative significance. An organization member is not just one who knows how to communicate and what that means, or who can access organizational media and indeed send messages, or who knows what appropriate action is and how to follow the rules; a member is someone who is actually a member, whose communication constitutes the organization rather than just seeming to do so—but their communication can only have such constitutive force by being organizationally meaningful, effective, and legitimate. Basketball referees Constitute the game by making calls, which have constitutive force and insofar as their calls are meaningful/legitimate and also insofar as it changes the context of the next call. Agency is, at its core, a transtructional relationship.

In parallel to the relation of the four transtructive modalities to agency, we can elaborate their rootedness in the notion of social practice. The most primitive model of a practice—a language game—requires "knowing how to go on." But the game is not just the rules—it is *playing*. Basketball refereeing is maintaining the game's Constituting order by (constitutively) making calls, manifesting the *power* to, for example, position oneself to detect violations and regulate the game, *understanding* the threats to an orderly game—for example, belligerent players—and the acts needed to maintain order, and displaying a *normative* commitment to follow the rules without favoritism. It takes little knowledge of basketball to realize that these dimensions intertwine—transtruct from one aspect to another. As in the specific practice of refereeing, practices too are, at the bedrock level, transtructive relationships.

Perhaps the most noted example of a transtructive rule, for organizational communication scholarship, is Giddens' (1984) conception of ideology (p. 33; cf. Mumby, 1988). Giddens himself explains his notion: "To analyze the ideological aspects of symbolic orders…is to examine *how structures of signification are mobilized to legitimate the interests of hegemonic groups*" (1979, p. 188, emphasis in original). Elaborating on this conception, Giddens advances several other tenets. First, he defines interests as "facilitating the possibility [sic] of A achieving his or her wants" (p. 189). He thus allows for interests to be objective, since courses of events can, in fact, lead to want-satisfaction. Second, the phrase "interests of hegemonic groups" is shorthand for interests shared by actors due to their group membership—for instance, an interest in preserving the status quo state of resource imbalance that allows privileged-group members to use resources to satisfy any wants they have. Third, ideology has two faces: it includes strategic discourse that can, for example, coopt, defeat, or destroy advocates of social change. But it also has a more prevalent and unquestionable institutional face, involving "symbolic orders [that] sustain forms of domination in the context of everyday experience" (Giddens) One of his central examples here is the idea-cluster around "personal privacy," wherein the turmoil of family life—especially the repression, mistreatment, and deprivation/profligacy families can involve—has in modern times been *sequestered* as apolitical, counterposed to the order, discipline, and productivity characteristic of public and especially industrial routine.

Other examples of very deep-seated transtructive rules are patterns—termed *structural sets* by Giddens—characteristic of specific social orders, where one sort of resource can be converted into another, like *money: capital (i.e., ownership of tools of production): power over labor*, for capitalism (1984, p. 186). He notes that this sort of "transmutation" can occur inside one of the modal dimensions, or across them. This one is a deep structural feature of the emergent capitalistic system. As in Giddens' example of privacy as ideology, the *meaning* of a term like *private property* supports wealth/*power* inequality by *normatively/legally* legitimating it as a matter of individual rights. A general structural set, perhaps characteristic of most societies through history, is *allocative resources=authoritative resources* since it is clear that this transmutation very frequently occurs in both directions.

It can be useful to analyze relations of specific types of power, meaning, normative, and constitutive phenomena—what we have called transtructional rules—as schematic tools to explain communication, and organizational communication in particular. However, communication is quintessentially a dynamic process, and a set of rules or static dimensional relationships does not, as a matter of fact, display that dynamism very well. One valuable result of a term like transtruction is that it is evidently dynamic: communication transtructs the modalities, as power begets meaning, which begets norms, which begets constitutive force. However, to find the apotheosis of communication's dynamism, we must turn to the concept discussed in the next chapter—our central concept, *flow*.

4

The Four Flows Model

Our four flows model of organizational communication is an extension and specification of structuration theory, explicating how communication has constitutive force, in general, and specifically for organizations. In this chapter, we articulate the model and argue that its generality and flexibility is valuable and perhaps necessary because organizations are constituted in more than one way, fitting more than one specified model of communication. However, before making that argument, we must explain several concepts, especially *flow*, which we think of as somewhere between a metaphor and, itself, a model or even an ontology (Seibt, 2009) for communication. We offer extensive, though certainly not exhaustive, reflections on flow as a means to see the conceptual perspective as well as the possibilities that flow offers to reflect on the communicative constitution of organizations.

4.1 Flow and Constitution

First, before we explicate the metaphor, a *flow* as we use the term typically refers to multiple communicative practices that are analytically distinct, though in fact often performed conjointly, and prototypically essential in the constitution of the organization. As we put it elsewhere, flows consist of "circulating systems or fields of messages" (McPhee & Zaug, 2009, p. 29). Messages, in this sense, can refer to units as big as, say the US Constitution or an official meeting transcript (McPhee et al., 2006) and as small as a derogatory word. However, *messages* does not really capture the processual, coherent nature of communication or the variety of analytic units it involves. *We believe that all organizational communication is, ontologically, necessarily part of a flow*, since a

The Communicative Constitution of Organizations: The Four Flows Model, First Edition.
Robert D. McPhee, Karen K. Myers, and Joel O. Iverson.

message with no varied predecessors or successors is surely not organizational. So, we substitute *flow* as an encompassing category, relative to and conditional upon an array of other flows. For instance, strategic decision-making and public relations are good examples of flow-immersed subprocesses. When organizational leaders make decisions that define the future direction of the organization to outsiders, and members of public relations communicate those plans, they, for example, clarify, alter or reaffirm the organization's mission and methods for achieving those goals. Such messages are contextually immersed and thus part of a flow constituting the organization for various stakeholders, including workers, the community, outside agents, and all the individuals that the organization serves (March & Simon, 1958). Likewise, when new recruits enter, are trained, and begin to perform roles in the organization, sometimes negotiating with supervisors or other coworkers about how they will perform the role, they constitute an important element of the organization by shaping what it means to be a member of the organization. While it is useful to understand these as flows, we must first note that the terms *a flow* or *flows* are perhaps confusing since we can distinguish a specified flow from a more generalized flow only analytically. The four flows we specify later are making specifically unique organizational claims and serve a specific organizational purpose. In the social systems of today, any purportedly distinct flow depends on and merges with an overall societal communication flow. It can be very useful to speak of "a flow" about a specific topic or starting with a particular message, and we do so below, but thinking of a lot of separate flows, one per organization or person or topic, runs against our general conception elaborated here, and implies an impossible task of exhaustively articulating every flow and subflow that most scholars would wish to avoid. It is more realistic and less conceptually dangerous to speak of individual streams as *currents* that might be thought of as *intermingled* in an inclusive flow.

Now, explicating the metaphor, what is a flow? We can identify several facets. The term flow obviously suggests that communication is like a river or some other moving body of water. It most often relates to fluid dynamics and is applied to phenomena like atmospheric dynamics and electrical currents. *The Oxford English Dictionary* defines *flow* as something that moves "steadily and continuously in a current or stream." This metaphor has been used before in various ways (Deleuze & Guattari, 1987; Latour, 2007; Mintzberg, 1979; also Castells, 2011: Urry, 2007), but primarily used by system theorists to characterize the passage of information signals through predetermined channels such as electrical circuits. However, our metaphor is based on very different assumptions. For instance, we accept, within limits, some of the ideas of process philosophies like those of Whitehead (1929/1985). Like any metaphor, it highlights certain properties of constituted communication, both ones that deserve emphasis and misleading or subordinated ones (Black, 1962). As a way of seeing, like glasses with colored lenses (Deetz, 1992), it lets us see certain things clearly while obscuring others. We discuss some of the positive analogies next.

Flow is a dynamic metaphor—a flow moves; it is liquid, not static. Observing it at a single point, we may have little idea what happens five miles downstream because its basic patterns can change from day to day in contextually constrained, but unpredictable ways. Contrary to the *Oxford English Dictionary* definition, we vigorously deny that communication flows are typically steady and continuous. A single flow can change from a trickle to a river from rainfall, snowmelt, or as other tributaries join it. If we are on shore, swimming in a flow, or in a boat, our observation point changes, too. Our position changes what is seen and unseen in the flow and we can be swept up by it. Relatively defined currents within it might, for some time, retain much of their identity and separability via temperature, velocity, composition, or other factors; they might infuse or be infused by other currents relatively slowly or rapidly. We find the multiple possibilities of the flow metaphor useful for articulating the complexities of organizational constitution as well.

The flow of organizational communication generally has a discernable direction, no matter how dammed up, whorled, and changed by obstacles, islands, etc. The main patterns of communicative flows are analogous to time itself and the varied dynamics of time, with some currents' forward motion affected by contextual obstructions like dams (e.g., remote workers' distance from office context; McPhee & Canary, 2009; Van Zoonen & Sivunen, 2022), or to the basic, cumulative dynamic of communication, whereby new meanings and events are stimulated and contextualized by earlier ones, and serve as context for later communication in multiple ways. In other words, communicative acts are related to earlier and later ones. Individual acts in isolation are less interesting than sequences of such acts within episodes; both can be directly related to past conversations or diverge. For example, surveillance by management can quickly shift grumbling into reciting the corporate motto. This exemplifies the production-reproduction dynamic of structuration and the dynamic character of the structurational hermeneutic. Some constitutive acts are routine and have continuing impact over time, similar to erosion, while others can be strikingly transformative, such as floods.

The flow metaphor can suggest more complexity: also contrary to the Oxford English Dictionary definition above, communication can appear to move in one direction while actually, bending, curving, moving in another, get eddied, roiled, or partly trapped in stable/stagnant pools, and suffer crosscurrents or counterflows (we discuss some of these ideas below as *contraventions*). A riptide is a good example—a flow that holds together alongside other currents that are very different in speed, direction, temperature, etc. Likewise, organizational communication can be ambiguous and can partly or fully change its direction. Different depth levels can flow at different rates and cause surface disruptions.

Flow is also useful for analyzing communicative constitution as discussed in recent organizational theorizing. In earlier chapters, we began to discuss organizational communication scholarship covering a range of phenomena centering on contradictions but more generally involving strains and disruptions of discourse and meaning (Putnam et al., 2016). Many researchers have articulated ideas about these concepts by using terms such as *contradiction*, *paradox*, *dialectic*, *tension*, and even a more technical sense of *disorganization*. We believe that the notion of flow can illuminate such phenomena, in part by focusing more intensely on ways the discourse featuring them is, as Putnam et al. (2016) note, dynamic. In fact, this property is so important that we want to introduce a term—contravention—that we believe is essential for capturing this dynamism which has amazing complications.

Contravention is meant to cover terms such as paradox, contradictions, tensions, and dialectics as they emerge and diverge in communication flows. For instance, contradictions like "You must follow the rules, and you must adapt to situations" and paradoxes such as "Following the rules is inevitably breaking the rules" can be expressed this way, as *standing* formulations, like standing waves (two similar waves flowing simultaneously in opposite directions) creating situations such as *leaders are dependent on followers* or Marxian notions of *forces of production contradict productive relations*. However, these almost always develop over time as pendular or conflictive manifestations, as secondary spin-offs of deeply contradictory structural principles, as collisions of incongruous interpretive schemes, or dynamic, flowing transformations, by specific agents or groups flowing into incongruities. These contradictions can be seen in the use of "free" with released prisoner A: "I'm *free* to join supportive relationships, find new options, or…" as opposed to released prisoner B: "I'm *free* of prison routines, but I don't know what to do, so I see no other option than to rejoin my network and commit crimes." In later chapters, we mention some other complexities within each flow. Additionally, in Chapter 9 on confluent and thus stirred-up flows, we develop these ideas, including contravention, to reorient theory in this more dynamic direction.

A flow can combine with other tributaries, carrying their influx along or getting roiled in new ways, but typically getting strengthened by the force of the ongoing motion. Flows can *combine* in at least two ways. First, the process of changing one flow can have influences upon the others. For example, changing organizational culture and policies to a more team-based approach (self-structuring) can also impact morale and identification with the organization (membership negotiation) as well as the activity coordination when members must work together. Second, comingling of multiple flows can be found in one communicative episode. When an organizational member announces a retirement, they may be simultaneously negotiating the end of their membership, leaving others to coordinate coverage for their absence, potentially revising the structure of that department, and changing the nature of external relationships and contacts. Each of these complexities combines with others, though we may select specific communicative practices for analysis.

4.2 Flows with Agency

Agency occurs when a human takes a stand—becomes anchored in the flow—and exercises the agentive powers discussed by Giddens (1979; see also Chapter 2 of this book) to change the flow of events. Alternatively, they can maintain the flow by reproducing its communication and action. The communication flow includes and involves *agents: they essentially both influence and are influenced by the flow*, as a fact prior to their agency. Newborns emerge as agents in the flow of interaction, analogous in a way to how new members emerge into communicative agency. As our earlier chapters argue, agency is conditional; an important condition, which affirms that it occurs as part of the flow of communication. Agency itself also flows, especially as flowing discourse creates or influences the challenges to agency listed in Chapters 1 and 2. Flows bring agents—insiders or relevant outsiders—into richer or poorer agency in part by locating them in contexts that expand or contract agentive power to avoid or suffer agency blockages. Thus, marketing managers participate in the flow of agency as they receive messages inviting them to important product decision meetings, or encounter and get recognized by important customers or clients. Such communication broadens the power resource array of the agents, even though it might also undermine their agentive power by overloading them or involving them in hopeless problematic situations.

Paradoxically, the agency of agents means they demonstrate power as they interact in the flow—contribute to conversations in ways that change the course of the conversations—despite its dependence on them. That is to say the flow constitutes the agents (and their organization), even while being constituted by them, as explained in Chapter 3. We already noted that the structurational duality view of communication is essentially paradoxical, except that the logic of it does not self-obviate—instead, utilizing the flow conception, we can see, trace analytically, the separate paths of conflicting logics and forces, as they collide in conflicts as well as in their logical development in interaction in nonconflictive sites (see the discussion in Chapter 9).

In addition, we can say that communication constitutes certain contextualizing, internally organized streams of practical human activity, of praxis, that are often called practices. We can see in a new way, and to quote Weick (1979), "know what we think." For example, professionals practicing medicine by performing an operation are participants in a flow including a current of coordinated communication in a surgical arena semipermeably bounded by the walls, sterilization routines, supply stocks, line of patients waiting to enter, are subdivided, etc., that constitute (especially, maintain or transform) its outside.

Significant organizational change impacts not only the organization, but also its environment. A flow can impact change beyond its containing banks like a flooding river, as some natural tendencies overwhelm, for example, attempts by human agents to direct or stabilize it. It can flood, or wipe out mid-stream structures like bridges or islands. Significant organizational change impacts not only the organization, but also its environment. Kelly et al. (2005) describe a syringe exchange program that was originally an illegal organization that secretly provided clean needles and advocated for policy change. Membership was voluntary and decisions were made by consensus. Once organization members became successful at altering the policy, the organization became legal and made major changes in its internal structuring with a more traditional board, employees, and volunteer coordinators. Many members left because of decision-making changes, conflict, and a different environment (less dangerous and exciting for some) as well as opening the possibility of competing organizations.

4.3 The Materiality of Flows

A flow typically carries nonliquid materials (sediment load or even other liquids like oil in water) along with it—silt, which it can drop to be sedimented, or tree-branches that can at some point block or divert the flow. It can be directed or transformed, as well, by obdurate rocks or islands, but wears away at all of these, often over long stretches of time. These suggest potentially valuable ways the metaphor explicates materiality, drawing our attention to the ways materials are processually constituted. As discussed earlier, *materiality* is itself a metaphor (as is material when used as an ontological fundamental concept; see Barad, 2003, but especially Seibt, 2009). Specifically, we concur that the practices of organizing occur in a material and social context that enables and constrains action. When personnel do not have a sufficient budget or supplies in the chain, or possess the needed skills or knowledge to complete tasks, their effectiveness impacts organizational processes. However, if the resources appear, they can themselves have communicative force; a worker's state-of-the-art monitor may have the same force in one current as verbal praise.

Structuration Theory (ST) gives us several main concepts useful for analyzing the idea that communication is itself material in more detail—an array of concepts that can supplement, even supplant, the jargon of materiality (cf. McPhee & Iverson, 2011). The first is a core concept of ST: *structure* itself primally includes *resources* that can be drawn on in action, and the fact that this concept includes material resources is obvious in Giddens' discussion of allocative power resources. We do not believe Giddens is discussing such resources (e.g., guns and ore) as antisocial objects existing outside of the flow of human interaction; such resources exist only as they are involved in an interpretive, enabling interaction flow so that they can be recognized, have meaning and significance, and mobilized in social activity. Even a glance at Giddens' (1981, 1985, 1990) writings critiquing historical materialism would utterly refute the impression that ST ignores or excludes material objects.

A second concept relevant to materiality is the concept of constraint. As one important instance, constraints due to the material human body include: we cannot be in two places at once; only so many people can fit, or fit comfortably, in a physically bounded room enabling face-to-face talk; only a limited number of people can hold the floor, or have their voices heard, in a collective meeting (Giddens, 1984). An organization's staff cannot limit information technology (IT) access too securely and still have it be friendly or useful to ordinary work interaction. Bleich (2013) uses an emphasis on the materiality of communication flow channels to ground his discussion of the myriad power-giving, or power-denying, results of constrained flow.

The idea of constraint is made especially valuable by its dialectical pairing with the seemingly contrary term *enablement*. For ST, every constraint on human activity is an enablement, and vice versa. Thus, we can communicate amazingly well using cellphones, but those objects constrain us from talk with people who cannot afford phones or have forgotten their cellphones...but those constraints can enable us to become conscious of the communication gap, and cellphone addiction, in society generally. The constraint/enablement duality impels scholars to search out the (biased) power-giving implications of (selective) enabling inclusion in organizational membership, coordinated activities, or extra-organizational interchange.

A final concept from ST, especially valuable for the analysis of topics labeled *materiality* is the notion of *conditions*, including material conditions. In particular, social interaction constituting organizations occurs under conditions of institutional structures like English, industrialization, and national security that are agent/resource complexes presumed and used in our lives—indeed, they require special effort to escape or alter. Flows, with their material contents, occur in such a context and environment. The flows themselves depend on the materiality of people keeping the flow going, acting, and employing resources. Enacted policies and structures such as bonuses or sanctions have a materiality as well. In addition, they potentially directly enact each of the four flows in ways that make separating the material and ideal difficult, far from encouraging Four Flow Theory attention to purely the social.

4.4 Flow as Organizational and Communicative

Returning to more general discussion: in this multitude of ways, the metaphor of *flow* changes traditional, common-sense views of organizations and communication. Many of the positive metaphor resemblances point to essential features of organizations, features that make them what they are, while leading us to notice some complexities of organizations. The flow also overtly opposes the *containers metaphor*, which implies that organizations are self-contained like boxes or clocks (Smith & Turner, 1995). Instead, *flow* highlights the strengthening and transformation of some currents and dissolution of others, the unintended, turbulent, but still constitutive results of communication, its power to select meanings that sweep away alternatives, and sometimes battle unintended consequences. For instance, conversations can require and generate strong boundaries of shared memory and purpose, and still have many shared and unintended consequences that decenter agency in context analysis. Interventions in any ongoing process require strong points of stability to even get started, but still mostly get swept away.

Indeed, the range of unusual and valuable notions implicit in the metaphor seems to us to warrant a stronger claim: if a model is essentially a representation of a set of objects/referents that suggest relationships among them, then the array of concepts implicit in flow deserve to be considered a model of communication (Deetz, 1992; McPhee & Poole, 2016). As discussed above, and in more detail later, it shifts our notion of communication in valuable ways by recontextualizing, the structural models of the speech act and the conversation-analytic adjacency pair, or the diagrammatic models of the human or concept network. In contemporary times, it is especially important to realize that a message—a post of a message in social media, or a strategic plan—does not merely go to its designated recipient with unaltered meaning, power implications, etc. Rather, it is an entry in the flow, and can by its nature be swept in all sorts of directions and admixtures. An organization is a broad-based attempted patterning of the flow, capturing and directing a cohesive, intendedly self-organizing mix—so attempted patterning processes are themselves part of the flow, not some divine agency outside it. Just like water drowning people in a tsunami or pushing at a hydroelectric generator, messages are inherently part of a power dynamic, and for any communicated message or interchange, the four flows model, and indeed ST, urge us to search out their power-resource roots and effects.

What are the implications of this notion of flow for communication analysis and research? First, it impels us to change, or refound, our theoretical vocabulary, as discussed further below. It is fine, and emphatically valuable, for researchers to continue to say "message" or "network" or "conversation" (or for that matter "human agent"), as long as we constantly keep in mind that these are contextualized by and conditional on a broader flow and sometimes maybe use the notions of flow and stream to ground our understanding.

Second, it impels us to look beyond any singular, simple communication routine, urging us to expand our study to the broader array of flows that are concurrent with it. While we are not advocating adding them to the four flows model of Communicative Constitution of Organizations (CCO), we do contend that the flows approach broadens understanding as articulated above. For instance, McPhee (1988, 1989; McPhee & Corman, 1995; cf., Myers & McPhee, 2006) argued that manager-subordinate dyads, and especially vertical triads of upper manager-lower manager-subordinate need to be recognized as the broader range of flows, even within the limited but incredibly important development of the organizational communication research focus of vertical communication (Barnard, 1938; Hage, 1974; Jablin, 1979; Weber, 1968). McPhee (1988) argued that such dyads or triads needed study in the flow of, at least, vertical communication from top to bottom, at each level of which dyads and triads operate differently.

Third, this conceptualization leads us to approach CCO in a distinctive way. Organizations are not singularly constituted, say by a founder or charter or initial utterance—those are impotent outside a supportive flow. To depart for a minute from the flow metaphor, if we think we should study the constitution of a building by attending to its implanted girders, we may think added studies are urgently called for: of the bedrock in which the girders are embedded, with all the cracks the embedding caused; of the scaffolding that surrounded the building, accomplishing its constitution, of the additional floors and extensions that are sure to appear. Thus, CCO points to a broad set of communicative actions that exist within a larger framework of constitution that typically remains unexplored yet is still present.

Overall, a flow approach to understanding the interconnections and relationships between communicative practices yields a useful metaphor and perhaps ontology. While we articulate many flows that could be developed, the four flows approach signifies a more specific theory than the generalized flow of communication. We propose a model involving four currents—which we more narrowly describe as flows—that are analytically distinct but multidimensionally confluent in constituting the specific social systems we call organizations. It is easier to think of this set of four flows as a model, and we aim, from here on, to illuminate the character and interdependences of the flows—after some reflections regarding the limitations of the flows metaphor.

4.5 Ways That *Flow* Departs from *Communication*

Despite the interpretive advantages of *flow* as stated earlier, there are a variety of important ways in which it, like any metaphor, can be deceptive that Black (1962) calls *negative analogy*, and the metaphor of communication as flow is no exception. By claiming flow as analogous to communication, specifically to the communicative constitution of organizations, we are not only pointing out similarities, but must unavoidably recognize, admit, and adapt to differences. We are quick to deny that communication and flows are even close to identical in their most vital conceptual elaborations.

For example, the flow of surface water is typically driven by gravity (as well as occurring over time). We do not claim that communication is gravitation-bound, natural, or determined by motivating conditions. Again, rivers have multiple tributaries coming together, like our four flows, but for rivers, those flows become quickly indistinguishable once together. We claim that our flows, while generally and notably confluent, remain analytically, and often processually, distinct. Again, many particular instances or examples of organizational communication have served us as prototypes to illustrate a single flow especially well. But almost always, a noteworthy instance/example of one flow in fact contributes to or has significance in all four flows—it somehow (in ways we can discover in analysis) orients members, is reflexively self-structured, serves to collaboratively accomplish something, and potentially alters the organization's place in a larger societal system. By expanding the dimensionality of researchers' views of any flow, or any focal communication current, we are using the flows metaphor to advance theorizing and inspect the complexities of the communicative constitution of organizations or single out phenomena from the flows of which they are part.

One paradoxical use of the metaphor is that we are conscious of it and can more easily step away from our use of it. Other elements of the flows metaphor attempt to reduce communicative flows to a much simpler concept than they actually are. Flows, despite the surface senses of the metaphor, are not simple, smooth, unidirectional processes—they can flood, be stopped or sundered, or establish new courses, much like organizations that can suffer goal drift or dissent about the direction. If a flow starts to zig-zag wildly or is confronted by a giant whirlpool blocking the whole current, or by a dam blocking the flow enough to turn it into a lake, the term flow potentially does not fit. On the other hand, these analogies might serve well to understand organizations, or be wildly unrepresentative. Organization members find that they cannot step into the "same river"—but sometimes the river gets fixed, stopped up, so stepping in repeatedly is, in a limited way, possible. For example, after-action reviews performed by various emergency response teams are designed to vividly recall events and review and learn from the team's performance (Jahn, 2019a, 2019b). While there can be varied flows, divided in varied ways that are more channeled, or divided by depth or other properties. A pull in a single downstream direction overwhelms the eddies, cross-currents, etc., which may be super-ceded (or energized) by the constant directional flow.

A flow of organizational communication is interconnected in many more ways than the currents or eddies of a river, even taking into account multiple crosscurrents. Episodes are of many types and are mutually relevant in innumerable ways, whereas a river is typically thought of as almost all water, with relations mainly stemming from physical proximity, with important but pretty limited cross-flows. In particular, a flow of communication, as well as communication in it, is *contextual*. Its meaning and significance depend on the current of communication it is part of, the whole flow containing it, and cross-cutting communication from other flows. Because of meanings constitutive of multiple contexts, organizational communication is more of a turbulent mixture than any river. Communication is inherently transformative, *making* the flow exemplify the adage that *you cannot step into the same river twice*. Moreover, organizational communication has constitutive powers largely as a result of these complex interrelations, so the metaphor of flow, taken in itself, is useful, but limited as grounding an account of organizational constitution. For instance, the fact that a river flow has banks could very easily lead us to a version of the now-discounted container metaphor.

The metaphor of flow should not and cannot fully displace some rival metaphors for communication in systems—instead, it reframes them. A key example of ST is the notion of *agent* or agency. As already discussed, a number of important negative analogies exist, especially related to the notion of the *organization as agent* (or plenum of nonhuman agents). Agents (humans) have the capacity to *understand* communication in its context of resources and to respond meaningfully by drawing on their contextual understandings of their circumstances and of their strategic direction, which their responses affect, and in turn, the rules and resources they *structurate*. Those capacities ground the ST explanation of how shared understandings, practices, and social change—are possible for human agents. ST also notes that agency is not an elemental essence *per se*, that it too must be constituted, arguably in flows of communication and practice. It suggests that human agents rarely have the power to divert the larger flow, and mainly get carried along by it. Contrariwise, agents knowledgeably communicating, *en masse*, constitute the flow and keep it going in ways responsive to context. As discussed in earlier chapters, agents also have the ability to "go on" (Wittgenstein, 1953). They can float along in the stream, more actively swim to reposition themselves, cling to other objects in the stream, or *occasionally* have the power to significantly affect the flow by augmenting it, or blocking or redirecting it. Similarly, individuals in an ongoing communication process are immersed in a stream, the character of which they can understand to a very limited degree. So, though flow is a potentially misleading metaphor, agency too is for us, as for Giddens (1984), often a constrained and subordinate, though a vitally revealing, metaphor for many crucial organizational communication processes. *Flow* helps us decenter agency, and is supplementary to it.

Some other potentially rival metaphors emphasize the repetitiveness of communication—those in the families similar, on the one hand, to networks, chains, and on the other hand, to conversational and discursive regularities. Undeniably, typical network models reveal the routine selective choices of agents to communicate with—to repeatedly communicate with some agents more than others (especially up or down vertical chains across ranks; McPhee, 1988) and to reply to those selected agents using the meaning-tradition constituted in earlier interchange. Conversation or retweeting is sometimes an interaction feature in enduring or long chains of relations, in which content or ideas are transformed and reiterative. Relationships are reinforced by recurrently involving the same agents. But in response, we note that the network and chain metaphors tacitly assume that network links channel/constitute the flow of electrical current, signals, messages, etc. Network and other seemingly nonflow communication patterns—the meeting, the announcement, the conversational chain—suggest narrowed channels of flow that very often get sedimented, although there may be multiple constitutive processes of flow in the history of a communicative relationship. Thus, between a company's CEO and his/her current Vice President of Sales, there may be both routine communication that constitutes the company in routine ways and acrimonious communication about whether to restructure the Sales Division. Of course, such communication often *leaks out* to sales managers and employees, other coinvolved executives, and even outside stakeholders. In the lens of the 4F model, leakages and their consequences occur, essentially, inevitably, perhaps intentionally and perhaps in ways opposed to some parties' interests. Such leakages *are crucial topoi for organizational communication research* and *have constitutive force for the organization*, too. An organization is thus the kind of thing wherein leakages, and attempts to respond to them, typically occur.

A relevant subterm of flow, perhaps better for understanding relational phenomena than link or imbrication, is *eddy*, a pattern of flow that varies from the main direction to cycle, whirl, or reiterate currents of flow. An eddy, like an agent or a relationship, could equally correspond to a problem or a topic constituted in and by the ongoing flow of communicative practice.

The four flows approach elaborates on how communication constitutes the organization, how practices of human agents produce and reproduce the organization, and in particular, how four conceptually distinct components (flows) combine in complex ways to accomplish organizational constitution. The analogy of flow moves past a static, functionalist view of organizations without slipping into an overly fluid view that organizations are simply communication. Rather, theoretically, the four flows model offers unique insights to the processes of organizing.

4.6 The Four Flows Model

Three questions seem immediately pertinent when we hear the term *four flows model*. Why flows? Why *communication* flows? Why multiple flows, and why four of them and these four? The previous sections of this chapter help to answer, we hope, the first question. While it is often analytically useful to objectify and discuss the boundaries, constant parameters, and repetitive patterns of organizations, it is vital to realize that such objective properties froth on the surface (or noticeable currents) of dynamic processes that initiate, stabilize, prioritize, and frequently transform the boundaries, parameters, patterns that seem like essential organizational frameworks. Process is itself a metaphor, but it extends too easily to regular movements of signals in containing media. Using flow is our attempt to work at a more basic level—the level of constitution of the organization.

For the second question, about focusing on flows *of communication*, we surely recognize that there are potentially many flow types, not overtly of communication, or of economic resources, for example, Marxian structural sets like supplies transformed into resources/means of production, transformed into outputs. Additionally, a structural set is based on money transformations: money transformed into budget, then into salary and expenses, into labor, which is transformed into products, into sales, and into profits (respectfully deviating from Marx). These processes represent flows that coincide with CCO flows as well.

How are processes like these related to communication flow? First, only communication can label the organization, refer to the organization or its supplies, budget, etc. with the needed level of reflexive agency. Organizations, through agents, *live* in language; it is the basic web or, actually, world (Gadamer, 1989; Heidegger, 1927; Ricoeur, 1981a, 1981b) or flow connecting people in social relationships and allowing for reflection about and reflexive monitoring of ongoing developments in their organizational lives. Second, a consequence of the first: people (agents if you will) are members or employees of an organization only through communication processes. An examination of an untenanted assembly line is a desiccated picture, mainly because no true communication occurs in it, but it is easy to find organizations that are essentially nothing but people communicating. Third, communication flows are necessitated by other communication, an idea we expand on soon.

As for the third focal question, why does our model involve multiple flows? We agree it is tempting to think of an organization as a single flow, analogous to a single river. Are we, then, contending that an organization is like four rivers? No, the flows we discuss are more like interacting currents within a river all along its length in a constitutive churning interflux. Each would be a flow, if water from the tributaries tended to cohere somewhat strongly rather than simply merge and become dissolved into the overall flow. But the other implication of flows is that multiple organizing subprocesses exist and are important, but have essentially varying implications for organizational constitution. The flows are like subcurrents or depth currents that carry along constitutive consequences. Organizations are not constituted in just one type of communication, so a model with just one type of communicative flow is not sufficient.

Before we discuss the question, why four, there is another feature of the model that should be discussed: why use analytic categories as large or inclusive as flows? Is it helpful to discuss all kinds of flows such as institutional positioning in a larger landscape, which includes other organizations of various types, but also isolated individuals, flows of goods, and money?

While we draw upon the model of Parsons (Parsons & Smelser, 1965), we amend that model quite drastically in advancing the proposition that an organization consists of four essential flows of communication. Parsons' scheme of four functions was especially meant for analysis of old-style social systems like nations, though it extended analysis down to subsystems. But mid-twentieth-century organizational theory tacitly accepted that very clear *functions needed* to be performed by subsystems that are necessarily present because the whole system requires them. Thus, leaders are present in groups because they are necessary to provide decisive guidance. Or theorists might say a system *needs* performance of a function like defending definite boundaries that help impose order, with that systemic need causing empowered leaders, consciously or unconsciously, to work to achieve boundary defense. But as we noted earlier, ST rejects the notion that the group is a super-agent that says or thinks, "Since I am a group, I need guidance and thus I will empower a decisive leader." Or "I, an organization-agent, need boundaries." No, groups do not say or think, or want or require anything—only humans can do that.

But if the flows do not reflect system-mandated functions, what are they? One possible answer is to employ the flows more as *sensitizing* categories for putative systems like organizations that feature *advocated* or *attempted* order, boundaries, and congruent meanings. Rather than assuming that cross-border relations, controlled work operations, and reflexive collective interpretations are necessary, essential features of organizations, we cast our net wider, to sniff out their flickering, partial, precarious, conflicted manifestation in communication flows—conceptions that display the order, and disorder, of organizations, but ground their accounts by acknowledging communication's dynamism and constitutive power. We thus vigorously deny imposing a top-down conceptual scheme on organizational communication. A flow is not something we presume, but something we find.

However, that said, the four flows model can sensitize us to identify necessary conditions, as long as their necessity resembles, say, the need for anonymity within the mob in *To Kill a Mockingbird*. No, the mob did not feel or express any need; rather, some (but not all) of its *members* needed anonymity, a need that was deconstructed when one of the hero's children called out a mob member, who tried to avoid recognition, but failing that, left in a fashion that induced the other members to follow (https://www.youtube.com/watch?v=HT4q5cg4FEk, as of 5/15/23). An organization lacking one of the flows may not seek it out, or motivate its members to enact that flow; instead, the flow's absence may lead members to find a substitute, or it may result in one of a number of sorts of systemic failures. Or the flow model may sensitize us to processes that even express the desired *absence* of the flow. For instance, "we let everybody who works here do their own thing," seemingly outlaws activity coordination, though we might watch further for communication that *coordinates* the independence of the activities—resolving conflicts or assisting with effortfully ignoring overt problems of individual members. A flow may be necessary, paradoxically, in ways that are denied in overt organizational discourse.

This brings up a way the four flows model is, we believe, attuned to necessity in a deeper sense, as well. It sensitizes us to watch for communication currents that include expressions of needs or problems or requirements involving a flow, or expressions of commitments, plans, and practical action responsive to expressed needs.

Articulated needs or responding operations may emerge as agents draw on a variety of sources, including externally imposed mandates, inter- or intraorganizational imitation, internal emergence, or cross-flow shaping. Expression of needs or operations, in flows, are not *necessary*, but their existence is the result of a sort of constitutive communication: *necessitating* communication. The sorts of power-production listed earlier are gross examples. Then, as power-developing processes, members make them swing into operation, reinforcing each other by enabling their continued operation. For instance, governmental external imposition is implicit in mandating messages like "To meet legal requirements, we have to include an information leaflet, X, that provides an array of information along with every prescription order for drug Y."

Necessitation is not a precondition forcing any specific organizational function or communication procedure; it is not a theoretically prescribed explanation, but the result of prototypical but observable communication that constitutes organizations by presenting a demand for, or discovering the utility of, such functions or procedures, and then communicating to meet the demand (in varied ways due to power distribution and context). The flows are, at this deeper level, more akin to questions or lenses for analyzing organizational communication that necessitates, or then seeks to achieve, putative necessary functions: they ask, for example, how a need for membership and its management become recognized and interpreted by power-elite agents, and then dealt with by members?

Thus, to be specific, membership negotiation is not the result of a mega-agent *needing* members. It is likely the result of powerful agents (e.g., founders) communicatively acquiring knowledge that suggests the utility of organized procedures for dealing with members and their interrelations, and then other agents (e.g., human resource managers) using those processes to build their own power by legitimately staffing the organization. External communication is not needed by the organization; it results from interactions persuading organizational agents (as just one example, company executives with experience at prior publicly held and socially supported companies) to notice its utility (necessity as communicatively constituted), or to respond to communicated demands—by, for example, governmental agents or stakeholders—that necessitate a complex flow articulating organization identity or developing brand loyalty. The four flows are therefore communication-oriented and constituting responses/reactions to issues whose prominence results from the communication that necessitates them. We can see a need for order as manifested in communication flows—conceptions that display necessitated (or accidental) order, and disorder, of organizations, grounded in accounts acknowledging communication's dynamism and constitutive power.

Two flow processes generate relations of the organization——clearly, organization-constituting relations—with its members (Flow 1) and its institutionalized environment (Flow 4). Two other subprocesses deal with the order, or sometimes disorder, carried by self-structuring metacommunication (Flow 2), and by locally generated ordering processes (Flow 3), *along with* their shadowing disorders.

We suggest that rather than seeing member recruitment or coordination or boundary maintenance as necessary functions for organizations—as strong beams supporting them—we think better imaginations are of them as murky well-springs or up-currents. There is the current, markable if we release dye into it, but quickly intermixed with other up-flowing streams that may support it, lending it vigor, but may just as likely dilute it or deflect it. A type or flow of communication may serve to enact and support authoritative organizational operations, as it serves such goals, it is liquid, easily mixing into other directions. Rather than fulfilling a system need, it may identify the need as a meaningful issue, generate multiple streams of discussion about it, and perhaps tend toward need fulfillment when not churned into confusion or diverted toward some other need. Organizations are constituted in this turbulence due to powerful agents collaborating, communicatively, enough to channel communication into the four flows that conspicuously contribute to organizing.

1. *Membership Negotiation*, the first flow, in which agents become organizational per se, with standing to be active or influential in various currents of the flow, so that their knowledge and expertise, their rationalization powers, their identification with the organization or facets of it all contribute (positively or sometimes negatively) to maintain their task and relational relevance, and thereby their constitutive significance. All through the processes of search, actual hiring and crossing the boundary onto the membership

roster, then socialization into work roles, sharing narratives with other members to position themselves, actual work experience, and perhaps exit—in all of those, both members and organizational others exercise agency about the parameters of their roles in tacit or explicit negotiation processes through which the organization as a multimember collectivity is constituted,
2. *Self-structuring*, the second flow reflexively develops and discusses three types of communicative phenomena: the formal (authoritative texts), the informal (cultural patterns), and the technological (infotech networks). These correlate because they shape, contextualize, and legitimate other currents of organizational communication, helping a sense or senses of the organization to emerge in the process of collecting and directing all four currents to give them constitutive force. For instance, implementing a computer system in a small firm involves Flow 2 decisions about who is connected and how well, and about who will get access to which information—choices before as well as during the implementation and computer-use processes—choices that *are* self-structuring to constitute the firm.
3. *Activity Coordination*, the third flow, allows for communication that gets things collaboratively done. Often this local, practical communication occurs in organizational settings, yet is not specifically controlled or authorized (e.g., classroom activities within a school). However, it can cohere and constitute the organization by collectively adapting, revising, or resisting Flow 2 structuring enough to allow (or resistantly reroute) situationally suited action.
4. *Institutional Positioning*, the fourth flow presents and constitutes the organization and member actions by multiple organizational members that may interact with a variety of others, *crossing* (actually, constituting) boundaries to relate to nonmember activities and social entities. These processes, whose vital significance is understated in current research, can include lobbying with a national government for the right to deliver assistance to earthquake victims and negotiating for rare-earth metals to allow production of computer chips.

Naturally, an important part of any episode's force as being part of the flow comes from temporally earlier, and spatially distantiated, episodes with contextual continuity in the flow that it carries, furthers, and reproduces, as well as other currents of constitutive communication. We accept the fact that these processes are well known to occur via communication, but we also transform the copious research about them. Our aim is to organize them and display their constitutive significance—a factor that remains to be explored. Each flow has a unique nature and manifests a facet of organizations.

4.7 Conclusion

In the chapters to come, we intend to show that together, the four flows communicatively constitute organizations in a compound, complex process (McPhee & Iverson, 2009). Each of the flows represents a different vital facet of organizations. Each flow comprises the necessary processes for creating and maintaining an organization. Negotiation of membership, self-structuring, activity coordination, and institutional positioning reflect the differing elements of an organization. The flows allow a conceptual disentangling of the communicative constitution of organizations, while recognizing their interrelated nature.

At the same time, the four flows interact—are confluent, overlap, and countercurrent in endlessly varied ways. Many communication acts accomplish more than one flow in equal measures. Similarly, like the confluence of two flows in a river, a communication event may be rooted in one flow, but evolve in such a way that one flow is evident. Countercurrents among flows are also common such that two flows can attempt to direct the organization in one direction while simultaneously pushing it in another all within one communication event.

We have a specific notion of communication in mind as we articulate this model, many features of which are described in earlier chapters. However, the Four Flows model itself is open to many images of what communication is, with minimal constraints. It can be accepted that organizational communication is message flow through prespecified network links, or processes of sensemaking being articulated and reconciled throughout an organization, or processes of power structures and imbalances, or conversation or ventriloquism involving nonhuman agents. But to be an adequate account of organizational communication, a theory or theoretic model must, at least in passing:

1. Recognize that communication, as it describes it, has constitutive force;
2. Recognize that there are four analytical separable types of communication, conceptually congruent with our *four flows*, that together are necessary to, and broad enough to, explicate the constitution of complex organizations through communication;
3. Be open to the kinds of *flow* phenomena that we described in this chapter earlier;
4. Be open to cross-cutting and mutual mediation among the four types/flows of communication.

In short, this list is offered as a template to illuminate the essence of organizational constitution.

The flows metaphor vigorously opposes models representing the organization as a fluid or other process captured within a container or pipe that demonstrates the clear boundaries of where the flows are and are not. Rather, the metaphor demonstrates the fluidity and action of enacting the social institutions of the organization. Further, we demonstrate that the four flows allow a distinction of theorizing organizations from other social processes such as friendship or a group of people at a concert. A model showing the distinctness of the complex organizations that dominate the model world is not just appealing but invaluable to understanding or theorizing about today's organizational communication. Each flow is complex and dynamic and enacts a different aspect of organizing.

5

Membership Negotiation

First and foremost, in order for an organization to exist, it must have some human activity associated with it. While nonliving aspects of nature can be described as active (wind, tides, and temperature changes), there is no (apparent) goal in these activities. Once goals are defined through agentic actors, the context is set for an organization to be constituted. Therefore, and as McPhee and Zaug (2000) argued, organizations do not exist without the activities of people. Those individuals must be more than a mere collection of individuals who might be enjoying an afternoon in the park or standing in line to board an airplane. We might describe these groups as collectives that are impotent in action. Instead, individuals must be connected in some way in order to play a part in constituting an organization. Their goals often differ, but their aims are linked in multiple ways, including their contributions, more or less conscious and chosen, to successful progress toward the widely understood, usually formally chosen, goals of the organization, the choice and development of which is the result of self-structuring, our second flow.

This complicated relationship between the goal of an individual and putative organizational goals is indicative of a broader conflict about the very being of both member and organization, apparent in the connotations of the term *member*. Deriving from the Latin *membrum*, a member was originally a body part or limb, a meaning preserved in expressions like "dismember a corpse." So, a member is part of an organization like a limb is part of a body—consubstantial with and a systemic part of the whole. Yet a member of an organization is also a human agent, with autonomous powers of reflection and rationalization that lets them articulate personal—or organizational—goals, and to realize that those are distinct. Those powers are crucial for organizational operations, which depend on members' thoughtful, skillful, and even critical devotion to activities. However, the

The Communicative Constitution of Organizations: The Four Flows Model, First Edition.
Robert D. McPhee, Karen K. Myers, and Joel O. Iverson.

organization is typically oriented to absorb the individual in varied ways, working best when members are fully *part* of the organization by guiding themselves wholeheartedly toward organizational goals. This contradiction, *member as an autonomous agent* versus *member as organizational limb* is the central tension involved in the nature of organizations. The contradiction takes on special zest when we recognize, as a tenet of ST, that the organizational whole is actually a collectivity, of other autonomous individual limbs! In 4F, such contradictions actually develop and unfold themselves organizationally in a flow of contravention, a dialectic in ongoing interaction. Specifically, individuals come to be organizational members in a two-sided process of *negotiation*, as individuals are persuaded, motivated, and rewarded to act, and see and evaluate themselves, in line with organizational expectations communicated by other members—representatives—whose expectations vary and who are involved in their own negotiations with the organizational *body*.

To demonstrate how members might have differing organizational goals and varied relations to the organization's mission, a business owner's goal in starting and developing a strategy may be based on the long-term building of the organization to potentially sell the company at a large profit or to bequeath the firm to her children. Meanwhile, the company's managers can be committed to leading their departments and employees toward achieving productivity goals, both for bonuses and promotions or to pad their resume for their next job. Still others may continue their membership merely because their employment provides a paycheck and health insurance for their families. Their commitment to stated organizational goals is weak at best. These are merely some of the goals individual members may have, some in line with the well-being of the organization and some that have little organizational benefit and may even negate it (cashing in on stock options or corporate takeover). Similarly, individuals who become associated with nonprofit organizations—whether they be volunteers who seemingly donate their time or paid staff—may or may not be fully committed to the avowed or formalized purpose of the organization.

The issue of member-organizations is complicated when we recognize that *member* is often treated like an identity category—somewhat analogously to *gender* and *class*, as well as intersecting with those categories. Intersectionality is a very broadly researched and theorized topic; one influential essay is that by McCall (2005), who discusses it as the complex intersections of membership categories, or category systems. Her work has been critiqued (Rodó-de-Zárate & Jorba, 2012) due to its overemphasis on static categories—a problem just like the one with *member* we are discussing. Here is one juncture where the idea of a flow of membership negotiation is very helpful. Identity categories do not work like concrete blocks in overall organizational discourse. Rather, as discussed further below, they are produced and reproduced, variably, across the distanciated organization in interweaving flows, all of which are crucial to members' identities and the constitution of organizations as identity-articulating systems.

As can be imagined from the previous examples, the goals of individuals differ in their focus and scope, but their activities are all tied to and are the context of the organization. Their connection to the organization may be financial, social, professional, emotional, or otherwise, but because they demonstrate linkage, they are members (Cheney, 1983a, 1983b). In each of these examples, they choose to be members of organizations because there is a benefit to their organizing. Or, in the case of involuntary membership (e.g., incarcerated individuals or drafted into the military), they have lost most or all of their agency and others have determined benefits to their organizational membership. However, whatever factors condition their linkages, they perform organizationally constitutive activities and thus are presumably elevated from the condition of being practico-inert.

As they develop connections, learn about organizational goals, master their work-activity context, and orient to the interpretive and value facets of that context, something else is happening: to some extent, they are entering and being absorbed by the power domain of the organization. In the larger organizations of today, the power involves communication processes that exclude most members, especially lower levels. Of course, newcomers typically lack social connections, which also might leave them out of these conversations. However, envelopment into organizational power actually works according to the dialectic of control: seminal organizational processes are oriented to achieve complete control, like a drill sergeant who demands their new recruits' compliance and imprisons the members in an iron cage—the term used by the founder of organizational studies, Weber (1946). Recently, distributed workers have experienced this type of extreme control when managers utilize monitoring software that sanctions workers based on keystroke speed and bathroom breaks. However, the organization also is oriented to need the cooperation of members employing their agentive powers of understanding and skill voluntarily—which gives the member some leverage for negotiating acceptable or even ideal working conditions. The dialectic of control, one version of contravention, is also at work as the most powerful organizational leaders are in a sense controlled by their reputations, vested interests, and self-regard to *work for* the organization, even driving themselves into poor health or disintegrating their personal lives.

With this backdrop, this chapter recounts the first constitutive flow, membership negotiation. We describe *membership negotiation* as the ongoing communication and activities that constitute members' relationship with the organization and their associated behaviors (McPhee & Zaug, 2000). In constituting membership, individual members' flows define how they experience and enact their membership with many proximal and distal outcomes for themselves and the organization. Individual member's communication and activities are linked to memberships of others because how one member performs their membership affects supervisors and coworkers. Conversely, how they are treated as members affects their attitudes and behaviors. Members can develop pride in how they as part of a workgroup perform their roles, or, for example, members might engage in competitive practices with their colleagues. They can perceive leaders and their goals as unified with them and their own, or they can perceive management as adversarial, someone to dodge or battle. Moreover, they are affected by the feedback they receive causing them to alter their behaviors or resist. Certainly, the membership negotiation flows produced by members at various levels of the organization are but one communicative current. This flow merges with the other flows of self-structuring, activity coordination, and organizational positioning, combining to influence as well as to produce each other, and to constitute the organization.

We begin this discussion of the membership negotiation flow, first, by describing boundaries of membership, then by elaborating how individuals are introduced to membership in organizations through socialization and one example of a socializing message. Like other socializing communication, the message is intended to guide individuals in transitioning from being unaffiliated individuals to being and acting as *members*. We discuss the purpose of the message given by a training supervisor to a new employee—to shape member behaviors—but because individuals have agency, we also describe new members' potential responses to this and other socializing messages ranging from learning and adapting to explicit resistance. Our conversation then turns to other aspects of membership negotiation such as employees' role relations with members closest to them.

We feel it important to emphasize at the onset, the vast majority of the research on membership assumes that the newcomer/member is of the majority race, adheres to the gender and class norms expected by the organization, and is negotiating inclusion in an entry-level job in a typical Western organization. Of course, this situation is far from typical of all organizational membership. Membership negotiation is very different in involuntary membership situations such as prison labor camps or for newcomers whose power relation to the organization is very different such as when a CEO is hired from outside a company compared to the entry of an undocumented day laborer. While we cannot account for all or most differences, we will attempt to offer examples of how individual diversity and diversity of situations can affect membership negotiation. Additionally, we should note that direct negotiation of an individual's membership is the tail end of a longer process of negotiation involving those members. Established organization members engage in negotiations targeting prospective new members. Such negotiations create conditions delimiting the direct negotiations. For instance, management must make organizational decisions, reflecting a socially established necessity, to hire a certain number of employees, with certain skills and credentials. They also must offer a normative salary range, place the new employees in certain departments and locations, and hold them to certain standards of performance. This type of larger process, creating a context in which newcomers and socializers feel the necessity to negotiate out their roles, has rarely been the focus of communication research.

5.1 Moving from Outsiders to Insiders: Socialization Toward Membership

Ordinary parlance, as well as the container metaphor we have critiqued, portray membership as somehow being *inside* an organization's boundary. We do recognize that *membership* implies that an individual has achieved a special status (defined in our Self-Structuring flow) relative to the organization, but while organizational membership seems relatively easily defined, boundaries that designate organizational insiders from outsiders can be vague. Employees, students, and individuals who formally join clubs, associations, religious organizations are easily identified as members by using lists. However, some individuals are less easily defined as members or non-members: gig workers who more or less work as independent contractors, individuals such as volunteers who rarely participate or whose participation has waned, company stockholders, adjunct lecturers and other temporary workers, and retired employees. Whether and how these individuals negotiate their membership—learning about and communicating to define their role, positioning themselves relative to others associated with the organization, communicating one's commitment and identification with the organization, and more—may be key in this determination.

Dobusch and Schoeneborn's (2015) investigation into "organizationality" using the communicative constitution of organizing highlighted the issue of membership. They aimed to offer a language-centered view of organizational identity processes through analysis of identity claims made during critical communicative events. The social collective that was the focus of the study, Anonymous, was a covert hacking operation described as a fluid social collective with no physical location, identifiable leadership, or formal membership. Instead, individuals who wished to associate themselves with Anonymous activated organizational "actorhood" through performed identity claims (Dobusch & Schoeneborn, 2015, p. 1007). More specifically, when websites were attacked, some individuals anonymously claimed that the attack had been conducted by Anonymous. Due to the fluidity of membership and secrecy of Anonymous, the hacker's membership and representation of the social entity for making the attack and/or claiming responsibility were questionable. Likewise, following another threat and declarative statement of Anonymous' responsibility, other "Anon" actors disaffirmed the announcer's membership or their ability to speak on behalf of the collective. Their study highlights questions about what constitutes organizations and also the definition of membership and who or what discursive process gets to declare someone a member—questions that make the notion of *membership negotiation flow* a potentially better one than static notions, human-agent-centered or not.

Membership negotiation involving new members with typical American corporations and similar organizations involves several communicative processes, and none are so prominent as organizational socialization. Organizational socialization is defined as "The process by which one is taught and learns 'the ropes' of a particular organizational role" (Van Maanen & Schein, 1979, p. 211). Socialization is thought by many to be foundational as it is typically one's first exposure to the organization and at a time that many newcomers find exciting, disappointing, and/or uncertain (Louis, 1980; Woodrow & Guest, 2020). Newcomers are socialized by supervisors and other more senior members in a process designed to introduce the policies and practices of the organization toward instilling with them an understanding of how to function and how to think more or less like *ideal* organizational members (Ashforth et al., 2007; Schein, 1990; Wieland, 2010). Communication and activities involved in socialization have important implications for current and future functioning and success of the organization (Reichers, 1987) because as newcomers enter organizations, they need to learn about how to perform tasks associated with their role and also about organizational rules and policies to successfully function as a member (Bauer & Erdogan, 2011; Van Maanen & Schein 1979). Organizational management also has a vested interest in training and developing the newcomer (Rubenstein et al., 2020) with the goal that newcomers settle into practices that will benefit the organization (Bauer & Erdogan, 2011; Haueter et al., 2003). Socialization is thus a two-directional process of necessitation, as both new members and representatives—formal and informal—of the organization learn and persuade each other that the membership of these newcomers will benefit both sides of the negotiation.

However, while newcomers can introduce innovation and new perspectives, they also pose a threat to the long-term stability of the organization. Past work experience is beneficial to newcomers, giving them an understanding of expectations about how to perform tasks associated with their role (Endacott & Myers, 2019). However, practices and understandings from previous experience may not translate well into the new environment (Davis & Myers, 2019). Newcomers must be clued into their new organization's "tried and true" established operating procedures that have consistently led to productive outcomes. By socializing newcomers, leaders encourage and better ensure consistency—causing new members to adopt desired attitudes and behaviors. However, their adopting these rules and procedures is not automatic. Newcomers may question and resist the organization's practices and policies. They might choose to observe others to learn which rules are legitimate and consistently followed, and which rules can be ignored. Newcomers can also be disappointed during and soon after socialization by unexpected realities that breach their psychological contracts (Woodrow & Guest, 2020), causing them to leave the organization a few days or weeks after entry (Lee & Mitchell, 1994).

Socializing messages and mentoring in the first few days and weeks after joining can be especially influential as newcomers encounter the organization and infer the necessity of finding, without being stifled by, their role within it (Miller & Jablin, 1991; Morrison 1993, 2002). Guidance from more experienced members often helps them resolve those uncertainties (Rubenstein et al., 2020). Memorable messages given to newcomers can guide them about what they should and should not do, often providing a more informal view of how the organization operates (Stohl, 1986). Of course, prior identity perceptions—message flows from outside the immediate negotiation context—affect the types and styles of these messages. New members of various races, but especially those from nondominant races, for instance, may receive messages that single them out, subtly—or not so subtly—disparage them, limit their access to important messages or negotiations, or express outright hostility—or, we would hope, messages of welcome and openness to communicative differences (Allen, 1996; Shenoy-Packer & Myers, 2013).

Some socializing messages attempt to instill common attitudes amongst newcomers that will guide them throughout their tenure. For example, a training supervisor may tell a new customer service representative that in our organization "customers are always right." This message can garner multiple responses and influence the membership flow in many ways. In these responses, evidence of the modalities includes differing meaning, legitimacy, and power with various interpretations and at varying levels to those who hear it. In fact, customers can have a voice in shaping elements of the organization, which might, at times, outweigh the voices of employees and affect members. For example, they can complain about an employee's work, which gets the employee reprimanded or fired, or offer praise that in many ways is similar to the praise they would receive from a supervisor, which contributes to an employee's promotion. Over time, the organization may come to be known as a place in which the customer is always right, causing customers to flock there, but with the unintended consequence of potential employees selecting to go elsewhere.

Messages given to customer service representatives, for example, can result in several potential interpretations and responses. First, new customer service representatives may hear the message—"The customer is always right." Context plays a foundational role in understanding the message (Giddens, 1976a, 1976b) and because the message was given by a presumed *legitimate* source—their new supervisor as part of their initial training—the words should have *power* in influencing the newcomers' attitudes and intended future behaviors. Not only has the supervisor been given the authority to provide guiding statements, but they also may have the power to reprimand or even fire a customer service representative who does not comply with rules and this type of guideline. In addition, based on their general understanding of the role in which they have been hired, newcomers frequently perceive the trainer's messages such as this to *mean* that *they must do everything* within their power to please customers. In transtruction, the meanings, norms and power of the statement are entangled and mutually elaborative—constitutive of their membership as a customer service representative in the organization. Members always put the customer first! As they enact their membership guided by the supervisor's message, the flows of communication and their activities *constitute* an organization that caters to customer demands.

Of course, it is more complicated because even in the midst of their uncertainty as newcomers, customer service representatives still garner agency. They may choose to loyally follow their supervisors' guidance, negotiating their roles as catering to their customers' every whim. In doing so, their membership in the organization is *constituted* to provide enduring service to paying customers and the flow of their communication with their supervisor and coworkers supports and promotes the customer-service objective. When they enact their roles as customer service representatives as thus described, they forge and/or replicate attitudes and practices that facilitate a culture of strong customer service. Their activities and communication with others in their workgroup reflect this understanding of their membership. Members may coordinate to achieve this objective (mingling with flow 3). As they perform this role, customer service representatives may need and request additional resources devoted to enhancing customer service. Resources could be devoted to rewarding customer service representatives who reflect this prioritized value, and some customer service representatives may be given assignments to oversee their customer service representative teammates, further mixed into both flows 1 and 2. The high service commitment becomes the expectation for these and other members and they come to judge themselves and others on that basis. Eventually, the organization may become known by outsiders and insiders for the high levels of unwavering customer service it provides (contributing to flow 4). However, this is only one way members can understand and respond to the supervisor's directive.

Newcomers' agency and choice to do otherwise can cause other responses to this statement by the supervisor affecting flow 1. The new customer service representatives could perceive the supervisor to have little legitimacy and power. They might wonder whether the supervisor has recent sales experience themselves which would help the supervisor to understand the challenges of the job. These and similar interpretations affect the meaning of the directive for customer service, which would cause customer service representatives to negotiate their membership much differently. They might choose to operate more independently, deviating from that directive and choosing to only appease customers when they believe it makes sense to do so, but not when it is inconvenient, and not when they do not particularly like the customer. As these customer service representatives exercise their agency, they communicatively construct their role to be more individually adaptive when it comes to serving customers. Among individuals who engage in these discourses, membership is constituted to reflect these perceptions. In this example, they might exercise their agency by focusing their efforts on cooperative customers and ignoring those that may be less enjoyable and profitable. However, people are not organizational members in a vacuum; in the next section, we delve into how life experiences and environment shape values that can influence membership negotiation.

5.2 Previous Experiences and Their Relation to Membership Negotiation

Individuals join and are members of organizations with experiences (past and present) that influence their perceptions and how they interpret communication and their organizational roles. Through communication and early life experiences, people learn about work and particular organizations that have the potential to affect them throughout their membership (Drucker, 1973; Gibson & Papa, 2000). Those interactions cause individuals to develop expectations and values that influence their choice about the organizations they join (Roe, 1956; Schneider, 1987) and become the basis for the meanings they develop, the norms they expect and power they perceive once they become organizational members. These values emerge as a result of interactions with influential others, but also interactions in the environment. Child development research has examined the effect of socialization children and adolescents receive that shapes their understanding of the world of work and what it means to be an organizational member (Goldstein & Oldham, 1979; Myers et al., 2011). In the field of communication, this area of research is termed vocational anticipatory socialization (Jablin, 2001; Vangelisti, 1988).

One of the most commonly cited studies about how socioeconomic status and other contextual factors influence the educational and vocational choices made by youths is Willis' (1977) book, *Learning to Labour*. Over the course of three years, Willis followed "working class lads" in Britain to learn about their resistance to capitalist ideals about the promise of a good education. Resistance theory, which is largely attributed to Willis, explains that the boys resisted capitalist claims that anyone was capable of being successful in society. Instead, the lads believed that only individuals who are born and socialized to white collar or knowledge work occupations are likely to have the resources available and believe that they are capable of roles that afford members any sort of social status. (This is, of course, a belief shared by many experts.) Rather than viewing education as an opportunity to advance to higher socioeconomic status, the lads treated teachers and educational systems as fodder for jokes, and ridiculed those students who buy into beliefs that they could advance. This sort of within-group ridicule by the boys elevated their status within their social group, but severely limited their potential to attain membership and status in solid careers.

At a baseline, it is clear that individuals enter and experience organizations with differing levels of levels of social resources based on physical characteristics which can enable or constrain their ability to negotiate their membership. Physical issues such as gender and race have long afforded White males privilege in negotiating their roles. Continuing pay inequity between men and women demonstrates part of this issue. Generally speaking, when men join organizations, they negotiate with the employer for higher salary, resulting in higher pay than women for the same jobs. This inequity persists because women tend to be reluctant to tout their achievements and be proactive in asking for pay increases (Babajide, 2021). As a result, the gap grows larger over time. Babcock and Laschever (2009) presented evidence about how women's social perceptions hinder their asking for higher wages and more resources. Women tend to rationalize that if they have to ask, they probably do not deserve the pay increase, better schedule, or promotion. Even in contexts in which men are the minority—in teaching, nursing and the beauty industry—they are frequently given privileges that women do not receive such as higher pay, better schedules, and overall higher prestige (Harvey Wingfield & Myles, 2014).

Race, too, creates unfair advantages for individuals of certain races (often White) in membership negotiation. Individuals from minoritized groups have long been discriminated against by organizations in everything from hiring practices to merit reviews in standards that were developed based on White Male standards, often referred to as institutional bias (Shenoy-Packer & Myers, 2013). Asian

Americans and Pacific Islanders, often thought of as ethnicities that excel in organizations, can have this stereotype work against them. They can lose their ability to negotiate their roles as individuals described in the model minority myth, which assumes that all Asian Americans and Pacific Islanders prioritize hard work and prefer to remain invisible in organizations (Chou & Feagin, 2008; Yi & Museus, 2015). Other seemingly unimportant individual characteristics can also influence member negotiation such as attire, physical body including weight and height, and attractiveness. Simply said, individuals who do not conform to the expectations of others in the organization and or industry are seen as less legitimate and their power to negotiate often is diminished. Organizations in which these issues are particularly apparent often position themselves (via flow 4) as entities that are not accommodating to minoritized groups, which of course, causes individuals from these groups to be less inclined to join, which can mean the situation is unlikely to improve.

Values and expectations follow individuals to the workplace and are reflected in their membership. Some research has found that individuals from working class families are frequently socialized to believe that *real work* involves hard physical labor and that supervisors hold significant power over employees (Gibson & Papa, 2000; Lucas & Buzzanell, 2004). As organizational members, when they are directed by their supervisor to perform difficult physical labor, the transtructive effect and their response are colored by their perceptions about the powerful position of the supervisor and that employees should expect to work hard and even sacrifice their well-being to be a good employee. They likely would accept the legitimacy of the directive, offer little push-back to management, and perform their role accordingly. However, even with those experiences, their responses are rarely unequivocal. Some may have had experiences that caused them to not trust that management is looking out for their best interests. They believe that the company is taking advantage of employees, eroding the members' trust in management. Alternatively, they may view jobs such as this as a short-term relationship without much commitment (Myers et al., 2011). Or they may be influenced by resistant workgroups or demonstrations by unhappy members. These workers may ignore, discount, or actively resist the supervisor's statement. We will discuss the implications for their membership negotiation in the next section of this chapter, but what about members who initially attempt to comply?

Returning to the example of customer service representatives, some may hear the directive given in their initial training about customers always being right with a more organizationally aligned perspective. Like some other customer service representatives, they initially perceive that the supervisor has power and legitimacy in the context and the meaning they take from the statement is to treat it as a guiding principle as they learn their tasks and perform their role. They see their role as customer service representatives in full partnership with their organization in striving to achieve the ultimate goal of customer satisfaction, believing that this goal will ultimately serve them too. They might be rewarded with recognition from supervisors, greater compensation, and eventual promotions. They enact the rule through their communication and activities with customers, as well as in their interactions with other organizational members. This contributes to the constitution of the management-shaped definition of the customer service representative role and contributes to institutional positioning (flow 4). However, once they encounter a combative customer and face the full meaning of the statement—the customer is always right—they begin to realize the effect that the guiding principle has on their membership, to feel the tension between their powers of agentive memberhood and the constraint of their already-negotiated role. The contravention involved here can play out in varied ways: they may continue to perform their membership much as before, but they may consciously or subconsciously begin to enact their role in less compliant ways. Alternatively, they lose sight of their agency and comply with their supervisors' directive without question. Others in the workgroups may have various feelings about their colleagues who comply, ranging from resentment to jealousy when the compliant members are favored for raises, promotions, and new opportunities.

5.3 Ongoing Membership Negotiation

Although membership negotiation is usually most active during the first few weeks and months of membership, communication, and actions associated with this flow have more distal effects on individual members and others. For the individual member, adhering to rules and guidelines influences the relationships they develop with supervisors and coworkers. Supervisors are more inclined to trust them to perform in predictable ways that align with official policies, and rely on them to instill and reinforce norms of compliance. With predictability and trust from alignment on this issue and others, they may become a part of the supervisor's in-group—those with whom the supervisor has a closer and more trusting relationship (Graen & Uhl-Bien, 1995). Members receive special treatment by supervisors, which further reinforces their membership as compliant organizational citizens (Ilies et al., 2007), while also rewarding them with slack to neglect some role duties or even take organizational property as their personal possession. For example, an employee may be allowed to take home technology to work evenings or weekends and never asked to return it.

Coworkers can also be influenced by exposure to their colleague's membership negotiation, and in this case, they may conform with the supervisor's directive for customer service. Seeing their colleague's acceptance and compliance can cause others to fall in line and not question the meaning of the statement, its legitimacy, or the supervisor's power to make and enforce the policy. The transtruction results in membership that is constituted with an organizationally focused orientation and approach to the role. Even if they initially question the statement's power, they might feel more pressure to give in when coworkers comply. They do not attempt to negotiate that element of their membership and, as they also perform the role with this ideal, they further reinforce this enactment as normative of membership in the organization.

Do the Rules of Membership Apply to All?

Martin et al. (1983) offer a memorable story that demonstrates assumptions that some might have about whether leaders must adhere to organizational rules much like rank-and-file members. The story involves IBM Chairman of the Board Thomas Watson, Jr., members of his support staff, and a security guard named Lucille Burger, whose job it was to ensure that only individuals with the proper security name badge entered certain secure areas of the IBM building. One day, when Watson and his team sought entry into a controlled area, Burger recognized Watson but noticed that he was not wearing the proper security badge, stopped him, and told him that he could not enter because his "admittance was not recognized" (Martin et al., 1983, p. 440). Watson's team members were shocked by the security guard's impediment, assuming she did not recognize the chairman of the board. However, Watson appeared to understand the fuller implications of the situation. He raised his hand, stopping his staff's protests to the security guard, but asked one of his men to obtain for him the appropriate badge. This story has been recounted by others (see also Mumby 1987) as it is a powerful demonstration of the importance of leaders communicating that they are not above the rules and setting an example for other members. With this communicative action, he affirmed the equality of all members, at least where security is concerned. Had Watson ignored Burger's directive to stop, most immediately, he would have undermined the security guard's power and legitimacy in enforcing security rules. He would have told IBM members that rules can be broken by some, inviting members to henceforth question the company's rules. The constitutive effects are significant for self-structuring (flow 2). Breaking the rule and communicating that the company's rules can easily be broken by some constitutes an organization whose members do not adhere to their own rules—at least if you are in a leadership role.

Individuals who reject rules or norms that they believe are illegitimate because they are overly restrictive often not only push back as previously described, but their nonconforming behaviors influence others. If members see their peers rejecting guidelines and either benefitting from that choice by not having to perform duties they find distasteful, or at least, not suffering consequences, they contribute these behaviors to their workgroup's norms, influencing how other members—current and future—enact the customer service representative role. Their large or small deviant interactions and behaviors can create *cross-currents*, described as discourses among groups of members that deviate from the dominant discourse set by leaders (Giles & Myers, 2020). As cross-current discourses continue, they can be empowered, causing more members to join their flow.

Individuals who participate in the cross-current can gain strength as opinion leaders in their workgroup, making them less reliant on supervisors causing them to further ignore supervisors' advice or directives. This can cause leaders to reassess polices and values of the organization. Although relationships between leaders, supervisors, and members might not be negatively affected, they can be less stable. When cross-currents gain strength, the resistant members can reconstitute the modalities of membership, and the experience of membership itself.

5.4 Members' Relationship to the Organization

The tenor of the membership negotiation flow decisively influences one's relationship with the organization. As Giddens (1991) argues, in the contemporary world individuals' identities and experiences of life have become directly tied to organizations and institutions. Individuals define themselves and others perceive them often on the basis of the organizations in which they are members (employees, volunteers, and other types of memberships) and their role within them. For example, individuals commonly introduce themselves to new acquaintances based on their organizational membership: "I'm a firefighter for the U.S. Forest Service" or "I'm a student at Arizona State University." This organizational link to personal identity is so much the case that individuals might remain employed in an organization, not because they enjoy the job or have any particular loyalty to it, but because they like the prestige it brings to them to say that they are employed there. However, one's relationship to the organization and perceptions of it can influence qualities of membership, including organizational commitment, citizenship behaviors, intent to remain in the organization, and notably, organizational identification—the process wherein individuals define themselves in terms of their organizational membership (Mael & Ashforth, 1992). Organizational identification is "interaction or other behaviors demonstrating one's attachment" (Scott et al., 1998, p. 303) and is the belief in shared common values, and the perception that membership in the organization is a salient part of one's social identity (Mael & Ashforth, 1992). Like other elements of membership, organizational identification is influenced through the structurational hermeneutic—when a member's flow reflects and is aligned with values espoused by organizational leaders and other members, the mere act of communicating and enacting those behaviors enhances the member's identification (Scott et al., 1998).

Drawing again on our example of the supervisor's unrelenting drive for superior customer service, members who comply may develop stronger organizational identification by enacting communication and behaviors that closely align with the defined organizational objective (Scott et al., 1998). Over time, even if they initially did not feel a strong desire to obediently serve customers, through their communication and actions, eventually, their values really are aligned with the organization (Tyler & Blader, 2003)—sort of a "faking it until you make it" phenomenon (Goffman, 1961; Hill, 1992). They negotiate their membership to adapt to organizational expectations, but also to accept the attitude and behaviors associated with the role. In the example of the customer service representative, they perform the role contributing to the flow as a devoted representative and may come to genuinely feel the role as performed. As a result of enacting the role, they may develop stronger relationships with their customers and more favorable relationships with supervisors. However, pressures created by this flow could cause negative effects such as burnout and turnover when members overcommit for extended periods of time and or they feel as if their extra contributions are under-valued (Irshad & Bashir, 2020; Kreiner, 2006). The potential effects are lower member commitment and citizenship behaviors and potentially, turnover. Also problematic is when members identify with the organization (or its leaders) to the extent that they engage in or cooperate with activities that might be deceptive, unethical, or even illegal (Conroy et al., 2017; Irshad & Bashir, 2020). Through this flow, these outcomes extend beyond the immediate effect on the individual member to diminishing loyalty and productivity by those who are subjected to the pressures felt and discussed in the workgroup discourse. Long-term, the flow can have lasting effects by constituting the culture of the organization.

5.5 Materiality

Material aspects of organizational membership—such as physical appearance, attire, office space, and workplace technology, just to name a few—play a profound role in membership negotiation. Proximity to supervisors and leaders can facilitate trust, enabling members to develop stronger relationships, and advantaging them for promotions (Stryker et al., 2012). Of course, members who are already recognized as trustworthy, particularly skilled, or have positive relationships with supervisors are more likely to be chosen by leaders for favorable locations near leaders (Pentland, 2012). The size and location of office space both communicate power and also are rewards. Those with higher profile offices are generally afforded more voice. Offices with more windows and a view or larger offices can benefit these officeholders because more meetings are held in their "home territory." Variations on these issues operate in many organizations; what is of note relative to membership negotiation is how these issues potentially pit one member against others and how management uses these issues of materiality to potentially reward some, but punish others.

A different situation emerges with open workspaces. Open workspaces have become popular in recent years with the aim of fostering stronger relationships and more collaboration between coworkers, offering proximity that can improve connectivity and relationship building (Knight & Haslam, 2010). However, open workspaces afford less privacy. Following a transition to open workspaces in a Finnish transportation company, Sivunen and Myers (2022) found that employees felt diminished value in their organization, which affected their identification with the company. For example, several asked why they bothered to work so hard only to be relegated to work in a large bullpen environment. Others were pleased because they felt that they had more access to supervisors who also worked in the open workspace. Thus, the meaning of the change influenced the legitimacy the workers felt and the power they perceived.

In contemporary organizations, technology's constitutive effects are undeniable (See also the discussion in Chapter 6.). Organizations that adopt the newest technologies often operate much differently than those that do not. New technology can make organizational operations much more efficient by collecting and sorting useful data and facilitating communication, which can change the nature of work and help members be much more effective. These qualities can be attractive for members and attract others to join. However, technology can be expensive to adopt due to the cost of the technology; also significant is the time required to train members on its use. Further, new technologies come with bugs or unforeseen issues that make adoption risky at least in the short run. Employees can also become attached to their older technologies and intimidated by having to learn and change routines. These concerns can cause leaders to delay adopting new technologies. However, this too, comes at a price. Members can become frustrated by out-of-date technology systems that impede their work.

Members can also be defined by technology. Some members easily adopt technologies and become identified by their ease and expertise in their use. They simultaneously negotiate their membership as up-to-date, even innovative individuals. Others in the organization seek out their skills, asking for their help to understand the capabilities and outputs of the new technology. Still other members are defined by their reliance on older technologies and systems; their image and skills sets can be harmed by their resistance to adopt. These individuals might have great cognitive abilities, and as leaders they can be at the forefront in strategy, but they can become reliant on others to perform tasks and risk becoming perceived as old-fashioned or limited.

5.6 Constitutive Effects

The processes of membership negotiation as described in this chapter create, transform, and even dissolve membership for individuals, and for organizations, too, inasmuch as having members is a constitutional requirement for organizations. In any one organizational context, some individuals may be joining the organization. For them, many contextual issues at the time of their entry—for example, the individuals involved in new member selection and training or the level of the organization's profitability at the time, and other environmental issues—can influence who is selected, their training, and attitudes of newcomers. Thus, the contours of the membership negotiation flow have reciprocal effects on self-structuring (flow 2)—who fills roles in the organizational structure and how hierarchy is communicated to members. The selection and training of new members also afford different levels of activity coordination (flow 3) based on the skills they are trained on and the experience they bring, which also shapes membership for others. In addition, those who become members and the values they hold, position the organization/institution (flow 4) based on how members enact their roles, which enables others to compare the organization to similar entities. For example, individuals might be selected for membership who have been poorly screened by human resources. They might have provided inaccurate information on their employment applications or have attitudes that make them poorly suited for teamwork or customer service. Mistakes such as this can affect flow 2 in their ability to achieve goals, how effective they are as part of a team (flow 3), and whether their mistakes create a poor image for the organization (flow 4).

Similarly, individuals negotiating their membership as they exit the organization are implicated in vacancies they leave in the various functional areas as seen on an organizational chart (flow 2) and how processes can be delegated and completed (flow 3) with implications for customers and other external audiences (flow 4). Members with extensive experience can choose to quit at once, telling their customers that management has treated them poorly. Large gaps in one department can have negative implications for achieving goals (flow 2), workflows (flow 3 as well as 2), and how the community views the organization and whether others will choose to join it (flow 4). Overall, these flows have a constitutive effect on how they transform the organization immediately and in the future.

5.7 Drawing on Membership Negotiation

Several studies have used membership negotiation as a construct to examine and discuss how members adjust to and integrate into the cultural and functional elements of the organization (Scott & Myers, 2010). These studies primarily focus on the early stages of membership and the interactions between the newcomers and others in their organizations relative to the effect of past work experience (Endacott & Myers, 2019), whether newcomer socialization influences membership negotiation and the organization (Stephens & Dailey, 2012), how communication professionals become familiar with coworkers and the diverse various functions of their organizations (Woo & Myers, 2020), and the effects of differing workplace flexibility policies (Nordbäck et al., 2017). McClelland-Cohen (2020) explored how individuals negotiated membership in a grass-roots organization that transformed to become a national organization affecting national and local elections. Although Bean and Buikema (2015) used the entire four flows model in their analysis of the decline and fall of al-Qa'ida, only one element of their analysis discussed the complexity of membership and affiliation in the terrorist organization in which membership was unclear and shaded, even to those within.

Prior to the introduction of the term, membership negotiation, these studies may have conceptualized their studies differently to examine how newcomers become assimilated into the organization. Organizational assimilation—defined as "the process by which individuals become integrated into the culture of an organization" (Jablin, 2001, p. 755)—shares much in common with the processes involved in membership negotiation. While organizational assimilation is a communicative process of interaction between newcomers and incumbents, it is a more limited term focused on the integration of an individual member. Membership negotiation allows researchers to fully appreciate and explore that membership really is a negotiation involving back-and-forth interactions. Unfortunately, most previous studies do not fully make use of the flow metaphor to demonstrate how members' interactions to position themselves in the organization, both functionally and socially, extend beyond the individual to include the other parties involved in the negotiation—supervisor, peers, other members with higher or lower rank, and either customers or other outsiders.

While it would not be suitable for all research, it is intriguing to reimagine organizational socialization and assimilation studies as membership negotiation inquiries. A recently published study by Jiang et al. (2021) found that newcomers who witness supervisors' abusive communication negatively affect newcomers' proactivity and, ultimately, their organizational socialization. Their negative socialization was operationalized as the newcomers' lower role clarity, task mastery, and social integration. While these findings are valuable, an examination of membership negotiation would provide an understanding of how the newcomers process the experience of observed abuse—for example, about how they feel after being positioned within the organization—perceptions and relativity to others. It could also examine how members' integration is constitutive of the organization—how are they shaping it now and for the future. Another example is Myers' (2005) study on the organizational assimilation of firefighters, a study that examined only the effects of the communicative and behavioral processes on probationary firefighters. It did not examine the booters' ability to negotiate their membership within their fire stations and with coworkers despite firefighters' traditions, which may have lasting effects on crews. Future socialization-assimilation studies should also consider how membership negotiation by individuals and throughout the organization are constitutive of roles, workgroups and, of course, the organization.

5.8 Conclusion

This chapter described the first flow, membership negotiation. It is impossible to consider an organization that does not have people associated with it. While some individuals associated with organizations might be suppliers, clients, silent stockholders, or regulatory agents, members are actively involved in engaging in processes that make the organization what it is.

As we presented in this chapter, numerous communicative processes are a part of this flow including—but not limited to—developing relationships with other organizational members and those associated with the organization, developing an organizational identity and positioning oneself relative to others; learning about, adopting and performing the functions associated a role; and developing a relationship with the organization which can include developing commitment, loyalty, and identification. Transtructions, the transformation of communication and behaviors to be constitutive, occur as individuals participate in organizational processes involved in membership. Individuals interpret meaning, norms, and power associated with others' and their own interactions, which become entangled with constitution. Through these ongoing communicative processes of transtructions, membership is negotiated for individuals, workgroups, and the people of an organization. This is but one flow that, combined with the other three flows, is constitutive of organizations.

6

Flow Two: Self-Structuring

A social collection of people—a crowd or neighborhood—might have some agents trying to organize it as a base for parties, riots, etc., but they have no coordinated goals or trustworthy means of achieving the goals. Such collections can develop into *organization* systems insofar as they are arranged, with interrelations maintained through explicit communication, in ways that facilitate progress toward explicit goals through their operations or mutual connection. Specifically, such systems are bounded enough: to define the term *member*, to develop and maintain legitimate ways of crossing the boundaries, and to make member activities explicitly relevant and coordinated with each other (the other three of our flows).

Organizations are *arranged* and become *bounded* in the first instance by communication that—through reflexive self-monitoring—studies, records, plans, articulates arrangements and boundaries, and in many other ways, structures them. Some authors extend this idea by holding that communication is autopoiesis, or *self-making, self-organizing*. All four of our flows, being constitutively enacted by agents, are in various ways self-making, self-monitoring, reflexively maintaining or transforming the resource amalgam of the organization—for instance, membership negotiation enfolds people and thereby makes something novel, a social system. But in the self-structuring flow, discourse goes past that to accomplish self-making through noticeable, intentional communicative reference itself.

Another point deserves early mention: an organization is, we must emphasize, like a city in Giddens' (1981) analysis:

> …a 'generator of effective space' [for the exercise of power], or what I have called…a 'storage container', that permits a [unique level of] time-space distanciation, [as the]

The Communicative Constitution of Organizations: The Four Flows Model, First Edition.
Robert D. McPhee, Karen K. Myers, and Joel O. Iverson.

> locus of transformation/mediation relations.... Power is generated by the transformation/ mediation relations inherent in the allocative and authoritative resources comprised in structures of domination. (p. 144, 92)

The flow of power, its bases, and its effects, is the special intent, often explicit, and certainly the outcome, of self-structuring by agents with self-monitored awareness of goals and other imperatives. And that is a distinctive way that organizations are unique: that agents are, ideally in a coordinated way, communicating to bring about structural constraints/enablements that will shape and direct actors' work in the system, and outcomes of that work, in a part or the whole organization. Researchers of organizations should look for communication of that sort, which will be a crucial part of organizational constitution.

We distinguish three varieties of self-structuring communication. First, obviously, is the sort of plan or other explicit formulation that is called formalized or just formal. This *formal structuring* category includes such elements as explicitly stated goals and rules; members' officially stipulated formal roles, activities, and interaction; deeds and contracts for property and supplies to be possessed or controlled by the organization; thus, prescribed boundaries, domains, and linkages among organizational communication and processes. Boundary discourse, in particular, occurs both between organizational *members* and with *outsiders*. It is useful in discussions of constitution because it both implies a social (and often physical) scope for the legitimate relevance of the other elements, and is the explicit and implicit assumptive foundation for their meaning and power. This broad usefulness of communication implicating the constructed notion of *organizational boundary* does not end up with a single clear, effective boundary for the organization; its ambiguities and gaps constitute it in their variety and inconsistency. But all of these elements—just like various sorts of boundaries—are sustained in multiple, mutually reinforcing flows of discourse that gain their authority from their overt legitimacy and, even more, from their allocative power over rewards and deprivations based on organizational [bounded] lists for membership, wages, hierarchy positioning, promotions, and other stocks of resources. Messages and interactions in this current of discourse structure and constitute the organization by themselves being resources, explicitly documented to be (in the ideal case) stable, clear, and reliable, drawn on and reproduced in organizational—and related—discourse. The flow is *necessitated* by agents who seek to use, or do purposefully use, the well-known formal structuring practices to make, and empower by legitimizing, transformative moves. For instance, like giving raises to members (a necessitating message would be "X deserves a raise, can we find room in the budget for that") or initiating new products ("We should offer something to compete with the Prius?"). Such messages, like others that self-structure, join other formality-relevant ones by colonizing all currents of organizational discourse, even though we must pay attention to processes wherein formal discourse is redesigned, overrun, eroded, or muddied in its production/reproduction.

The second variety is the *system of organizational information and communication technology.* Actually, the "system" is a conglomerate of networks and resources, partly overtly chosen and directed in empowered decision processes. This conglomerate is then designed and embodied either, *first,* by information system engineers who implement the hardware and software media constantly transformed by systems and versions. Information systems are necessitated by powerful agents' recognition, mostly flowing from engineers and salespeople, that such systems are useful for solving problems or supporting new organizational initiatives. But the conglomerate is, *second* and increasingly, elaborated either by members connecting and augmenting the systems with person-to-person linkages—or by empowered organizational actors seeking power to do surveilling—rerouting and mining, collecting, and commodifying the flowing information channelized by this augmented network. They can do this with organizational technology or their own technology. The resulting network constitutes the organization in three ways by (a) being divided, usually inconsistently and problematically, into *legitimate organizational* vs. *other* technology-mediated flows; (b) mediating practical relations among members and activities relative to organizational goals; (c) least visibly, mediating efforts at all hierarchical levels to transform the network into a resource for select groups, within the organization or without.

Third is the intermingled system of interactional and relational phenomena that typically are not authorized or labeled, but noticeably *characterize* the organization; these are conceived and studied as *organizational culture.* Organizationally distinctive cultures include features as diverse as badges and logos, typical clothing styles, traits like a friendly or aggressive atmosphere, and root norms of acceptable, respect-worthy, and organization-serving action. But they also are *culture,* perspectival and practical resources characteristically enabling and constraining members as they conceive, articulate, and figure out how to react to events in or outside the organization. Agents seek resources to make sense of their situations, and such quests for shared meaning, and/or interactions that help shared meanings emerge, are *necessitating* organizational culture as a medium of self-structuring. This cultural interpretive frame includes styles and themes of practical production of the formal structure and the organization's information communication technology (ICT)—it engulfs, in a word, the other two varieties of self-structuring as a sort of internal confluence. Cultural themes also tend to be appropriated by members in expressing and constructing their personal identities.

In this chapter, we elaborate on each of these varieties of self-structuring and describe the communicative self-structuring process that constitutes organizations. By even presenting these as alternate modes of self-structuring, we are avoiding the notion of a super-agent "structuring itself," or of organizations as super-agents seeking rationality, etc., and instead emphasizing the constitutive communication practices, reinforcing and contraventive ones among them, through which all self-structuring happens.

6.1 Type 1: Formal Structuring

Organizations are overwhelmingly depicted in popular culture as loci of power-laden control and constriction of people's options. One important way organizational members' actions are guided is by articulating formalized rules and authority relations—by *formal structuring*—that leaders create, communicate, and sometimes enforce. The *formal structure* thus created is a distinct variety of the structurational resources drawn on by agents to act and communicate. Formal structure is prototypically overt, *out there*, in explicit discourse, typically depending on written resources. Formal rules (Don't smoke) and job titles (President or Outside Linebacker) are the first sorts of formal structure we think of, but we should remember that lots of other types exist, as discussed below. Especially important for giving punch to all these formal structures are more specific policies and procedures for applying the formal labels, rules, and other resources, as well as for reflexive monitoring of the effects, good or bad, of all the formal structuring.

Knowledge of formal rules and how to obey (or disobey) them is an important structural resource, but a simple, material piece of paper with rules written on it is of course not a resource without a user's practical knowledge. But real practical knowledge about handling formalized discourse requires that discourse to exist, to be known. Formal structure, while often generally overt, can be secret—available only to select members.

Often, *formal* rules are thought to simply control members, curtailing their freedoms. However, rules and structuring discourse can also helpfully guide members about what behaviors are expected and rewarded, not just those that merit reprimand or even termination.

Moreover, due to uncertainty or past experiences in other organizations, members expect a rule to exist—"What's the rule here about smoking?" In doing so, they are seeking out formal structure. As viewed in structuration theory, as members engage in behaviors that follow rules, they practically interpret those rules (which includes learning, recreating, and reinforcing them), thus making the rules more enduring, more sedimented, and difficult for members to break.

One current in ST theorizing about organizations emphasizes the organized and organizing message assemblages that constitute and reconstitute institutions (a topic that will be more fully explored in Chapter 8). For our purposes, a study by Schrodt et al. (2006) about divorce decrees (formal, though not organizational) illustrates the different ways formal self-structuring communication works. They note that the decree can function as a *contract*, allowing parties to hold one another to observe its general dictates, sometimes enabling smooth coordination but sometimes constraining adaptation to circumstances, or as a *guide*, grounding communication that stretches or even contradicts the letter of the decree. Just so, around any formalized text, there is always a web of communication in which its rules are followed or adapted or even ignored or purposely violated—all of which belong in this flow as self-structuration producing/reproducing the formalisms. This idea of texts or formalisms *structurated* by the flow is thoroughly analyzed by an important wave of studies of organizational communication genres (cf. Orlikowski & Yates, 1994; Trace, 2011; Yates, 1989), wherein genres of texts, despite impermanence and stylistic appropriation themselves (described well in Bazerman & Bonini, 2009, as well as Im et al., 2005) have been shown to give meaning, orient, ground collaboration in, and stabilize or structure the surrounding flow. In response, "because genres are enacted through a process of structuring, members are always negotiating, interpreting, and improvising in ways that allow for changes to their organizing structures" (Im et al., p. 571). This process can alter the generic form or its prevalence. These ideas are reconceptualized in flow terms later.

The presence of this sort of interpretive web results from a basic contradiction plaguing any system of formalized rules such as an organizational mission, say, or an activity schedule, or list of excellence criteria for an employee. These rules must be applicable in some situation, but any specific situation includes constraints that taint and twist the rules. For instance, the generality and imperative force of any element of formal structure tends to contravened by its application by members seeking to structure (feeling and expressing a necessity for) freedom, local adaptability, or personal power.

Outside pressures communicated through outside messages that are not consistent with the work prescribed in the rules, still necessitate attention to the rules but persuade us to deviate. For instance, a doctor's prerogative of professional control over patient treatment can subvert nurses' professional roles or an immediate response to patients whose condition suddenly changes (Nicotera & Clinkscales, 2010). But, when members judge organizational rules as overly restrictive or wrong, they may choose as empowered agents to ignore or break the rules, for example, by feeling entitled to harass other members and urge or pressure their colleagues to do the same. Such behaviors still reproduce the harassment rule, as a broken rule, now liable to be mocked and flouted in many other situations. Rule-breaking can result in members being called out by supervisors or others who view their deviance from the rule as a violation. In that case, the member has a choice to either adjust their behavior, switch to more surreptitious violations, or to evaluate whether they wish to resist conforming to the rule or leave the organization. If they are successful in resisting organizational pressure to change their behavior, the rule and the organization are likely to be reshaped in ways adapted to their behavior. But whether regularly flouted and dead, or revised in a more solidly enforced new text, the original formal rule is still a resource, used by members to frame the new situation. Most importantly, the rule organizes behavior—in most but not all cases, coordinates behavior—in reliable ways.

For instance, organizational communication scholars and others have done extensive research on firefighting and rules, as well as other structures such as Incident Command and High Reliability. They explore how these structures are implemented, their unintended consequences, and their transformations—that is, their structuration—in the overall armamentarium available to firefighting organizations (Ford, 2018; Thackaberry, 2004). In particular, the US Forest Service has a codified set of safety directives that "participate in everyday activities through structuring action. Safety documents remain active as members reference them in their day-to-day activities…." (Jahn, 2019b, p. 238). Jahn posits that such rules: (a) guide planning of daily tasks, (b) highlight problems and roadblocks requiring action and adaptation, (c) supply a codified knowledge stock about how to adapt to "handle and avoid similar hazards in the future" (p. 238), (d) are transportable to other members and situations, (e) give communicative resources for critique, advocacy, and dissent, and (f) are enmeshed in a dynamic web of related documents and an application/change cycle. They were necessitated as organization members sought ways to prevent unsafe actions that could have disastrous consequences. Though useful in all these ways, the rules were found too inflexible to guide optimal firefighter action when put into practice within a dangerous and dynamic context, and focusing on safety rule violations stifled safety dialogue rather than enhance safety.

Jahn goes on to describe how these rules, articulated in the usual rigid way, are reframed in a revised set of documents (which are formal structure) called Doctrine, which holds that the rigid-seeming safety rules should be seen as "not absolute rules (but principles that) provide guidance in the form of concepts and values,…general guidance that requires judgment in application. Therefore, while authoritative, Doctrine is not prescriptive. Doctrine is about tools, not rules" (USFS, 2005, p. 10, 12, cited in Jahn, 2019b, p. 241). Moreover, even this formal structural statement about how to view the old rigid rules—a statement that expresses well the view of structuration theory (cf. Scott and Trethewey, 2008)—does not stand on its own. It is part of a formally stipulated procedure, crafted largely by social scientists, for investigating, assessing, and learning from putative disastrous mistakes, a procedure that avoids casting blame in favor of finding sources, at many hierarchical levels, for accidents that might result from even the best professional judgment on the spot. But a structurational approach goes one step higher, to urge that this learning-seeking stipulated procedure, too, is a resource that may both enable positivity and growth, yet constrain identification of truly reprehensible bumblers. We should note that formal structural proclamations favoring variety and dialogue can be applied—produced and reproduced—in wildly unpredictable, perverse ways. "Let a hundred schools of thought contend" was a famous proclamation by Chinese Communist leader Mao Zedong, though it was followed very soon by official action to snuff out about 99% of the schools.

Formal structuring in modern organizations—the kind that has swept through much of the world—creates a controllable, potentially rational (within its own logic and goals) order among the people drawing on its resources. Even for rank-and-file members, structuring rules and information lets them understand their role and power, typically, to perform their own tasks, cooperate with others (unless prohibited), and identify with their organization relative to the outsiders they encounter. Weber, Simon, and other groundbreaking scholars have noted that formal structuring also distanciates employees, legitimizing unique powers for members—a sphere of action that is "theirs," and equipment to exercise work powers within it—and leading them to see things from their own sanctioned viewpoint. They learn, via structuring, to ignore collateral damage of their own and others' activities when structuring guides and sanctions them to do so. Obviously, this separation has to be partly overcome, in communication, to negotiate membership, coordinate activities, and act to support the organization's societal position—but preferably only in channels open relative to structuring.

6.2 Organizational Goals

Formal structuring constitutes, most overtly, one or more orienting, legitimizing goals recognized by members. In the previous chapter, we described how membership negotiation intermingles with, in varied ways, inclusion in the flow of communication about the organization's goals as an aspect of organizations per se. It is vital for giving all members a sense of where the organization is going, what actions and outcomes are worthwhile, and why the members are attending to their roles at all. Membership negotiation is constitutive for a deeper reason: its necessary contribution to and involvement with self-structuring (our flow two), for example, self-structuring via organizational goals, which, as we shall explain below, constitutes organizations, too. Systems such as armies, small-scale or nation-state governments, and corporations are prototypical in recent history throughout the world, mainly because of their effectiveness in pursuit of their unifying goals and collateral impacts on other parts of society.

Documents or conversations that generate, maintain, and apply, or even contest organizational goals are manifestly self-steering discourse: they focus activities and communication on the goals, ideally making the activities help achieve them. Of course, other terms for and types of "goals" exist: objective, profit, desired outcome, target, etc. One especially good example of a goal is an organization's mission statement. For instance, the US Forest Service has an explicit mission:

What is the Forest Service mission? "The mission of the Forest Service is to sustain the health, diversity, and productivity of the nation's forests and grasslands to meet the needs of present and future generations." (https://www.fs.usda.gov/about-agency/meet-forest-service)

This statement is condensed from a lot of other subgoals and versions. One is detailed as follows:

Our plan contains four outcome-oriented goals for the Forest Service.

1. Sustain Our Nation's Forests and Grasslands.
2. Deliver Benefits to the Public.
3. Apply Knowledge Globally.
4. Excel as a High-Performing Agency.

https://www.fs.usda.gov/strategicplan

Goal statements like the ones just cited have a special character: they are authoritative and articulated in a way meant to be decisive. Down through all but the most recent history, that has meant they are written. Written text can be stable, more than talk, and can be preserved and protected from rebels or criminals. Written goals can be worked on or amended. They can be duplicated, distributed, and certified as genuine. We can see written or other stabilized goals as attempting to impose fixation in the flow of organizational communication. *Then, to be relevant in any organizational way,* organizational words and actions must exhibit some relevance to, and at the extreme, be obsessed with, achieving the formally articulated goals.

But we must note that *goal,* like *mission,* is a concept that is problematic in multiple ways (Iverson, 2010a; Perrow, 1961, 1970): without question, *official* goals must be accompanied by a flux of communication supplying interpretive connection to practice (for instance, specified and operationalized in policies or in what Perrow calls less overt *operative goals* [1961, p. 855]). He also notes a variety of types of goals, including *product* (e.g., quality) versus *system* (e.g., overall profit), written in highly public versus practical planning documents. Even explicit, official goals may be (a) vague, (b) paradoxical, (c) stated variably across documents or contexts, or (d) nonconsensual, and thus taken as illegitimate or provocative. They vary from one division of the organization to others, so that local goals seem more important than the system goals. They also vary politically as those in authority see varying threats or opportunities and thus articulate and interpret them in different ways. Additionally, they drift with the passage of time and new developments elsewhere (March & Simon, 1958). But in conformity with the specifically organizational power system, individual members can or must use communicated goals, with all their flaws, to guide and evaluate their own as well as others' behavior.

ST encourages us to ask about a goal's presence in rationalization and accounts and overt expression (or tacit implementation) as a reflexive resource, not a static document, drawn on in action. All the flows of an organization's communication, including goal communication as well as all non-goal discourse enacting the other three flows, get empowered, pulled, and constricted, judged and legitimated, discussed or avoided, and contextualized by the goals. Contrariwise, we must remember that an organization's goals, no matter how overt and simple, get washed and wrung with the other three flows in the mangle of communication, as well as the mangle of resources/practices incorporating extra-organizational structuration. We will present the recent international emphasis on corporate social responsibility later in Chapter 8 as relevant to particular organizations as subjects of organizational communication register, elaborate, and reproduce that institutional system. All of these, phenomena that broaden the range of goal reproduction, are potential foci for 4F research, though they certainly have been broadly explored in valuable relevant work (Cheney, 1983a, 1983b; Conrad & Cheney, 2018).

The goals, and the flows carrying but also oriented by them, are prime examples of organizational self-structuring. To steer all the flows—to work as orienting guides in membership negotiation and activity coordination, and interpretive banners in institutional positioning—goals would ideally be overwhelmingly consensual, influential, and clear. But as just discussed, they aren't. Yet, despite the flaws, articulating a goal is a powerful way of making sure that a goal is upheld in later action and communication, and able to organize power resources for achieving it. Accepting and applying a goal in context equally empowers an employee, as a guide to direct their attention and action, and just as importantly, to account for it in coordinating or evaluation contexts.

6.3 Organizational Boundaries

There is a considerable temptation to define organizations as collections of people and activities located inside clear social and even physical boundaries. As an example, think of the military politics involving national boundaries in Eastern Europe or the southern US, or disputes over ownership of a logo or chemical formula. Yet boundary stipulations, in even moderately complex societies, rarely hold water according to their face value design. For instance, a cardinal type of boundary stipulation—the list of members—is inevitably flawed. Such lists are never up to date so as to recognize people in the process of leaving, moving across subunits, or being hired. A member does not always correspond with a single organizational role: members can simultaneously be located in two hierarchies, reporting to two types of managers—this has been called a matrix organization. Or they can be acting managers of a unit without the definite powers of a full manager.

Just so, liaison members, with a formally stipulated presence in two units or even organizations and thus living in inside-outside eddies of communication, inevitably draw on structural resources from both units, easily creating contraventions and undermining normal boundary-creation practices. They are typically agents whose explicit responsibilities answer to multiple collaborators, managers, or powerholders, supposed to find ways to maximally serve the interest of both or all at once. And, equally challenging to the standard conception of boundaries, members can be traitors, such as the idealistic secret leakages of Edward Snowden, informing the public of illegal violations of citizen privacy by US government agencies. Other examples include family and spouses of members who belong to organizations with strong cultures who are acculturated through organizational osmosis to those cultures (Gibson & Papa, 2000).

There are some commonly understood guidelines for stipulating boundaries: they should be clear, relate to visible aspects of the phenomena being bounded, create homogeneous groupings (Galbraith, 1973). ST would say: easily produced and reproduced. But we should keep in mind the contrary aspects of boundary construction: Some boundaries are meant to be crossed, and are articulated to organize crossing—helping new hires cross into membership is a vital correlate of member/nonmember divisions. Sometimes boundary-crossing is a source of creativity. Sometimes boundary maintenance has ethical and societal implications. For instance, drug companies commonly control their drug patents tightly, using this monopolistic control to keep prices high. But at some point, corporate social responsibility (discussed in Chapter 8) may be a factor influencing that tight boundary around the company's patents, and induce the company to allow production of generic versions, with a royalty. Further, organizational boundaries can be drawn in ways that are first power interest-dependent but evolve to become contrary to the organization's power interests.

In short, despite being distinctly imperative and often written, boundaries, like other self-structuring communication, may start as clear lists and walls but are quickly transformed, as an essential part of self-structuring, into porous, negotiated inclusion or separation of members, activities, and resources within versus outside, so as to (misguidedly) invite representation of the organization as a *container*.

6.4 Rules, Goals, and Other Formal Structuring

As we delineated earlier, there are, in addition to goals, *a torrent of varied* other types of formal structural stipulations that, while maintained or transformed in their own communicative currents, energize, redirect, and constrict the other organizational flows of communication and, generally speaking, structure communication and behaviors associated with the organization. Some other forms, noted earlier, include formal role systems such as job labels and descriptions; formal divisions such as departments and teams; other formal relations such as required reporting communications; in addition to lists and inventories, accounting labels and records, templates, policies, implementation procedures, and more, which all may be written in a formal style indicating a claim to authority. These other forms of formal structure have a special effect: they *articulate* the formal goals, or missions, or success criteria, or payoffs to powerful stakeholders such as owner, in ways that contextualize relevant people and their activities.

For instance, sometimes organizations create subgoals, and formally set up organizational subunits such as divisions, workgroups, or project team assignments to pursue them. These subunits, often diagrammed as an organization chart or in ranks like Executive Vice President for Development (a subdivided function), are another sort of formal structure. For instance, here is a statement of a goal, and a set of departments, across government agencies that structure a formal unit to deal with interagency issues of wildland fire:

> Wildland Fire Leadership Council (WFLC): The WFLC is a cooperative, interagency body dedicated to achieving consistent implementation of goals, actions, and policies … [through] high-level dialogues between federal and non-federal entities to set strategic direction for national fire management. The Council consists of… the Chief of the U.S. Forest Service; the Department of the Interior's (DOI) Assistant Secretary for Policy, Management and Budget, the Directors of the National Park Service, Bureau of Indian Affairs… The Council is coordinated by the Department of

Agriculture's Deputy Undersecretary for Natural Resources and Environment and DOI's Assistant Secretary for Policy, Management and Budget. https://www.nifc.gov/sites/default/files/redbook-files/Chapter08.pdf

As the second sentence indicates, this council aims for "high-level dialogues … to set strategic direction for national fire management." Then it lists the formal divisions that must be involved in the dialogues, and stipulates that the DOA's Deputy Undersecretary and the DOI's Assistant Secretary are at the top to coordinate dialoguing in the whole council. This formal structuring statement is more explicit than most delineations of structural hierarchies in saying that the flow among the people on this council is communication. The structure itself is a sort of meta-communication—its words create an organizational place for the dialogues that constitute relations among fire management executives.

An opposite sort of example can be found in the early days of Eventbrite, an events-management technology service, whose "mission is to bring the world together through live experiences, through a powerful, broad technology platform was built to enable creators to… seamlessly plan, promote and produce live events, while reducing friction and costs" (Eventbrite.com, 2023). When it was founded, its organizational hierarchy was gossamer. As described by Julia (the now-CEO) and Kevin Hartz,

JH: Some of our close friends, who had built a few businesses together, gave us this great advice: "Divide and conquer," they said. "Never work on the same thing at the same time." And that was our golden rule. …When we started, I had a nebulous title of president, and Kevin was C.E.O. That was obvious, as he had built companies before. But at the beginning, it's all kind of fake.

I was doing a little bit of everything, but by that point, we had found the customer support lead, the marketing lead, the finance lead. I was not functionally critical. [So] So I decided to focus on people. … .(Gelles, 2019, p. 4)

KH: We also had this perfect triangle where I would work on the product side and hand the designs and specs to Renaud. He would implement them and push the product out to our customers. Julia had a great pulse of the customers and would get their feedback, then filter that back to us. We had this very tight development and release life cycle.

JH: As the business grew we continued that divide and conquer strategy; we looked for areas of the business that matched our individual skills and weren't overlapping. If you have a cofounder, one of the benefits is you'll get from point A to point B two times faster." (Shontell, 2012)

It is instructive to notice the constraints lurking under the surface of her self-understanding. Her perception was that she needed a stipulated—potent, and eventually a formally labeled—position in order to have a (solid, i.e., legitimate) role in the decision-flows of even the nascent three-person interpersonal company. The sense that that position, not her sheer competence or presence in the company from the beginning, grounded her ability to avoid debates about whether she should have a decision voice, how, and when. The sense, to extend the understanding, that formal structuring would legitimately eventuate in an executive position leading to, possibly, CEO-ship. What you hear is constitutive interweaving in the flow of self-structuring communication, with obvious implications for her membership negotiation, activities in coordination with others, and power to constitute relations outside Eventbrite. This is necessitation at work, a formal structure created because it is argued, by powerful agents, to be needed.

The main structural principles of the early Eventbrite were that *golden rule*, and the *perfect triangle* of major subfunctions the rule implicated, which developed, in later years, into separate formal units led by a Chief Officer. (Julia's focus on People led to a Chief People Officer who channels the organizational culture.) Even though nebulous and often ignored, those articulated, stable principles—topoi of necessitation—were wellsprings for structuring the clear work relations, and later formal documents and groupings of employees, that mushroomed as the organization thrived. We should keep in mind that organizations, specifically ones that have formal structures, conquered the world several centuries ago, and are maintained as the supreme powers dominating our lives today. Perhaps artificial and fake from one point of view, they can still be earth-shaking.

6.5 Emergence of Ideas of (Formal) Structuring

As scholars have explored the origins and growth of the relational form known as organizations, they have noticed and focused on some important organizational communication phenomena characterizing and constituting the organization as a form.

Anthony Giddens, in tracing the emergence of organized power systems, emphasized elaborated forms of record-keeping to tally up arrays of agricultural and other products for taxation purposes, for example. He also highlighted the role of devices for marking and recording divisions of territory, to settle issues of ownership and control among powerholders.

A founder of sociology, Weber (1968), is widely regarded as the first author of the idea of *bureaucracy* and even *organization* due to his analysis of bureaucracies such as the Catholic Church and military forces, emphasized their dependence on decisions that were able to embody and employ organized power resources, as a consequence of respected legitimacy because they were rational and legal, in the interpretive context of agents in the organization and in the institutions supporting it. Equally, he highlighted how rational decisions depended on bureaucratic systems of officials transmitting information up vertical hierarchies.

The Nobel-prize-winning scholar Simon (1945; cf. March and Simon, 1958) is noteworthy for his analysis of how organizations perform rationality. They do it by *satisficing*—by dividing up roles and guiding communication in ways *good enough*, not perfectly, but effectively and practically for the organization's purposes. Satisficing is of course a form of necessitation, involving decision processes that agents carve out of ideal rational stipulations because they find adherence to the good enough ones necessary or valuable to avoid impossible demands. But they might also develop since the slack they provide lets power be divided up among department heads.

The communication scholar Beniger (1986) analyzed the growth of far-flung industrial systems such as railroads, and found that they depended crucially on *communication-based control* that could integrate and coordinate those systems. *Scheduled information transmission* (e.g., telegraphs and railroad timetables), which eventually served as foundations for economic empires, had to carry facts for coordinated and trustworthy adjustments that could overcome the problems of complexity and dynamic change.

The business scholar Zuboff (1988) reconceived the notion of organizational control to include two varieties: First, *automated control*, typical of blue-collar work, is reconceived as highly skilled, immediate, and even visceral hands-on labor operating complicated machine tools in complex situations. Second, *informated control* is conceived as remote, distanced, abstract work usually by white-collar employees. But unlike century-old white-collar work of typists and ink-spattered ledger-keepers, informated work is performed within a context of elaborate and sensitive information transmitters. Informated work has the power-centralizing advantage of letting managers surveil employee activity key-stroke-by-keystroke based on identical information feeds instead of managing people acting with skilled, sensitive presence.

6.6 How Formal Structuring Constitutes Organizations

Many sorts of formal structure have seemingly commonsense ways of doing constitutive work. An organizational goal of some sort has to be present, or people flounder and their discourse becomes irrelevant. If we look at an organization chart, we are strongly tempted to say, "This is an organized set of people and relationships"—which is exactly what makes an organization what it is.

We should not quite make that leap. As we argued earlier, and as we will see in the *culture* section, pieces of formal structure like these can't be relied on at face value. For one thing, they are constituents of the organization's culture, setting it off, more or less, from organizations that purport to be totally informal (Pacanowsky, 1988). Second, goals or charts are ideals: we already discussed the research showing how goals get extended, reinterpreted, argued about, drifted away from…so the statements are sometimes hollow, or too simple, to be realistic. They can be what an organization is ideally thought to aim for. However, as abstract ideals they can serve well in a vocabulary useful because it is authoritative and consistent across the organization (McPhee, 1985).

Third, rules and policies are part of a dynamic process of interpretation, use, enforcement, and revision that can last minutes or generations. Clear rules like

"Don't smoke in this building," are easy to follow, to notice noncompliance with, and to sanction, often by a command to go outside. But sometimes, rule clarity evolves into a tangle of issues and debates. A good example is the US Forest Service Doctrine, described above. A more relevant example is the formally stipulated web of communication. In classic bureaucracies, messages were supposed to flow only up or down, with problems between jobs A and B needing to be pushed up for resolution to the official at the peak where the vertical chains for A and B connect. Thus, if a communication class and a math class are assigned to meet in the same room and time, the clash would have to be resolved by someone in higher administration who oversees both departments. (And, even in notably *innovative* but centralized universities today, problems that are similarly localized sometimes do get pushed up to, or get interfered with by, such high-ranking executives). In more modern, practical organizations, communication is formally mandated to flow in multiple directions—but in reality, it can flow as needed, easily from one problem-solver to another, and way beyond to others who can contribute to their solution. This positive flow may, however, be limited because the parties are ignorant of the best resources, but also diverted or blocked by formal, technological, or cultural forces. (Mintzberg et al., 1976 elaborates such complexities found in multilevel organizational decisions.) Such a problem-solving flow can be formally required, encouraged, or just allowed by formal stipulations—but *no rule* is a self-structuring move just as much as *Rule X* is and may constitute the organization as a flexible, loose, sloppy one.

Thus, like goals, the array of other formal structural elements—rules, charts, financial figures, and accounting procedures—tend to have, or refer to, a directional quality, sometimes strong and sometimes very weak. Some (No smoking in the building) are simply mandates of general stipulations in the larger society, related to the larger societal goal of health but intrinsically to work or authority arrangements (unless they get politicized), and can be adopted or discarded without any organizational effect. But, despite its inclusion of paradoxical, counterproductive formal examples, including red tape and fine print in contracts, and despite being inescapably afflicted by contraventions (the other flows, illegitimate activity that still serves organizational norms, and definitely disorganizing communication), they have a constitutive quality. All organizational activities are, if never exactly rule-bound, still rule-relevant, creating a *rule-ish flavor* that spices organizational communication, memberhood, and relationships.

6.7 Formal Structuring and the Four Dimensions

Formal structuring is a way of emphasizing that documents such as mission statements, for example, have authority. We can see formal structure's value in a richer way by using the four dimensions that frame all communication, as discussed earlier. *Interpretive dimension:* Structures are given meaning in discourse announcing and applying them, placing them in a larger context recognized in the fourth flow, only to roil it by placing in it a new thing—an organization—with its own direction. And then the goals, like other structural elements, transform the meaning of other discourse by labeling it useful—and elucidating how, or labeling it irrelevant, usually without mentioning why. The interpretive flow dimension is therefore relevant to the goal. Once a goal is stated, it can be questioned as related to broader goals. For instance, employees of Norfolk Southern might have questioned whether the goal of cost-cutting by eliminating all but one or two engineers per train served the higher goal of public safety, and thus avoided the monstrous chemical spill in East Palestine, Ohio in 2023. Indeed, an explicitly stated goal may become influential in the organization's culture, a process described as the cultural self-structuring flow below. Just so, the other modes of formal structuring exist to provide interpretive templates for valid organizational action. For instance, the Doctrine document gained legitimacy by being promoted and understood as more flexible and less punitive than the rules preceding it, and still more legitimacy by being applied and hammered out in group discussions. *Power dimension*: Goals are the epitome of discursive power tools. They exemplify the ways formal structuring justifies members pushing or pulling others in mandated directions (or constitute a floor for reorienting, resisting, or deviant influence). To do that, they steer the provision of personnel and management, material resources, and authorize activities by subordinate employees. *Norms/ egitimation dimension*: By articulating goals, especially the mission-statement/ financial-charter kind, members create a validation frame for all other organizational discourse. *Constitution dimension*: as we have just recounted, the organization as a social form grew and emerged as people, inspired by goals, learned and spawned the convoluted, organizational systems we see today. For instance, Eventbrite became an organization as its founders worked together, finding and articulating rules to guide and govern their cooperation. At their very taproots, organizations are what they are by being self-steered, especially through formalization.

6.8 Type 2: Information and Communication Technology

It is probably a mistake to speak of the communication technology (the usual current acronym is ICT) of an organization as a system. More realistically, ICT in a contemporary organization is a conglomerate of networks and resources, partly overtly chosen and directed through legitimate, empowered decision processes. The legitimate part of the conglomerate is then designed and installed by information system engineers who articulate a convincing necessity for purchasing, developing, or hiring a system of technical and human technician resources as they fashion and run the organization's hardware and software media. Equally necessitating are factors like rivals' profitable or fashionable ICT innovations, in overblown reports by professionals as well as networked executives.

The recent focus on AI is one example of this phenomenon: fashion as well as proven capacities are currently driving widely varied uses of AI in many sorts of enterprise (Cascio & Montealegre, 2016). Many of these involve simple data processing. Others, like Alexa, allow control of technological processes by vocal or visual cues in everyday language. Still others involve ordinary-language exchanges between human agents and programmed response apparatus. The same sorts of AI devices in wide consumer use are widely employed in organizational contexts, as supplements to communication among employees or with outsiders such as customers. But, equally often, the connection between technology controllers and users of AI devices is not communication even if we interpret that as a very indirect, mediated connection since all of the interpretive context at either end is stripped away by the medium. For instance, AI facilitates the analysis of masses of data to discover trends in more sophisticated ways than statistical analysis. Despite the fact that this big data capability is at the heart of some of AI's most striking successes—expert chess play and human-like verbal output—big data analysis is the *I* part of ICT—it is Information Technology. It comprises communication only in the narrow sense of being a channel between the designer/owner/parameter-chooser and the recipient of output like the name belonging to a *recognized* face or the audio message, "Your prescription will be ready for pick-up at…." In this section, we will be sensitive, as much as possible, to the difference between information and communication processes, but since the first amplifies the second while making its origin and implications opaque, we cannot sever the bond between them in our analysis.

But with the connective potential of ICT comes powerful and necessary constraints, which can be manifested as counterarguments (against the perceived necessity of, say, any IT feature) or tacit counterpressures. The first is sheer cost, including material communication media, technical support work, and varied supportive infrastructure. Second is the urgent threat of technology overload on members' attention, psyches, training levels, and social relations (Edmunds & Morris, 2000; Lee et al., 2016). Third is the issue of vulnerability, for example, hacks by malicious agents, as discussed below. Fourth, ICT are, due both to their complexity and to the mismatch of technology and users, especially likely to engender unanticipated and undesired consequences—communication breakdowns or influences by unintended parts of the network. Fifth is the fact that to satisfy the empowered interests in an organization, even the best or most transparent practical ICT design is always re-oriented to reproduce, with some distortions, the power and task structure of the organization, and then it can either reinforce and serves hegemonic parties (possibly in very limiting, unprofitable, or transformative ways), or becomes a medium for power struggles.

6.9 Bases of ICT

One foundational *information-processing device* that comprises ICT is a computer, an enlightening conception of which is a Turing machine. A Turing machine is actually a theoretic conception, a description of the minimum necessary features that would allow a machine to do what computers do—process information. It is essentially a tape—a string of signs, for instance 1011100...—and a mechanism that operates on the string. An easy visualization is that the mechanism is the transformation of an input string operating on it to create an output string. But the input string isn't just the raw material operated on by the mechanism; it has two other main features. First, the input string (and, as an important feature, the output string *also*) controls what the mechanism does to create or change the output string. For instance, if a sign on the input string is a 1, that can "tell" the mechanism to write a 1, or tell it to write a zero, on the output string, according to a simple rule. Second, the rule governing the mechanism can be complex in certain ways: for instance, governing which direction the machine moves on the input tape. (And we should recognize that there is actually only *one* tape, as the input gets operated on to be both product as well as, reflexively, instruction). Generalizing, ICT is novel in potentially being both the target of operations—data entry, etc.—and a medium of control, an exponentially increasing resource of agentive power. In particular, formalizing the organization by creating a metalanguage of communication often involves labels—*member*, rank, tenure, required communication linkages—that can be easily surveilled and recorded via ICT.

It is worthwhile to distinguish three levels of ICT phenomena that constitute organizations in different ways: *core*, *peripheral*, and *consumerization*. The core is the keep of the organizational castle. This includes the technological operations that, from the viewpoint[s] of powerful interests, demand vigorous protection due to their value for organizational functioning and vulnerability to corruption or exposure. (We note that such a core, if it exists, is dynamic and layered; also, there are probably multiple cores in any organization, arranged by different powerful interests.) ICT allows for varied access controls to guard officially owned computers, routers, or websites, with access achieved through passwords or recognition processes. But the minute we allege the existence of something like a core, we need to emphasize that a well-contained core is impossible: its boundaries cannot be impermeable if its resources are to be useful to guide or inform any internal or external activities. Security is contravened by the need for utility. In particular, core information or processes need ineluctably to connect, to some degree, with the internet—ICT-grounded organizations (i.e., nearly all organizations) are so essentially open that isolating them from social media and the Web would usually both starve them of resources and cripple their productive impacts. Even electrical failures or denial of service cyberattacks typically disable an organization, mainly because they clog its nourishing interchanges with the environment. Cascio and Montealegre (2016) call this "ubiquitous computing," but make the important point that even an earlier notion of Web connections, which they call "strategic communication," achieved interorganizational flows that transfigured the sense of organizational boundary.

But equally importantly, having admitted that, we should also emphasize the counterpoint: members of an organization *can* roughly, equivocally distinguish a core set of "its own" network hierarchically placed agents/media/information stocks. The constant hack attempts experienced by governments and other organizations are deemed important because they afflict both organizational *ownership* of core information, equipment, and processing operations, as well as organizational *control*—the transtructed power that is the essence of organization itself. Using core capabilities and access, empowered members can engage with the organization's "own" messages (including, e.g., private formal structural documents and data); they can also open and process lower levels of peripheral or consumerized communication/information records that subordinates and outsiders think of as their own. For instance, a university *owns* all the emails sent using its accounts, by students or whoever, and it can capitalize or "weaponize" the information they contain.

ICT can indeed be a medium of powerful and centralized control by a high-stratum core. But then, in a reverse counterpoint to ICT centralizing tendencies, technologies have recently allowed many member activities to be increasingly shared in a *peripheral* activity domain with fuzzy boundaries (Cascio & Montealegre, 2016). For instance, a meeting with a speaker *officially* holding the (physical or virtual) floor can face an audience multitasking, providing mediated feedback, recording his/her words, and conducting more or less legitimate back-channel conversations and texting exchanges about the speaker or words being spoken. Sometimes these are purely supportive, like a stage manager or Zoom host organizing the display, sound arrangements, etc. However, ICT has increased the capacity for varied sorts of peripheral communication exponentially.

One sense of *peripheral* is "physically distant": work operations now less often take place in an organization's factory or central office, as work from home has joined field operations and work/life travel routes "on the road" (since physical travel is facilitated by, not replaced by, peripheral ICT.) Indeed, the prime example of how technology can shape organizations is distant work, exploding during the pandemic years, which actually is a total extension of the computer-mediated cooperative work arrangements widely present in organizations since 1980, if not earlier. Organization members are not tied to any physical location, and often negotiate freedom from any rigid schedule of work hours, and scheduling of tasks within a work role is often freer, as well. A related benefit for many workers is the range of technically available supports for work, schedule management, cooperative work, and general network and relationship building. On the other hand, technical instruments are enablements that bring with them constraints and costs. Famously, the power to work at home or from anywhere, with no rigid schedule of hours, means that employees can be treated as on-call 24/7, while also being less trusted outside face-to-face managerial scrutiny. But whether distant or in an organization's location, the possibility of distance work indicates an immense growth in flexibility, enough so that official job roles, functional areas, and even to a limited extent hierarchical levels, can (though they rarely do) wither in significance compared with new formalisms like task group and problem responsibility assignments.

In addition, peripheral networks can be structured by features like expert or lurker roles, subgroups focused on topics, and liaison members linking, in varied ways, distinct sub-net topical clusters. An example describing these features is

Trier and Richter's (2015) study of *organizational online networking* in a global engineering conglomerate, in which members do organizational work and relating through Web-based media, including social media—the websites, Facebook pages, etc. mentioned above. Trier and Richter (2015) find that this network is "a multi-dimensional phenomenon with multiplex" idiosyncratic meanings and "relationships that are unbalanced, primarily consist of weak ties, and are subject to temporal change" (p. 465).

One more overlapping complication at the peripheral level is that distant workers, resisters, and opportunistic members, indeed most members these days, can or must "Bring their Own Technology (BYOT)" (Stephens, 2018), augmenting and constraining the system even as it is constantly being transformed by its central current of systems and versions. When work depends on devices owned by members, the problem of unequal processing capacity becomes important. A special example of this is collaboration among parties through personal devices that differ in their capacities—across national boundaries, for instance. Keeping this slapdash system going is a major problem for systems managers and technicians. The resulting network constitutes the organization because it enables constantly evolving communication among membership ranks, thus practically and both overtly and tacitly, mediating relations among members and activities.

The BYOT phenomenon has sometimes been called *consumerization* because it involves devices purchased by consumers. But we wish to emphasize a different sense of consumerization: An organization's technology easily can include a Web, or other mediated, presence that allows non-members to engage with interactive online facilities—to sign up as members or Facebook links, purchase products, access and manage accounts, or enter portals to receive, for example, sensitive medical information. Sometimes these facilities, while designed as organizational boundary connections for consumers or other organizational publics, are useful means for members to perform their own role activities: a Facebook page for membership can include a function for, for example, interactive work on a manuscript, or a client can share control of the computer screen with a consultant to interactively solve the client's problems.

6.10 How the ICT System Constitutes the Organization

ICT, as mentioned above, is not a system unless we speak in the broadest possible terms: there are no definite boundaries, no definite relations, and no limits to interactions. ICT is part of various flows—indeed, it is the medium of lots of communication. But the technology per se is *not* essentially communication produced by agents: it is "material" information, comprised of signals and their media, and could exist and function without any living agents, like a solar-powered machine in the middle of the desert. To answer the question of how ICT constitutes the organization, we must relate it back, emphatically, to formal communication.

Part of the constitutive force of *formal* structuring is that it—as agentive communication—enmeshes the organization by displaying and arranging its unity under an organization name and top leadership, by stipulating certain agentive communication relations and contents—who should discuss a problem or even be aware of it, and what information or sources they should include, and by a special relevance as directional, imperative context for all organizational activity. Formalism traverses and relates all parts of the organization, facilitating (in an idealist's vision) unparalleled transparency, consistent directedness, and accountability reaching all its subunits and members' practices. But then, with its contravening practices and routines of use, ICT structuring is, in a muddy, wildly magnifying, and distorted way, the flip-side mirror image of the overt, power-enshrining organizational formal structure. It is a patterned medium of power. Formal workgroups and project teams can have their own Facebook pages and Zoom hosting sites (all organizational property, all with goal- and rule-relevant communication). While the impact of ICT is a matter of agentive use, its production/reproduction is a conditional "function of the material components comprising the artifact, the institutional context in which a technology is developed and used, and the power, knowledge, and interests of human actors (developers, users, and managers)" (Orlikowski. 1992, p. 421).

However, as already noted, ICT implementation ushers multiple hierarchy dimensions into a prototypical old-style organization. The first transformation of hierarchy is the emergence of a new power group—the information technicians, designers, and ICT administrators themselves, concentrated in a dedicated ICT department or dispersed across functional and hierarchical loci. This new group has special power because it wields and governs the essential surveillance operations. Second, the ideal, clearly designed ICT system is disrupted by new software advances, computer purchases, and changes in the organization's domain—new power tools, the new technologized periphery—a disruption like what happens with every new version of an iPhone or similar smartphone disrupts many routine features of earlier phones. An organizational instance is a merger or acquisition that typically involves absorbing or overpowering the technical system of the victim organization. However, the employees of the influx are usually initially muddled and disruptive, continuing their own culture and technical orientation peripherally to formally legitimated ICT. Formally empowered agents of the consuming organization must work to install, or hook up, the subordinate ICT just as agents must negotiate membership of the new employees. Last is the reverse influence of the peripheral network on the formal, as technology-based social capital and capabilities give unequal, often disruptive, power to agents in unequal ways that may not match their hierarchical positions. In the extreme, nonmembers (consultants and knowledgeable users) can have power that is greater than, and disruptive of, managers and executives.

The complexity of ICT's power-structure mirroring is conveyed well in Stephens' (2018) structuration-based model of dialectics of control (constraint, but therein enablement) of member activity that draws on (often personally owned) mobile devices in organizations. In a duality with the enabling powers of structurational individual agency, Stephens describes constraints maintained or transformed via interactional emergence, interpersonal relationships, customers, groups, and hierarchies. She dissects the materiality and expectations constraining (but, never forget, also enabling) their agency. Her research illustrates the power of structuration-guided research to illuminate both well-known power influences on new foci (e.g., mobile devices and their use), and transformed constellations of influence resources.

This ICT result, contravened reproduction of the formal communication flow, is *one* feature of ICT as it constitutes organizations. A *second* feature is the specific but ever-increasing variety of organizational practices and subgroupings that are enabled by communication technology. The study of ICT in organizations has been plagued by the disturbing distinction of human vs. material agency (already discussed), whereby scholars are lured to focus on the human at the expense of the material, or vice versa. Of course, organizational communication study immediately muddles this distinction with its attention, epitomized in the term *socio-*, to discourse and relationships (neither being overtly human or material), and ICT adds a transformed emphasis on the phenomenon of information—concepts already highlighted in century-old studies of organizational formal structuring, as noted above. One attempt to re-envision the human-material distinction has rested on the notion of affordances. This idea was articulated by Gibson (1966) to overcome the human-material split; its use has led to a variety of insights (arrayed in a valuable way by Treem & Leonardi 2012) into what we would call the ways material resources (ST stresses them being both allocative and power-controlled) are drawn on by agents.

We think of an *affordance* as basically a handle: it tacitly facilitates a sociomaterial operation transforming some focal object like opening a door or (collectively) composing a manuscript. However, it has widely been expanded to encompass dimensions of mediation of resources drawn on in action. But the affordance idea invites new complications, as the critical scholarly literature (Oliver, 2005; Parchoma, 2014) reveals: it has an unclear ontological status and equivocal action-relevance.

The concept of affordance has inspired truly valuable and innovative organizational communication research, an array of scholarship too broad to summarize. But, like our response to the general issue of materiality, we think a valuable alternative conception is the set of concepts offered by ST. An affordance is an enablement; it comes with constraints. It can be part of the presumed context of action, and thus an unacknowledged condition of it. Its use may thus be deeply tacit or habitual. Or it may be skillfully manipulated, subsidiary, or even focal in sensory, practical, or discursive consciousness, as a resource. However, at least, the notion of affordance signals the important and varied utility of ICT, as a constitutive aspect of organizational communication.

In the face of this degree of blurring, organizations can resort to Byzantine arrangements to capitalize on the productive potential of ICT by possessing, managing, and sanctioning phenomena that are off their physical premises. Surveillance, the *third* constitutive feature of ICT, is emphasized by Giddens (1990a, 1990b) as a major constitutive feature with impacts on modern life that flow far outside the boundaries of surveilling organizations. Developers of surveilling media argue, in organizational decision arenas, for their *necessity* in the name of profit or competition, or probably appeal to the pure delight managers may have in obtruding into employee life. For instance, NPR interviewed a woman whose

> employer has started using software called Time Doctor. It downloads videos of employees' screens while they work. It also can enable a computer's webcam to take a picture of the employee every 10 minutes.
>
> "If you're idle for a few minutes, if you go to the bathroom or whatever, a pop-up will come up and it'll say, 'You have 60 seconds to start working again or we're going to pause your time,'" the woman said. (Allyn, 2020)

The ICT network thus constitutes the organization by serving as a medium of indirect, opaque communication exercising control by powerful, technology-wielding managers and other agents.

Equally powerful in shaping organizations is the *record*-creating aspect of surveillance: the fact that, whenever a technological device is used or even present, it can make a record of all conversations and activities using it, or within its operative range, with the data immediately recorded or transmitted to varied outside agencies, to be collected and sold as a surreptitiously created commodity (Zuboff, 2019), or to be distorted and used to harass or intimidate its sources. One well-known example of this potential, with promised general social benefits, is the police bodycam: such cameras have surveilled and produced records of policepersons brutalizing the disadvantaged, despite their awareness of the cameras. Of course, the dialectic of control inevitably leads to bodycam use that hides brutal practices, or is used to justify them as responses to perceived threats. However, surveillance generally is covert, with victims sometimes knowing they are being surveilled but unaware of the scope and variety of uses of surveillance data. Thus, Zuboff (1988) describes how ICT, *informating* work, enables managers to train or collaborate with subordinates on tasks, even while watching and evaluating the subordinates' performance. Her more recent work, though (Zuboff, 2019), reports on the capacity of surveilled records of peripheral or of consumerized interaction, sometimes even if they are stripped of personal identifying signs, to provide valuable information that if catalogued can identify individuals simply using activity patterns, they are part of. And of course, no matter how much a company or other organization protests that they have returned or destroyed data about a person, there is a great likelihood that the data remain, stored in an obscure file, still part of the organization's information capital.

A *fourth* and final feature of ICT as constitutive of organizations, concomitant with its utility stretching deep into an organization's stock of power, is its vulnerability and need for defense. Among the structural foundations of an organization's

ICT are layered protection processes to guard against, for example, spyware and ransomware, hacks of customer accounts—all defending it in necessarily varied ways. The contradictory phenomena, of openness to agentive input and instructions but operational, opaque, reflexive closure that is essential but constructed by ICT technical agents, crucially constitute ICT but thereby afford a double vulnerability to an organization. ICT can be destroyed or overwhelmed from without, like any other power resource. But it can be infected to become self-destructive or otherwise perverted from within.

All three layers of ICT, described earlier, are gateways for interactions that accomplish, get things done—composing messages, computing tax returns, sanctioning members—or crucially support workers in basically agentive accomplishments—performing surgery, composing a chat-assisted manuscript…. (no chatware was used to create this book—perhaps you readers wish that it had been!) However, the three layers are, therefore, self-contradictorily, open doors that facilitate information extraction or disruptive or exploitative outsiders. The ability of a borderline-core member like Jack Teixeira, a Massachusetts Air National Guard member, to expose secrets about military operations is one level of vulnerability, but openness to peripheral interaction can allow spyware and ransomware to invade ICT, and even loss of a personal password might allow hackers to, for example, place false Amazon orders from consumer accounts. And since the consumerized level can be used for peripheral operations, and because operational connections often must input information (and potentially viruses) to core information stocks, each level of vulnerability leads upward. And the vulnerability of ICT to illegitimate exploitation is all the worse due to that cardinal use of technology: Surveillance, and the storage of unlimited information about the unwary, potentially employed not just by it and its information customers, but also by unfettered information thieves.

From above, part of the constitutive force of formal structuring is that it enmeshes the organization in varied ways. It unifies by stipulating an organization name and top leadership/ownership. It also mandates a mesh of communication relations and contents—who should discuss a problem, and what information or sources they should include. It even formally stipulates some attributes of ICT—its operators, some of its rules and required features, and formal ownership of hardware, software, and information stocks. As a manifestation of the overt structure, the main point of ICT is to enmesh the organization, by accomplishing flows of electronic signals and discourse between intended participants in a conversation. The mesh also includes links to databases and staff supporting the participants, and from the direct discursive interchange to those who record it, hook into it, or surveil it. Similarly, the ICT system, too, operates under the organization's name and manifests organization rules—or breaks them–in the arrangements of its designers and users. There are well-known differences between the use of a cellphone to get work done, using it to achieve a practical and livable work-life balance, and using it surreptitiously to contravene organizational interests. But, as we repeatedly note, surreptitious activities also constitute the organization as a system that may be weakened by them, or with effort detects and mitigates them. Additionally, the ICT reproduces the organization as a power system, a facility for task procedures and the exercise of control. ICT, in an ontologically distinct way, informs the organization and makes it what it is—that is, constitutes it.

6.11 ITC and the Four Dimensions

ICT is a way of emphasizing that, for example, technological practices as well as hardware are vital—"the medium is the message." We can see the value of mediated communication in a richer way by using the four dimensions of structuration: *Power Dimension*: ICT allows, supports, and encourages so many facets, old and new, of organizational essence that many of its power implications are blatantly obvious, extensions or amendments to formal structuring. Equally, it is itself a medium and focus of power exercise and power struggle, with rival groups and interests seeking to slant, rule, or flat-out appropriate it as a materially based resource. *Interpretive Dimension*: everyone knows what Zoom means, and its enabling and constraining effects, among which is a new intensity of demands for multisite and multicultural interpretive powers. Zoom is an important instance of ICT, but its blatant meaningfulness is just one example of the interpretive impacts of generations of ICT. *Norms/legitimation dimension*: ICT carries with it a set of presumptions about appropriate use ("faithful" use as described by DeSanctis & Poole, 1994), which in a way validates other organizational discourse that it *carries*. Inside the typical norm-imbued organization, any member using ICT today has experienced the manifest or latent *rights and wrongs* of its use. *Constitution dimension*: As we recounted in the section on formal structuring, "the organization" as a contemporary form grew and emerged as people discovered and elaborated the ICT resources typifying the convoluted, organizational systems we see today. Speech itself may have developed from sounds used to coordinate and control hunting practices, and each communication-technology novelty was, in its essence, a technology for organizing social activities. In elaborating and constraining its own ICT system, the agents of any organization are growing the organization itself.

From its roots, organizational communication studies have emphasized one sort of practical guidance for communication: how to write a memo, how to have a conference with your boss, and how to manage your subordinates. In an early, pretechnical way, all of these are ICT issues; contemporary ICT facilitates or substitutes for tasks like these, but also magnifies the reflexive analysis and control over them.

6.12 Type 3: Culture

It is easy and tempting to think of organizational culture as something that organizations, or more correctly, their individual members (and outsiders), *have*—a variable with different values for different organizations. For instance, a baseball team's cap, or a national flag, or an official uniform or preferred dress code—all certainly display a link of the possessor to the team or nation, a link that everyone would say is (at least partly) cultural. Similarly, organizations can possess distinct sets of acronyms, codes of conduct, and heroic leaders that overlap with the varieties of formal structure listed earlier. In fact, it makes perfect sense to say that the whole formal structure articulated in official documents is itself a part of an organization's culture—as is the ICT, its material presence, and its use as resource. One mark of variable culture is that another organization can possess the same cultural element. For instance, organizations borrow one another's cultural possessions all the time—color schemes, or names. Thus, the sports-team name *Cardinals* became, in 1899, the name of the football team now located in Arizona; a year later, the name was used by the baseball team now located in St. Louis; the duality was especially troublesome when both teams resided in St. Louis. An organization's technology, and agents servicing it, may be the product sold by another organization, and thus duplicated in other organizations.

But many communication scholars regard *culture* as a root metaphor (Smircich, 1983): an organization's culture encompasses the articulated interpretive scheme and practices, inclusion in which makes a member part of the culture. A logo, or a notable leader, or position description, are cultural elements due to the icons or personae having distinctive meaning within a shared web of meaning, practice, value, and trust drawn on by, for example, organization members. Encultured members can count on other members, with high reliability, to know in detail, for instance, the expressed priorities and distinctive accomplishments or mistakes characterizing notable organization leaders—a view about the Tom Bradys or Nancy Pelosis of a specific organization. A particular formal rule can have lots of different imports—it can be interpreted broadly or narrowly, and involve harsh or trivial penalties, as enforced in one enforcer's style rather than another's. In many ways, *culture* is a theoretical concept similar to Giddens' *structure*. But since structuration is our root theory, we use *culture* in a more focused way.

A widely respected definition of organizational culture is Schein's (1992, p. 12):

> A pattern of shared basic assumptions that the group has learned as it solved its problems of external adaptation and internal integration that has worked well enough to be considered valid and, therefore, to be taught to new members as the correct way to perceive, think, and feel in relation to those problems.

Some of these terms could be like variables—making one assumption versus the opposite, for instance. In addition, later in his discussion, Schein explicitly mentions material *artifacts* like hat colors and logos as important cultural elements—even more easily regarded as narrow variables (in some organizations members worship their hats, in others, not). But artifacts can also include features like training manuals and meeting schedules, as long as they are studied in the light of their meaning and significance for "the correct way to perceive, think, and feel." But even regarded as separate features, Schein's concepts have clear communication implications: Cultural assumptions are shared, have been socially learned in the course of group problem-solving (communicatively), and then are taught. One common reaction to new communication technology, for instance, is to be baffled by the new technology and continue using the old, even while noticing and labeling the early adopters and truly overwhelmed members. Moreover, the sorts of cultural communication just mentioned involve a definite notion of reflexive construction of paths of action. Culture includes: assumptions members can make without thinking about it and count on to be shared. It includes values manifested in solving problems regarding the world outside the organization, and regarding conduct and relations among its own members. Thus, it requires and lauds some communication channels between members while discouraging or repressing others, elevating some members to be leaders, and others respectable followers or backstage support staff.

Additionally, Schein holds that culture provides direction about problem-related behavior, thoughts, feelings, and typical artifacts, direction valid enough to be taught to new recruits. Culture, then, is a prize candidate for the category *self-structuring*, because first, a plethora of organizationally relevant activities have patterns generated by culture. And second, all of those elements of culture are the structurational rules and resources that are drawn on and reproduced by members.

An important constituent of organizational culture is the set of ideas and practices covered in the prior sections—culture subsumes and interprets formal structuring as well as ICT processes. Cascio and Montealegre (2016) note a stream of research viewing ICT as "fundamentally social, grounded in specific historical and cultural contexts, and dependent on specific meanings and contingent processes (p. 362). Though they warn against underestimating the specific properties and effects of technology as it is intertwined with the communicative. For instance, take ICT monitoring:

> attitudes in general, and attitudes toward monitoring in particular, will be more positive when organizations monitor their employees within supportive organizational cultures. Supportive cultures allow employee input on the monitoring systems design, and focus on groups of employees rather than singling out individuals, and on performance-relevant activities. Theoretical and empirical researchers have identified three additional features of monitoring systems that contribute to employee perceptions of fairness or invasiveness (Ambrose & Alder 2000; Kidwell & Bennett 1994a, b). These are consistency in how data are collected and used, freedom from bias (e.g., selective monitoring), and the accuracy of data collected. Conversely, when monitoring systems are perceived as invasive or unfair, organizations run the risk that employees may not comply with rules and procedures, slack off on the job, or engage in deviant behaviors (Alge et al. 2010, Zweig & Scott 2007). (Cascio & Montealegre, 2016, p. 357)

As another, more human, example, the US Forest Service attempted to deal, some time ago, with a stark culture-defining conflict between fighting fires in a *risky*, heroic, glamorous way versus action that is careful, coordinated, and part of a *controlling* (ideally by a designated manager) communication web. In response to the conflict and its deadly consequences, fire leaders, social scientists, and experts from varied fields came up with a code of 10 rules, treated as standards for safe behavior (Jahn, 2019a, 2019b). (Notice that formal rules like these are Formal Structuring, and see the mention of this example up there—but here we explore the cultural significance of the changing cultural rules.)

But forest service leaders received and eventually noted the practical outcome of applying these rules: a reproduced conflict between rules and on-the-spot practical necessities. Firefighters' adaptation to such necessities, going against the rules, was a recognized meaning shared as part of the culture. An unfortunate result, also recognized as a threat in firefighter culture, was the prospect that rule violation would be harshly interpreted as criminal and sanctioned in court—though such penalties were objectively rare. Generally, the culture involved communication currents contravening the formal structure-promulgating communication. But then, culturally sensitive leaders perceived, and responded to, the necessity for a revision of the formal rules into the—formal but looser—Doctrine, codified in a handbook, but not as rigid rules. Rather, they are restructurated:

> as principles, values, concepts, and tools that require worker judgment. The purpose of these "principles" was to "empower" adaptable action by individuals in a "thinking culture." The notion of judgment was threaded through leadership training and accident investigation documents as well.... Management envisioned that future notions of safety rules as "principles" would use member expertise and judgment in risk management activities, while making sure members avoided "reprisal" for accidents, as was associated with the past notion of safety rules as procedures. (Jahn, 2019b, p. 242)

Thus, the rules were adapted, within the formal structure, to be more consonant with the overall culture, abler to fit in with it, and presented as resources useful for firefighters whose experienced, expert judgment was respected. They are available for wildland firefighters' understanding of right conduct, as well as for sessions reviewing accidents.

However, we can go to the other anthropological root-metaphor notion of culture, as a web of contextualized interpretive and practical resources that is shared and self-enforcing (so that culturated organizations, in maintaining or transforming their cultures, are self-structuring.) Items like a bureaucratic rule or promotion criterion, or even a general goal, have an impact because they emerge, get positioned, get spread, and get sedimented (Bastien et al., 1995) They draw meaning, have practical implications that go beyond narrow problems, and themselves stream meaning out to the rest of the organization's conversations and culture. They also tend to be appropriated by members in expressing and constructing their personal identities.

The Forest Service's Doctrine, flexible and user-friendly though it had become, still had to join the overall flow of culture, in dealing with the aftermath of tragic accidents happening after Doctrine was articulated. As one way this could happen, the Doctrine-application process was altered to include an added feedback loop, whereby leaders themselves how to articulate the Doctrine in a more flexible, supportive way, and to reconstruct accident investigations into learning reviews, educating both firefighters about ways to apply Doctrinal principles in safer ways, and leaders about how to make Doctrine documents more realistic and how to lead learning reviews.

However, this account understates the transformation in wildland firefighter culture, which the Doctrine partly initiated, but which morphed an earlier culture into another. In one sense, there was an explicit series of changes in firefighter rules. Second, one could notice an obvious cultural change because the rules and their practical application have cultural significance. But a third longer look notes a change in the very meaning of "having rules"—a change in the relation between the rules and the people, which amounts to a transfiguration of the constitutive force of formal rules, under the lens of organizational culture.

The earlier culture has been described by Jahn (2019a, 2019b) as centered in a "rationalist safety paradigm" in which wildland fires are well-defined problems to which a definite *best* response should be made. A set of firefighter rules can usefully guide, and govern, firefighter choices, so that *wrong* responses can be eliminated through sanctions and training. The transformation in the interpretation of the Doctrine, already described, is a

> …shift toward understanding what comprises "normal work" [and] is a monumental one; it reflects an ontological shift from considering that most hazards are knowable (i.e., a rationalist view) to embracing that hazards are emergent, and that problems might arise unpredictably regardless of worker diligence. (Jahn, 2019b, p. 243).

That is, it shakes the whole web of judgments and interpretations in the culture. It is not simply a set of rules/principles, nor a more flexible and respectful way of applying them. It is a re-visioning of firefighter identity, team relations and structure, and relations between firefighters and higher-level managers. It moves toward being an *ontological shift* in a more basic sense, too: the standard image of organizations is the "rules and hierarchy" system of communication, so much so that it is hard to imagine another way to achieve clarity, generality, and trust. The Doctrine shift is a relatively minor shift, probably transient, but even a minor shift in the deep rationalist paradigm flow of wide-ranging communication is important. For example, the former practice resulted in blaming and sanctioning the lowest level members for violating a safety rule, but Doctrine recognizes the work is too complex for firefighters to obey every safety rule at all times. The shift is the result of communication that is still formal structuring, insofar as it rearticulates old formality-based reasoning by using the old formal rules to elucidate just what the new style of reasoning is.

The metaphor of communication flow makes especially good sense of the idea that organizational culture is actually cooperatively enacted by members (and involved nonmembers) as they draw on structural resources to take part in organized work, or relational activities that are not exactly work. They participate in the flow, able to transform it in ways that may or may not spread and endure. In addition, the resources that a member or group finds useful tend to be disseminated out to others, not because sharing is mandated, but because ideas and tactics are ready grist for conversations. Ideas get shared even in the formally stipulated interaction in the Forest Service learning reviews—even in the ultraformal ones focused on statistics of effectiveness, expense limitation, and firefighter retention. The conversations, of course, flow carrying along issues (like wildfire-fighting safety procedures) that perhaps become widespread, and receive remedy, through more communication.

6.13 How Culture Constitutes Organizations

If we take the four flows to all be constituents of an organization's culture-as-process, then it constitutes an organization in all the ways they do. We can see a *strong* culture of an organization as *being* it—organizations are cultures, pure and simple, so of course, a culture constitutes its equivalent organization. However, the other two types of culture have cultural constitutive force, too: having one's membership relational web conflictful or messy still means one is *in* the web. Another option is to see "cultural" phenomena as *embedding* the organization in a sense related to Flows 1 and 4, since most cultural resources are simply drawn from the wider culture—no organization starts out fresh and innocent. Even Eventbrite, discussed earlier, had a cofounder with experience creating other organizations, and friends who suggested the Golden Rule. Then, constituting a single organization is at the root a matter of boundary structuration—Schein's "external adaptation," and "internal integration" as well. Members, individually and then collectively, must constantly, in each second and contextual focus of their work, answer these questions: What practices and materials that I/we work on or communicate with, are characteristically and legitimately ours, the organization's, and which stuff isn't us? And how do I, with my colleagues, operate this stuff in sync, overcoming the problems to produce and reproduce a form of life? An organization's culture tacitly gives ongoing, practically applicable answers to these questions, and that flow of answering culturally and communicatively constitutes the organization. The example of the new firefighter Doctrine, accompanying a shift in the kinds of answers to the two questions just outlined, is thus a constitutional shift.

6.14 Culture and the Four Dimensions

We can, finally, see the import of communication's *culturalness* more richly using the four structurational dimensions. *Interpretive dimension*: Culture's essence is interpretive, as is amply and explicitly discussed above. It gives, and is, a web of meaning for agents as they understand and react to events and problems. *Power dimension*: A culture gives value and prominence, often informal and context dependent, to some individuals, relations, and activities over others—though it gives meaning and practical impact to the formal structuring, too. The quote by Julia Hartz, mentioned earlier, says cofounders *speed the work*, but that assumes correlated orientations, skills, and work styles, and thus doesn't need to take account of spats, divergent interests, and turbulences of divorce. (For a contrary example, see the business empire founded by Marty and Wendy Byrde in the Netflix series *Ozark*.) For that matter, the titles of CEO and President can be "nebulous" and "fake" as culturally interpreted and enacted, like the job titles at the early Eventbrite. But CEOs have special power-based, often unintended, influence over culture. *Legitimation dimension*: Communication flows that have cultural significance are thereby legitimate or not—laudable, tolerable, or worthy of negative sanction. The Forest Service Doctrine principles acquired legitimacy through the "learning reviews," but the balance between the actions practically necessary in the judgment of professionals "on the ground" and the rationalizable [the members hope] conduct judged in "learning reviews"—that legitimation balance is a sterling example of culturally based. *Constitution dimension*: It has been discussed at length, just above. The Forest Service cultural and formal-structural constitution obviously transtructs the other three dimensions—meanings, power resources, and legitimate judgments of conduct.

6.15 Conclusion

From the perspective of *this* chapter, and in many discussions of organizations in many disciplines, self-structuring in all its varieties is *the* defining characteristic of organizations, and its instantiation in any one organization seems to epitomize that entity as being an organization. Indeed, organizations *are* new, peculiar social arrangements, bestowing on their elites, through this second flow, capacities of control, ownership, effective operation, and territorial spread that have enabled them to dominate the world. The three types of self-structuring articulate formal along with in-practice organizational values and goals, fitfully guide member activities toward those goals, and filiate its vital varied sorts of relations. And, perhaps most fundamentally, they demarcate the boundaries of organizational inclusion—belong or not? Connected or not? Savvy or not? But in the other core chapters, this book articulates three coequal perspectives—the other flows—that are, but in other ways, constitutive, and inextricable, for understanding organizations.

In many cases in organizational life, members and others act as though the organization's formal structure is or completely depicts the organization. If someone asks, "What is Ben's job?" the answer might well be, "He's a systems engineer," or "manager of the assembly department." And this answer locates Ben in the formal structure and indicates his place, even his role, in the formal-structural design of the company, and thus, a lot about his place in its control/power/normative system. The critical Foucault might well give the same answer, meaning by it his positioning in the visibility/knowledge/power arraying of the organization. That same question probably would not elicit Ben's place in the ICT network, perhaps because of its complex dynamism, but perhaps in the future "Ben's job" will always be accounted for, partly, by Ben's place in the ICT web of connections. The culture of the organization would probably not be used in describing Ben's job (though it might be in radically stratified societies), but a response that includes culture would answer the question, "What's it like to do Ben's job?" These systems supply answers to the basic questions because they tap the foundationally important constitutive power of the interrelational arrays. However, in the other core chapters, this book articulates three coequal perspectives—the other flows—that are, but in other ways, constitutive and inextricable for understanding organizations.

7

Activity Coordination

Organizations exist to get things done and accomplishing the various goals associated with the organization is dependent on members' activities. Thus, a primary benefit of organizing is to draw upon the knowledge, skills, and actions of more than one individual, combining inputs from more than one team, more than one department, or even more than one organization. To facilitate this, organizations are designed with structures such as goals, objectives, standardized practices, and reporting relationships to guide activities toward meeting those purposes, described as the structures of Flow 2. According to McPhee and Zaug (2000), while these resources are necessary elements of organizations, the structures that are a part of self-structuring cannot completely direct the activities of individuals in every situation, especially when activities involve new or novel conditions. When new members join or they are promoted to new positions, or when new processes are created or refined, activities must be coordinated. In these situations, individuals engage in emergent communication and communicative activities that may not be predefined or that require more or less continuous communication between members to ensure tasks are adjusted, improved, and successfully and/or efficiently completed.

Described in this way, activity coordination may appear to be a unified effort with all members willingly joining together, beneficial to the organization and members promoting teamwork and synchronization to meet goals. While this discursive flow can facilitate these ends, members or groups of members have various levels of agency about what they will or will not do and how they cooperate. When they do not comply, their resistant or divergent communication is almost always properly analyzed within the activity coordination flow, too. Defiant messages from one member can start slow (with a trickle), but their ideas and

The Communicative Constitution of Organizations: The Four Flows Model, First Edition.
Robert D. McPhee, Karen K. Myers, and Joel O. Iverson.

communication can be joined by like-minded others, eventually leading to a larger, more formidable flow. These communicative activities typically do not reiterate existing organizational structures and are intended to organize to shake up the system. While this may not appear to build the organization, this flow is also constitutive of organizations, adding complexity, tensions, at times, a distressing muddle, but potentially positive change, contextualized by other flows, can still amount to organizational coordinated activity.

In this chapter, we discuss the ongoing and spontaneous communication associated with members communicating to engage in linked activities that constitute organizations, Flow 3. McPhee and Iverson (2013) define activity coordination as the "interactive episodes during which members integrated in a single organizational locale or working sphere adapt to situational contingencies and the relevant acts of other members" (p. 112). This discursive flow is necessary to accommodate moment-to-moment situations in which two or more members must agree or at least be knowledgeable about the other's current or planned actions.

We should recognize that activity coordination commonly depends on minimizing or constraining disruptions or intrusions that might destroy the responsiveness or the fluidity of coordinated activity—in other words, a sort of boundary is established, sometimes by formal dictate or other means. One commonplace locus of coordination is the operating room in a hospital. Great care is typically taken that all the right members—perhaps necessary professions but even better, professionals who have worked together before and know each other's individual styles, all the needed equipment and supplies, and adequate lighting, power, and water supplies are present; in addition, contaminants, unruly outsiders, etc. are excluded. Of course, organizational conditions often are not prototypical: surgical operations must take place under conditions of war, pandemic, and natural disaster, or the perspectives of varied professionals clash. In such conditions, communicators may act not just to coordinate internally, but to minimize or circumvent the disruptions or mutually adjust their standard practices well enough for the work at hand, like for instance, the fire crew captain and firefighters discussed later. Perhaps of greater significance is that coordination arenas are, in most organizations, open to crossing flows. For instance, critical care units receive patients from surgery, along with notes about them, and have to discover the implications of the surgery for later care. The critical care site is essentially operationally open—its work can only get done by importing—patients, records, oral clarifications…so its activity coordination has a different character, and the practical boundary allowing focused coordination is permeable.

Activity coordination occurs in different ways in different functions and at different levels of the organization. At the top of the organization (e.g., owner, chief executive officers, presidents, and vice presidents), this flow is especially evident as leaders coordinate by discussing new or emerging goals (structural changes) that may require activity realignment or refinement throughout the organization (Carton et al., 2014). The flow also is surely a daily occurrence as supervisors and members communicate how tasks should be performed or when they simply tacitly display acceptance and understanding of the changes in context the work of others presents to them. In addition, members respond to the communicative agency of other members, or to blockages of agency, especially when members report updates on their activities, and when adjustments must be made. And, of course, whenever members must work on a joint task or tasks tightly intertwined, synchronous coordinating communication is almost the essence of work. However, at all of these levels, the streams of communication have multiple sources and communicative results. In this chapter, we discuss how the communication of members at all levels of the organization engages in activity coordination. Our focus remains on how this flow is constitutive of the organization through conlocutions and transtructions that occur within that process. We begin with a review of research on coordination, sometimes known as collaboration. Highlighted is coordination in high-reliability organizations. We then discuss transtruction through activity coordination communication and sociomateriality through workspaces and technology. The chapter ends with a discussion about activity coordination in workgroups, recent activity coordinated research, and future opportunities to investigate the communicative constitution of organizations through activity coordination.

7.1 Research on Coordination

Activity coordination occurs throughout the organization—at all levels and in all functions. As a flow, it is communication that allows and inclines members to cooperate and synchronize their actions with other members (Thompson, 1967). It also allows members to pool resources and to adjust creatively to novel opportunities or problems that were not previously covered in the organization's self-structuring (Van de Ven et al., 1976). Little research has examined *activity coordination* as a unique construct, so we begin our discussion by reviewing literature on *coordination* that occurs in organizations and workgroups.

Generally, coordination is thought of as the situation-sensitive integration of individuals' communication and activities to meet organizational goals (Rice et al., 2017). Thus, elements of activity coordination can involve individuals making preparations for the coordination such as determining what expertise will be needed for the coordination, inviting those individual members to participate, and scheduling a time to complete the task. An organization's activity coordination can also involve individuals outside the boundaries of the organization such as when the project manager places orders with suppliers who bring building materials to the construction site, or job candidates upload employment applications to a website, setting the stage for the search committee's review and deliberation.

Coordination is often sparked by *uncertainty* and *interdependencies*—when new or unique situations arise and members must determine how to respond together to align their efforts (Thompson, 1967). Coordination is achieved by pooling members' contributions, sequencing their actions, and reciprocating individual activities through which they can strengthen potential outputs (Van de Ven et al., 1976). In these ways and by communicating with others (verbally and/or nonverbally), individuals can direct, monitor, confirm, collaborate, and make decisions to resolve uncertainties when member goals and tasks are interdependent.

The success (or lack of success) of coordination is associated with several issues. First, and perhaps most simply, individuals who need to coordinate often rely on material items or tools to help them co-orient. For example, individuals might study a map to select a location to meet after a hike or a project team might review a flow chart to ensure that everyone agrees on necessary processes (McPhee & Iverson, 2013). Such tools—sometimes called *boundary objects*—can help individuals visualize the starting point and desired outcome, often with a sketchy path in between (Star & Griesemer, 1989). (For instance, the ICU patient mentioned above is a boundary object in the ICU for doctors, nurses, and other medical personnel.) Second, activity coordination outcomes are typically dependent on a shared understanding of approach and the desired outcomes. Because coordination relies on individuals more or less agreeing about what, how, and when activities must be accomplished, individuals who operate with similar resource knowledge (information, skills, and material resources) are more likely to understand the need for coordination and how they must align their activities with others. Thus, individuals who participate in a *community of practice* (groups of individuals who have similar knowledge and learning processes [Iverson & McPhee, 2002; Lave & Wenger, 1991]) can more effectively and efficiently coordinate their work than individuals with diverse backgrounds (Ballard & Gossett, 2007). Some communities of practice fluctuate between periods of inertia in which little activity is accomplished within the group and periods of urgency and productivity prompting extensive coordination among members, known as punctuated equilibrium (Gersick, 1988). Individuals within these groups may have different areas of expertise, but because they operate with similar understandings and objectives, they can prioritize their activity alignment to complete periodic tasks and projects. Cross-functional teams are often created in organizations because their diversity of knowledge and perspectives can facilitate idea generation (Kellogg et al., 2006). Just as true, their lack of shared experiences (and even goals) can make it difficult to understand each other's perspectives about what needs to occur and to synchronize work practices (Neff & Stark, 2004). Individual members of cross-functional teams commonly have at least some competing goals and this can make collaboration tense and activity alignment difficult (Ghobadi & D'Ambra, 2012). For example, members from the research and development department may argue for more lead time to develop a new product, while members involved in customer service may push for quicker product development to meet growing customer demand. Still, even diverse groups that seem to have little in common can coordinate their activity, in several ways. One is by the use of boundary objects, described earlier. The actual point of calling them boundary objects is that they are points of common understanding that can be used by teams separated by boundaries.

There are several skeins of theory and research that elucidate the notion of boundary objects. The phenomenon of affordances, discussed in the last chapter, is one. Affordances prototypically mediate, through tacit knowledge or what ST terms practical consciousness, the appropriation (Poole & DeSanctis, 1992), by individual human agents or univocal collectivities, of material objects as media for task activity. But affordances often also mediate, through overlapping uses of materials by groups or even individuals with varied perspectives. A map documenting locations and properties can be useful to firefighting crews in knowing where to devote their efforts, while commanders personally coordinate their work.

Another revealing example of the breadth of implications of a practice of coordinating focus on a boundary object is called by critical and decolonialist scholars the *tecnologia social.*

> To be called a *tecnologia social*, at its heart there must be some type of tool—[material (an artifact, a device) or immaterial (a methodology, a way of doing or organizing)]—capable of being conceived and implemented. The conception and implementation of a *tecnologia social* occurs through a political process of sociotechnical reconfiguration which involves the reassignment of meanings, values and interests through the interplay between artifacts and practices of social groups, so as to "redesign" scientific and technological knowledge [in a] sociotechnical reconfiguration…according to the interests of the social groups involved in a societal issue (Dagnino, 2009) … without attribution of primacy to Western knowledge forms]. … From its origins in Gandhian resistance to British imperialism, *tecnologia social* calls into question the hegemony of occidental technologies, the center/periphery relationship, and the purported superiority of occidental knowledge being framed as natural and imposed as universal. (Saldanha et al., 2022, p. 5–6)

A *tecnologia social* is a concept that centers on a community of practice focused on a material or immaterial object, which can become a stabilized standpoint facilitating activity coordination, while simultaneously carrying anticolonial implications in wider currents of all four of our flows. Members simultaneously coordinate on a task, invent relations between local practices and scientific techniques, and develop ways to protect the integrity of the local—all in a flow of communication that must be constrained (by awareness of local/colonial differences) but cannot be predetermined. While Saldanha et al. refer to sociotechnical reconfigurations as "*processes*," but of "imbrication of social and material elements" (p. 3) in, for example, "broad discourses" that are "evoked" (p. 9)—discourse thus, here, insinuates a structuralist brick wall that waits somewhere to be evoked. However validly intended, we think the alternate image of the flow of resources enabling, constraining, and reproduced in convergent and divergent structurational streams is another revealing, obsessively processual lens.

Two fundamental domains of resources for coordination were discussed in the last two chapters. Membership negotiation is blatantly a process of determining the parameters wherein members' positions and practices are ripe for working in sync. Similarly, all of the factors discussed as self-structuring, whether formalisms or ICT or culture, more or less intentionally have a mediatory function in the interest of activity coordination—indeed, the essence of organization, identified differently in the different flows, is valorized by its significance for coordination, seen as the essence in descriptions of organizations as mechanisms for "coordination and control." A blueprint or list of rules or organization chart, to mention examples of formal structuring, are each signally useful as members—or outsiders—determine where they are in social space, to know how to act in sync.

Perhaps the broadest perspective about the substantial factors—objects, vocabulary, etc.—that ground conjoint action draws from activity theory (Engeström, 1999), which gives an encompassing array of factors that are valuable in cooperation to develop ongoing shared goals to become activity systems—socially constructed groups organized to accomplish a shared purpose. *Structurating activity theory* goes on to describe the process by which individuals with different areas of knowledge and resources as part of an activity system engage in activities over time, and thereby generate, draw on, and reproduce structural resources to mediate activity-oriented toward a commonly desired outcome (Canary, 2010a, 2010b; Canary & McPhee, 2009; Hansen & Canary, 2015). Coactivity media in general include these categories:

> *mediating resources*, including nonmaterial resources such as language and material resources such as technology. *Rules* are social norms about how to conduct oneself within the activity system, including interaction norms and common practices that are used to accomplish activity. The *community* is the group of actors involved in the given system. The community might be a collection of specialists involved in a common activity, such as speech therapists, or a cross-functional team of professionals with varying areas of expertise. The *division of labor* includes both horizontal task assignment and vertical hierarchy within the system (Canary & McPhee, 2009, p. 153).

Structurating activity theory aimed, in particular, to elaborate the coordinative or mediatory capacities of these local group media as large-scale coordination occurs across time, space, and organizational hierarchic levels. Members' understanding of the issue and mediatory factors can cause them to approach the problem from dissimilar, conflictive, and domineering viewpoints and methods, but agreeing on a desired outcome and recognizing mediatory resources enhance the likelihood of cooperation in the coordination.

But just as important as the challenges of coordination, some members may actively choose not to adapt and generally not cooperate in efforts to synchronize their activities. Choices about whether and how much to comply with activity coordination draw attention to agency. In very general terms, agency is the ability to act (or choose not to act). Because of members' agency, they can reflect on their actions from the past and project toward potential outcomes when making the choice to coordinate their activities (Emirbayer & Mische, 1998). If they believe that coordinating with their colleagues and fulfilling their supervisor's directives will benefit them immediately or in the future, they are more inclined to put their heart and efforts into the tasks. They effectively strengthen the flow of activity coordination in the workgroup with ripple effects to the rest of the organization. However, agents can choose not to cooperate, for reasons tied to the organizational coordination task either directly (e.g., they think they know best) or indirectly, for example, in the case of a family emergency calling them away from work, or if they choose to work in their own self-interest.

Following Giddens, and as described in the chapter on structuration theory, agency involves an ability to be reflexive about one's actions—coordinate one's activities with others or not--to evaluate and make a choice. Many critical theorists beginning with Marx have argued that structures found at the macro levels of society are a primary force directing individuals' actions. Individuals who must rely on drawing a paycheck are under the control of the capitalist system and have little choice but to comply and contribute to activity coordination. Although supervisors' control over employees cannot completely be discounted, even when individuals must perform under the strict direction of leaders and rules, and with direct feedback from co-involved coworkers, individuals can choose how they interpret rules (Giddens, 1979). Members can communicate and coordinate their tasks in ways that give themselves from small to larger levels of autonomy—the dialectic of control (Giddens, 1979). Members can (and do) refuse to align their activities by direct refusals, by completing part of the task, or by completing the task with little concern for the quality or speed of their actions. Much like the challenges of agency mentioned in Chapter 2, activity coordination has its own set of challenges. Noncompliance also can be caused by: (a) deficiencies of the agent(s) such as inadequate motivation, skill, or time; (b) deficiencies of communication media, for example, lack of a common language or common routines that would allow for mutual adjustment or structural communication blockages such as bureaucratic red tape; (c) deficient resources such as budget, tools, or skills that block task accomplishment; (d) countervailing currents—communication that, for various reasons, intentionally disrupts or counterorganizes against cooperation or the joint plan from being enacted; (e) and, defensiveness because members lack trust in leaders' or colleagues' purposes in directing, influencing, or encouraging activity coordination.

While these and other obstacles can mean that coordination is less efficient or even impossible, coordination of activities and the flow of communication that makes it possible is an essential element of organizing. Indeed, some might say this is the *raison d'etre* of an organization. Without activity coordination, members would not be able to collectively problem solve complex problems or develop new processes and practices when a variety of knowledge is required. As individuals within the organization communicate with these objectives, they create a reflexive, ongoing, disseminating stream of reoccurring, familiar conversations that become understood by members as necessary to accomplish major and minor tasks that must be completed with the help of others. These reoccurring interactions become chains of interaction episodes, or flows of activity coordination (McPhee & Zaug, 2000), creating structural resources that can enable member action to move the organization forward (Boden, 1994).

Also drawing on a structurational approach, Zackrison et al. (2015) proposed a model of organizational coordination that included elements of uncertainty and interdependencies but also included knowledge and routines as structures which they termed mechanisms and outcomes of coordination. They argue that knowledge works as a mechanism of coordination when members draw on *resource knowledge* (information, skills, and materials) and *relational knowledge* (who knows what and how members should react to a situation) to guide decision-making and activities. Both types of knowledge work as mechanisms facilitating activity coordination as members are able to make better-informed decisions, draw on acquired skill sets, and are able to anticipate how colleagues respond. In turn, each of these mechanisms increases the likelihood of better outcomes.

Myers and McClelland-Cohen's (2024) review of coordination examined processes and accomplishments at the dyadic/group/organizational level as well as the interorganizational level. They conclude that despite the need to exert status and power, coordination often requires building trust among team members, workgroups, and organizations. They recounted research by Hollingshead et al. (2011) about how coordination can fail even in tightly coupled teams due to accuracy errors (inaccurate perceptions of others' skills or level of expertise), omission errors (inaccurately assuming someone else is handling a task), shared errors (when members disagree or are unclear about who is supposed to perform a task), urgency errors (when a member believes a task is more urgent that it actually is and takes on a task for which they are not qualified), redundancy errors (unnecessarily repeating a task that was or is being performed by others), and validation errors (when individuals do not participate and take responsibility for the group's actions) (Hollingshead et al., 2011). At the organizational level, information sharing within the organization is affected by (a) the amount and quality of team communication, (b) members' appraisal about whether the information shared has value, (c) communication norms such as whether sharing information among members is organizationally encouraged, (d) organizational support for attaining/distributing information, and (e) social ties including interactions among members (Gross & Kluge, 2012).

These and other points made by Myers and McClelland–Cohen demonstrate workgroups and organizations develop norms for open and continued communication and build practices and guidelines to facilitate those interactions (structures), they constitute workgroups and departments that effectively coordinate. At the third level, when organizations join together for interorganizational collaborations each organization arrives with different missions, goals, and structured practices. Similar to the obstacles involved in coordinating individuals, different organizations may be represented by cohorts lacking in commitment or the ability to participate Requisite skill levels, or being hindered by other interest groups in their own organizations between organizations, especially across cultures, language, and communication media differences may pose problems. And, of course, a joint task may simply mismatch with the array of talents and resources within the collective effort. Tensions can run especially high as the organizational representatives work through these differences and assess each other's potential to contribute and simultaneously jockey for power. In these situations, organizations are more successful when they rely less on their own structural routines and are open to at least temporarily following the norms of other collaborating organizations (Woo, 2019). Such collaborations can even strain the notions of *boundary* and *organization*, as when a putative organization like *Anon* (Dobusch & Schoeneborn, 2015) had conflict over the validity of membership, even as they coordinated hacking activities that definitely mediated both activity and contestation. Their extreme example shows the relation of the third flow to the second (partly by its absence, which is basically what puts into question its "organizationality"—how Anon is an organization) and, manifestly, the first flow, where membership assertions and coordinated action merge.

7.2 HRO Activity Coordination

Activity coordination and its essential role in organizational constitution are especially noteworthy in high-reliability organizations (HROs). In HROs such as such as healthcare facilities, police and fire departments, and nuclear power plants, to name a few, team members must continuously coordinate their activities in error-free ways to avoid accidents or injury to themselves or others (Perrow, 1984; Weick & Roberts, 1993). Most high-reliability teams include interdependent members with specialized knowledge who communicate through words and deeds to interrelate their activities (Weick et al., 2005). Elements of the HRO context such as organizational culture in facilitating activity coordination (Roberts et al., 1994), trust and relationship development on workflow negotiation (Clelland & Zarankin, 2012; Myers & McPhee, 2006) and relationships between members affecting the development of swift trust and member to member connections (Yang, 2014) have been investigated for their unique coordination properties These, and studies on reliability in HROs and HRO teams (Bierly & Spender, 1995; Myers, 2005), point to activity coordination between members as the essence of maintaining reliability to avoid disaster.

Research and theorizing about HROs and HRO teams focus on unique aspects of the precise and reliable communication between members to coordinate their activities. For example, Weick discussed the necessity for "tightly coupled" communication and coordination between members (Weick & Roberts, 1993), which requires members to be in continuous communication to report even the slightest anomalies and what they are noticing in their situation to avoid distortions and misunderstandings (Martinez-Córcoles & Vogus, 2020). Weick and Roberts (1993) argued that in order to be reliable "the coordination among activities is explicit and visible" (p. 357). They argued that at their best, teams can work with *collective mind*, which they described as "a pattern of heedful interrelating" (p. 357), enabling members to seamlessly engage in coordinated activity. Others describe *transactive memory systems* that can be used to coordinate and accomplish goals (Hollingshead, 1998), or *shared mental models*—"a cognitive architecture that enables effective coordination and collaboration in work teams" (Gross & Kluge, 2012, p. 403). Accordingly, knowledge can be held within a group and communicatively shared to coordinate their activities as in communities of practice (Kuhn, 2014). The examples we refer to above—of mediating objects and constraints (including challenges) valuably expand on these theoretic strains.

The term HRO was initially used to describe organizations whose goals were primarily designed to avoid accidents, in contrast to organizations that prioritize competition and profitability (Roberts et al., 1994). The term HRO is now commonly used to define a category of organizations, rather than to describe the practices they use to achieve reliability (Cantu et al., 2021), which is evidence of the constitutive nature of organizational practices. Although the tasks of HRO workers clearly involve activity coordination, and for a workgroup and organization to attain HRO status, there must be a flow of activity coordination, studies have not drawn upon this flow to frame and investigate the practices of HROs. Nevertheless, it can be argued that an organization that becomes known as an HRO does so on the basis of how well its members are able to establish and maintain a flow of activity coordination to avoid accidents and catastrophes.

Even though the consequences for activity coordination in HROs might be far greater than in most other organizations, the processes by which the organization is constituted through coordinating communication and action remain the same. To demonstrate, we draw on an exemplar from Roberts et al. (1994) study about the organizational culture in two nuclear aircraft carriers that enables them to maintain reliability. In the study, an officer recounts the daily meetings of the ship's department heads. He reports that the meetings often include interactions such as "By the way, I've got an ammunition onload tomorrow so I'm going to be using this area. … And then people have an opportunity to question you in an informal way about why you're using the hangar bay, were you aware we have another onload tomorrow?" (p. 157). These conversations coordinate the department heads, who will then coordinate the crew members under their command. As Roberts and colleagues claim, the conversation serves to reproduce the hierarchical and social structures of the ship (Flow 2) and it affords opportunities for disagreements and negotiations about roles (Flow 1) and how activities should be coordinated given the tight space on the ship and the need to accommodate more than one onload tomorrow (Flow 3). The transtructive process occurs as: the Naval context provides power to the statements; the leadership roles on their aircraft carriers establish legitimacy; and because of their familiarity with their roles, they understand the meaning of the conversation, which in transtructions constitute reliable action. As described earlier, when workgroups and organizations in which they are embedded consistently exhibit reliability, they are constituted as such.

While high-reliability tactics are demonstrations of consistent communicative practices that contribute to the activity coordination flow that can define the organization, other organizational practices and structures can restrict or dam the flow. *Silos* are a special type of flow problem. Silos are clusters of individuals in an organization that do not contribute to the overall flow of the organization, especially in coordinating activities. Silos emerge in areas of organizations that infrequently interact with other areas of the organization; instead, members focus only on issues and practices in their area and are blinded to concerns in other areas (Vantaggiato et al., 2021). Their lack of interaction can be related to the functions they perform, such as members of the production department who work more or less independently of other departments and do not regularly interact with other departments for goal-setting or problem-solving (Vantaggiato et al.). The lack of information sharing between areas of organizations results in an inability or a lack of motivation to work together to achieve objectives and advance the organization. Activity coordination flows can become disjointed and without momentum, affecting the growth and development of the cluster and organization too. Other blockages to the flow include novel problems that make it difficult to determine the best path forward or misunderstandings that result in an inability or lack of willingness to coordinate.

Next, we describe processes that occur in activity coordination and their transtructive results. We demonstrate the process with an example of communication between supervisors and subordinates as part of the activity coordination flow.

7.3 Supervisor-Subordinate Activity Coordination and Transtruction

As mentioned earlier, an organization's formal structure of rules, positions, documents, etc. can facilitate coordination. They typically generate a vocabulary for talking about tasks and responsibilities, saving considerable time and resources that might otherwise be devoted to disputes over relative authority or proper procedure (McPhee, 1985). In particular, in traditional organizations with highly centralized structures, communication was theorized to be primarily vertical, with most communication from supervisors directed down to their charges. While most no longer accept the assumption that supervisor–subordinate communication comprises the majority of interaction, it remains a focal point because supervisors' directives and monitoring control a great deal of members' activities toward achieving organizational goals. In less-bureaucratized cases, communication between supervisors and the members they oversee mostly occurs as a result of *in situ* events with far-reaching effects on practices and outcomes. When changes are implemented or unplanned circumstances arise, supervisors often communicate to align members' activities to accommodate the new situation.

To demonstrate the third flow (activity coordination) and its constitutive effect, we analyze the common occurrence of interaction between a captain of a firefighting crew and her firefighters. When the fire crew arrives on scene and the fire is a minor one, performing in normative ways, they can chiefly rely on standard operating procedures (self-structuring) or established practices to guide them to complete their tasks aligning with the work of fellow crew members. However, when the fire performs in highly irregular ways or the terrain is unusually challenging, new procedures must be worked out involving communication between captains and firefighters and among the firefighters themselves. In the situation of a wildfire quickly spreading because of wind which threatens a housing development, the captain may devise a plan intended to cut off fuel with a fire line. She coordinates their effort by saying, "We need five of you to start a back burn at the top of that ridge." The five firefighters hear this message and perceive elements of the message in many ways. First, they understand the *meaning* of the message. The supervisor wants them to prioritize certain actions that she thinks will minimize damage to the community. From her message, they also receive confirmation that the rest of the crew is dependent on them to quickly begin their work because of the fire's movement. Because of their captain's position to oversee their crew, most are likely to believe she has *legitimacy* in directing them and pointing out that they should attempt to perform their tasks quickly. They may also recognize that tied to her statement, is her legitimate concern for minimizing the fire's destruction and her directives to coordinate their activity are needed. As firefighters under command of the captain, she has *power* to push them to successful completion and even authority to reprimand them if they do not respond to her command with urgency. Rather than develop their own plan, most firefighters will follow the caption's directive. Of course, they still retain the agency (and power) to resist her request and adapt their behaviors to fit their own assessment of the situation. As they do, they can be reflexive about their actions to watch for safety issues of which the captain might be unaware. If they question the captain's judgment, they may disagree and challenge the captain's legitimacy and power. This can create confusion as some firefighters side with the captain, but others defy. At the extreme, they can even quit on-site. In *transtruction*, these elements—meaning, legitimacy, and power—are combined and *constitute* their response, in this case, creating an effective (or ineffective) fire line and working with haste to do so. These transtructive elements intertwine to characterize the fire crew as part of the firefighting organization, and draw on the power of constitution. The communication from the captain relies on that constitutive power to contribute to activity coordination flow.

The communication and resulting action are part of more continuous flows of communication directed toward mutually working together to create the fire barrier and signal their completion to the captain. As they complete the series of new tasks associated with making the fire break, crew members contribute to the discursive flow in various ways, suggesting, for example, different ordering of processes or by taking responsibility for certain tasks. As they engage and contribute to the overall thrust of these focused tasks, their interactions can become normalized and patterned into an overall flow of activity coordination focused on fighting a fire that is driven by wind and that is nearing a housing community. These flows of activity coordination merge with other currents related to fighting fires in their region and they become *constitutive* of a firefighting organization with a successful track record.

As should be clear, context affects the meaning of the fire captain's activity coordination communication and the transtruction of the message. The adaptive and novel abilities of firefighters is sparked, if not shaped, by their understanding, in the broadest terms, of their situation. Relational histories play an important role in individuals' coordinating their efforts by their effect on trust (Clelland & Zarankin, 2012). In some environments in which captains are known to be abusive, the firefighters might have presumed that their supervisor's message was to exert excessive control over them rather than allow them to perform the work with a level of autonomy. Because their captain has previously exhibited self-serving behaviors that do not benefit the crew, they perceive the power of her words as coercive and illegitimate, and as maintaining a crew's poisonous atmosphere. Together, the meaning, legitimacy and power of the coordinating message constitute an action that can be much different from the previous example. Using their agency, they might comply by creating the fire line starting at the ridge, but they might not work exactly as directed, and even mutually coordinate their own efforts with this as their goal. Thus, the transtruction intermingling their response to the captain's attempt to coordinate their activities has different outcomes, affecting the other crews working the fire and the firefighters assigned to the incident's ability to contain the fire before it enters the housing community.

7.4 Materiality

The influence of materiality is easily identified in activity coordination. As described earlier in this chapter, a map, flow chart, or diagram are common material objects that become integrated in activity coordination to help members align their efforts. Even the object of focal effort—a sick patient, a paper undergoing shared text processing—can be part of the communication flow, both because of its meaningful features and because issues such as disagreement and the like can be like a springboard for cooperative discourse. Other resources can be central in coordination including operations manuals, which enable members to coordinate efforts affording distanciation. Thus, workers in a plant in Chicago can create components of a cell phone that will fit with producers in another country, right now and two years from now. Similarly, training drawing on resources such as medical knowledge and equipment enables physicians to have similar and successful results in replacing knees in Chicago or San Diego.

Certainly, technology as a material resource is at the core of much activity coordination that occurs through video and other digital channels. For example, using specialized software enables airline schedulers to create a plan bringing together airplanes, pilots, flight attendants, and other personnel to successfully operate a commercial airline flight at desirable times, and using a limited number of gates in the airline system. Technology can also be as simple as a sign-up sheet that enables members to sign up to bring snacks to monthly meetings. Another popular focus of the study is the effect of open workspaces that can encourage more spontaneous interaction (Pentland, 2012), innovation and creativity (Congdon et al., 2014), cohesiveness (Stryker et al., 2012), and the ability to collaborate their efforts (Fayard & Weeks, 2011). However, open workspaces can also impede communication and coordination when workers feel as though their conversations are too transparent and will be shared with all others in the work area (Sivunen & Myers, 2022). In each of these examples, more interaction can work to derail activity objectives.

7.5 Activity Coordination between Coworkers and Transtruction

The activity coordination that occurs between members is equally constitutive and is reflective of much of what is accomplished in organizations. As previously described, in many situations when members must complete interdependent tasks, they rely on a standardized set of rules to guide their work, which often eliminates or at least reduces the need for ongoing communication. When a workgroup is given a new or unique task such as responding to a wildfire with new maps or without their usual equipment, or other elements of the context changes, the novelty of the situation requires exchanges of information and agreement about how to proceed in order to complete tasks.

Drawing on the above example, this type of firefighting (workgroup) activity to fight a wildfire typically requires coordinated effort, and working quickly—as stressed by their captain—adds to their activity coordination pressures, potentially necessitating even more coordination. Even when the five firefighters are aware of each other's role, skills, and responsibilities, they must communicate to agree on sequencing to complete the necessary steps of setting a backfire. Member #1 says to member #2, "I'm going to start over there, then you'll need to start there and walk toward me." Member #2 responds, "Yeah, I can do that, but make sure you first check our location on the map." In this brief exchange, #1 asserts his responsibility as first in on the line, giving him initial ownership of the task. He perceives the need to establish his role relative to #2 and direct how they will proceed. #2's response is based on her recognition of the *significance* of #1's statement—#1's position as first in the fire line and, therefore, his understood responsibility to start the work and the *legitimacy* of his desire to ensure that the work smoothly progresses with #2. She also is aware of and respects the *power* of #1's statement to take responsibility for the initial stage of the job. The context—unified goal of the firefighting organization, crew, and individual firefighters—shape the modalities of the statement and by which it is understood by #2 and others in the crew. They are, after all, members of a fire crew that has been given the task of creating a fire line in a timely manner. The message's meaning, legitimacy, and power in activity coordination are intertwined with, and are constitutive of, coordinating the activity. Beyond that, these activities are also constitutive of a fire crew that can effectively complete these tasks and organization that includes crews and firefighters that can successfully defend their community from fire. Once these individuals repeat similar activities with their crew members, and especially after similar situations have occurred and these activities are coordinated over and over, their activities become more and more structured. Activities that are structured (part of the crews' repertoire, repeated, or even documented) begin to contribute to the self-structuring flow, especially once it becomes standardized and documented. Thus, their activity coordination interaction to build a backfire to protect a group of houses contributes to an overall durée of the fire crew and the firefighting organization—defining members' roles in the organization, structuring roles, practices and potentially shaping policy, and defining what the organization is.

Jahn's (2019a, 2019b) study investigated the United States Forest Service's (USFS) introduction of Doctrine—an effort to change the uses of safety rules in leadership training, fatality investigations, and on-scene decisions and activities. The new doctrine was implemented to communicate to experienced firefighters that safety rules that had once been strictly enforced with policies to hold firefighters responsible when safety rules were not strictly followed could be more flexible. The meaning of the message was that firefighters have legitimate knowledge and could be trusted with agency to make judgments on-scene to adapt their actions without fear of liability. The Doctrine changed the meaning of safety policies, legitimized firefighters' own expertise and power to make judgments, transformed perceptions about the job, their membership. In the process, they potentially had a transformative effect on the USFS. The constitutive effects for the organization are realized when it is enacted.

As the above example demonstrates, research on activity coordination includes evolving ideas about organizational rules and policies and also members' ability to draw on their own agency to resist or transform rules into ways of working. Several recent studies point to research opportunities to highlight communication's role in constituting organizations, such as the federal government's use of data repositories to support interagency use of life cycle assessment data pertaining to buildings, transportation, construction and more (Kahn et al., 2022), boundary spanning between multinational organizations (Santistevan, 2022) for revolutionary ideas and products, and the role of social media enabling coordination and the development of transactive memory systems in virtual teams (Yoon & Zhu, 2022). In each of these instances, the role of transtructions and the communicative constitution of organizations should be focal.

7.6 Conclusion

Research on coordination between members has always been a popular area of research that has now expanded exponentially to include online coordination (Hand & Gorea, 2018) and coordination through technology (Wickersham et al., 2018). Despite the potential ways that the flow of activity coordination can be applied to investigate member-to-member communication and actions in organizations, research with this focus remains sparse in the field of communication. Studies in this area have the opportunity to include not just the coordination of activities for particular tasks or between members, but to explore how single incidents or single coordinating relationships can have more impactful influences on the ongoing discourses that permeate workgroups and organizations. Material resources have significant effects—sometimes determining whether coordination is possible at all—but often influencing coordination's success. Of course, members always have the agency to choose whether to cooperate in the coordination. At times, they may choose to outwardly object, comply with resistance or potentially hide their noncompliance, at least for a time. The constitutive effects reflect these levels of compliance for the strengthening, demise, or status quo, and with uniqueness of the particular organization. Overall, the flows of activity coordination have a far greater effect than is currently recognized in most coordination studies shaping interactions and also members' ability to respond to change, make decisions about and implement improvements, and perform reliability.

8

Institutional Positioning

Our first three flows demonstrate that organizations involve or consist of members, structures, and coordinated activities. While early scholarship has focused on the organization as a bounded place where communication happens internally and reaches out externally to other organizational containers, the container metaphor (Smith & Turner, 1995) has been problematized for overly reifying the organization, ignoring the permeability of those boundaries, and ignoring the deeper implications (Putnam et al., 1996). Yet, organizations are legally and communicatively treated as entities. The tensions between understanding organizations as entities and yet acknowledging that their existence depends on constitution by people in a social world of meaning require further exploration. Undeniably, an organization is a social entity that functions as a recognizable whole situated within and through a larger societal context consisting of multiple organizations, collectives, and individuals. Indeed, organizations interact with others (individuals and collectives) collaboratively, in conflict, and in complex ways. Institutional positioning recognizes the communicative flow that both constitutes the organization as a whole and as an interacting part of the larger social system.

In this chapter, we discuss the macro level of communicative constitutions of organizations by exploring the fourth flow, institutional positioning. This flow represents "communication positioning the organization in larger social systems" (McPhee et al., 2014a, 2014b, p. 80). Institutional positioning recognizes the constitutive nature of the organizational system through its actions, which both distinguish the organization from others and legitimize the organization as an entity (Putnam, 2022). In addition, at some level, all communication that is *organizational* (i.e., the other three flows) is thereby engaging in institutional positioning. Due to its encompassing nature, institutional positioning is present

The Communicative Constitution of Organizations: The Four Flows Model, First Edition.
Robert D. McPhee, Karen K. Myers, and Joel O. Iverson.

at varying levels. Additionally, since it includes research that references an organization as an entity, whether in relation to other organizations or to other flows, such as membership negotiation (which implicitly answers the question, "joining what?"), institutional positioning permeates organizational research. As a result, in this chapter, we focus on a few major and prototypical currents. Though not exhaustive, this chapter is intended to explore a wide range of institutional positioning facets. For this flow, the terms institution and positioning require further exploration.

8.1 Institutions and Organizations

Giddens (1984) broadly defines institutions as "the more enduring features of social life" (p. 24). At that level, institution is far from a synonym for organizations, but represents multiple levels of social system that exist across time and space. Instances include *Democracy*, the *Free Market*, the institution of *Western Medicine*, and the institution of *Advertising*. This expansive definition recognizes that "organizations exist in human societies that already are organized…Without an institutional backdrop, any but the most primitive human organization is unthinkable" (McPhee & Zaug, 2009, p. 41). Instead, the place of an organization within the broad institutions is enacted and is inextricably tied to the constitution of the organization.

To define communication taking place institutionally, we must pay attention to the ground-breaking work of Lammers and Barbour (2006): "For analytical purposes, we view institutions as constellations of established practices guided by formalized, rational beliefs that transcend particular organizations and situations" (p. 364). We would amend or supplement this definition in several ways: most important is that the constellations are *systems of individuals* sustaining the practices by producing and reproducing them. Medicine as a practice, for instance, would not react to the Tylenol scare as a set of abstract rules, behavior patterns, and standards; rather, medical *personnel* would react by communicating among themselves, and in technical flows with medical organizations. Our other supplements are:

- holding that the *constellations* typically include dedicated supportive organizations (law schools for legal institutions, international organizations like NATO for diplomacy) and
- emphasizing that the *beliefs* can also be informal, unstated, and even irrational (for instance, beliefs about the dangers of COVID-19 vaccines).

We believe that these supplements accord with the intent of Lammers and Barbour (2006).

We also believe it is useful, for the purpose of developing our own perspective, to suggest revisions of their well-articulated theoretical propositions to be more in line with our sense of the structurational fourth flow. Specifically, we certainly concur with their Proposition 1, that "communication (communication systems) sustains (produces/reproduces) institutions" (p. 364). Though, we note more explicitly that institutional *practices* include, crucially, communication flow. Their Proposition 2, that "Communication aligns organizing with institutions" (p. 365) could be usefully rephrased by noting that the four organizational flows involve a broader, less well-delineated intermingling of interorganizational flows, sometimes in submissive ways, sometimes in violent discord (for example, Folger et al., 2021). We generally agree with Proposition 3, that "Institutions operate… through formal communication" (p. 365), but our self-structuring (see Chapter 6) discussion emphasizes the critical and varied ways in which any formal document depends on a flow, smooth or riptide, of supplemental interpretive communication, often informal. Analogously, the US Supreme Court supposedly applies the Constitution, but its opinions get reproduced in a wide array of moments outside the court such as doctor-lawyer confrontations about reproductive care. Proposition 4, that "The success of boundary-spanning communication depends on…institutions" (p. 366) is laudable in its insistence that "individuals do [the boundary-spanning] on behalf of an organization" (p. 366) and we find its insight about the special focal point of boundary-spanning very valuable (though, notably, the boundary-spanning is both producing and maintaining/potentially transforming the institution). Finally, Proposition 5, that "Institutional hierarchy is manifested in organizing" (p. 367) importantly connects institutions to power (im)balance both between and within organizations, and to our Self-structuring Flow in particular.

We recognize institutional positioning can refer to multiple expanses of social system organizing. Larger institutions, such as the military industrial complex, or the institutions of healthcare, insurance, etc., are indubitably positioned relative to each other, partly by organizations created to do that sort of positioning. On the other hand, we also need, in this flow, to recognize and theorize such relations of the institutional/organization system in their manifestation through (and constitution by) the communication of organizational agents at the level of individuals who are not members—those who are either members of other organizations or who are members of *the public* or *the customer base*, both of which can usefully be regarded as systems in which institutional positioning is necessitated, as we elaborate later. However, we primarily focus on the level of communication by agents of organizations per se. What we want to emphasize is that such communication—agent-to-agent, across boundaries—takes place *institutionally*—what Lammers and Barbour refer to as "institutional communication."

Organization member communication with outsiders cries out to be characterized using one or another institutional vocabulary: it may involve buying and selling (in the language and practices of capitalism), or providing services by state-employed workers (in the language/practices of governmental assistance), dispute resolution by courts (in the language/practices of law); or contact between representatives of different governments (in the language/practices of diplomacy). Recognizing that institutional positioning can even occur inside organizational boundaries, we can look to the institution of management, especially leadership.

8.2 Positioning by Individual Agents

We must emphasize that ST grew as a social theory partly because it recognized both *interaction*, with its structural enablements and consequences, and *institutions*, conceiving the latter not as governmental departments or international systems (though those are important), but as concepts given analytic form by structural principles (domination, signification, and legitimation) and their subcurrents. Structural features such as these are systemically produced/reproduced/elaborated, not just of interaction or organizations, but also in currents of, for example, knowledge (organized in professions, universities, and mass-political practices enabled by social media) and power (organized weapons manufacturing systems, national military resources, and global alliances). Due to our concentration on complex organizations as unique independent systems, oriented largely toward the exercise of power (mainly economic), but requiring, and enabled by, systems of signification and legitimation, here we do not explore macrosocial theoretical conceptions—capitalism's relation to democracy—*per se*. We make that choice mainly because there is also, and more to our point, a plethora of scholarship regarding communication between organizational agents—members but other organizationally empowered actors—whose interaction crosses organizational boundaries to representatives or members of other organizational systems in their systemic roles, as well as to the general public. Such work often focuses on individual interaction with *outsider* individuals, with two provisos. One is that institutional positioning often, in orienting to the general public, also must involve currents oriented partly toward the members themselves, since they are also members of the public. They perceive and respond to broadly directed message flows that advertise, for instance, the organization's socially responsible work. A second point to note: very often these days, border-crossing individual interaction, like the rest, gets mediated and distanciated from other individuals by ICT, mass media, social media, and external systems such as artificial intelligence. This kind of agent-to-agent communication across boundaries is our target.

Scholars and laypeople continually refer to organizations, professions, nations, and historical eras as entities that have impacts, effects, traits, character, and even recognizable identities. Above all, they are seen to possess communicative *voice* that lets them make announcements, enact attitudes, or even claim to have legal powers, concerns, and rights. Similar agent-like putative powers let them make, sell, and promote products, employ members, have characteristics like bureaucracy and culture, and facilitate coordinated activity. References like this are so common and multifunctionally useful that we cannot avoid them, especially in this chapter. We will mention and use *Apple*, various *US Department of…*, and even reference "the organization communicating"—to be understood as shorthand for *systems* of communication by individuals. Messages that organizations emit or exchange are actually uttered by people (or collaborative groups) who "speak for" the organization. But when an individual "speaks for" an organization, no higher-level agentive entity authorizes them by "speaking through" them. Rather, such people draw on individually available systemic resources (including, ideally, legitimation by legal and ethical norms), and in speaking, construct a new interpretive context expressive of the individual resources.

Further, we note the linguistic difficulties in exploring the more generally macro concept of institutional positioning. While much of this chapter refers to "the organization" acting, just as many people do in conversation, media coverage, and scholarship, we are not alleging agency. Human agents have agency, or the capacity to act otherwise and reflexively monitor their actions. Yet, organizations, even if referred to as systems, are treated as if they are individual actors. This language game (re)produces the organization and positions it within social systems, but it also tends to mask the underlying processes of individuals communicatively constituting organizations. However, we contend this discourse that speaks of the organization acting is precisely part of the communicative constitution of the organization and necessarily comprises the institutional positioning flow.

Two important ideas guide our analysis. First, the *effects organizations have*—their products, pollution, jobs, salaries, red tape, emergent friendships—*are the results of people interacting*—the flows of communication. ST reminds us that all institutions and macro-entities—including organizations—rest crucially, in their very nature, on broad currents of communication and coordinated activity. The four flows are necessary, and their enactment is necessitated by communication that requests or motivates it, and that reproduces it—maintains or transforms it. Organizations, conceived in this organizing, generative way, do have external, even institutional outcomes and implications like the wages paid to employees, products competing in the marketplace, supplies and property appropriated for private use, and collectives enabled for cooperative work in designed and well-supplied worksite. Additionally, negative outcomes such as famine as organizations hoard the foodstuffs they own and pollute the rivers and air. Organizations, systems of interacting people, along with the material and other resources involved in their activity, do have effects just as any other systems have.

However, ST demands that we study, and otherwise constantly keep in mind, a special second current. Organizations—the *interaction systems—generate and disseminate a construct of the organization as a coherent entity*, an image to which we can attribute identity, needs, voice, ownership rights, free-speech rights, and more. To be precise, it is important to acknowledge that constructs or images of organizations are myths, by elucidating how they are constructed, or projected as coherent, usable images. Organizations are enacted *initially* by the communicative work of cooperating organizational members, which soon draws on the societal-structural resources of organization-creation, for example, organizational documents, negotiated contracts about employment, and supply purchases.

Communication streams enabled by these resources involve specific groups, of employees and outsiders, who collectively imagine *the organization* as a construct, display it as an image, represent it (and see themselves as its representatives—or masters), and lay claim to the outputs it generates. We advocate "explor(ing) the array of communication that influences how individuals—members and non-members— perceive the organization, its identity, mission, collaborations and other conceptions of the organization in its environment" (Iverson et al., 2022, p. 75).

8.3 Four Facets of Institutional Positioning

The general character of positioning combines both identity and place in a macro sense. For this chapter, we focus on four conceptual facets of institutional positioning, and two extended examples of corporate social responsibility and crisis communication that demonstrate the interconnected nature of institutional positioning.

Our four conceptual areas include:

- First, the constitutive process of creating an organizational identity and its symbolic existence, such as legal recognition, advertising, public relations, and marketing that directly relates to the organization—for example, executives making speeches directly or indirectly describing the organization, or image ads. This section focuses on the organization's identity.
- Second, and related, we explore the organization, thus identified, and its actions within the social system. This area emphasizes the positioning done by agents who relate at the organizational level to the agents of other organizations such as salespeople, clients, executives, or union leaders. Additionally, actions such as Presidents signing treaties and organizational involvement in the social context.
- Third, we examine processes implicating the organization (through its agents) in communication to individuals on its behalf, internally to members as well as externally. This section emphasizes that institutional positioning occurs even in communicating to the members of the organization, boundary spanners, and those decidedly outside the organization. Examples include cashiers at Costco doing business with customers, clothing buyers negotiating with designers for Macy's, and Customer Service Representatives interacting with members.
- Fourth, we examine institutional positioning, not simply organization to organization, but positioning themselves relative to other organizations qua their complex networks and layers. Collaboration, coalition, and competition occur across a complex landscape of social organizations and institutions.

8.4 Organizational Identity

For organizations to have a measure of coherence and meaning in the social world, their identity and apparent agency do not simply exist, but must be constituted. Identity of an organization entails the collective image of the organization. Organizational identity focuses primarily on the ontological questions regarding the nature of an organization (Cheney et al., 2014). While some approaches treat the identity of an organization "as something intrinsic, solid, and reliable that sets it apart from its surroundings," others see it as a social construction or a combination of those perspectives (p. 697). Structuration theory as well as the four flows model allow us to recognize the value of both approaches. Organizational identity is linked but distinct from organizational identification and identity work (Larson & Gill, 2017) and a part of institutional positioning within the broader framework of "creating, developing and maintaining institutional identity in a perpetually changing and evolving broader society" (Duffy, 2016, p. 76).

Institutional positioning provides a means of understanding how organizations engage in actions to distinguish themselves to justify and sustain their existence. Some of those actions relate to legal recognition such as incorporating or filing for 501c(3) status with the Internal Revenue Service. Organization members communicatively constitute the beginnings and maintenance of the organization as a legal entity. However, identity can exist beyond legal recognition. For example, *Anonymous* has an identity but is not a formal organization (see Chapter 5). Collectively, the International Red Cross and Red Crescent Movement enacts a global identity as a disaster relief and peacekeeping organization "dedicated to protecting human life and dignity worldwide, thereby promoting lasting peace" (Mercier & Reid, 1990, p. 194). Each national Red Cross or Red Crescent organization works to enact that identity through their responses, positioning not only themselves, but the collective identity as well.

Organizational identity is well established as a concept (see Cheney and Christensen, 2001) along with organizational image, public relations, and a host of other fields. BMW has developed branding as *the ultimate driving machine*. Hallmark has cultivated identity based on the phrase, "When you care enough to send the very best." Hallmark has extended that image of emotive action to their media channels including a known genre of Hallmark movies that can be considered their own category similar to westerns or other movie types (Braithwaite, 2023).

One context is the naming of the organization. Selecting a name for an organization, such as a university, signals not only the existence, but what type of organization is intended to be identified. We have analyzed Trump University (Iverson et al., 2022) as an attempt to present a pyramid scheme as a legitimized organization for learning. Additionally, name changes are attempts to rebrand, reposition, or reidentify as an organization. Facebook became Meta to incorporate its new product of a virtual world while keeping Facebook as an application within its organizational system. The extent to which the name change to Meta has changed its positioning is unclear, but it is a communicative act to reconstitute the organization as different. Further, organizational identity can be an attempt to establish the separation and declaration of existence as Karhili et al. (2021) contend for the Islamic State:

> The group's former leader and so-called Caliph Abu Bakr al-Baghdadi declared the organization's new name "the Islamic State" on June 29, 2014. In a speech announcing the decision, al-Baghdadi renamed the group by declaring the eradication of its group's former names like Islamic Sate of Iraq and Islamic State of Iraq and al-Sham (Levant) to unite under "the banner of the Islamic State – the banner of the Caliphate" (Baghdadi as cited in Roggio, 2014, para.3).

The visual appeals and media use are enacted to establish the organization's legitimacy as well as to maintain claims of authority over official state powers. Karhili's analysis of visual images used over time demonstrates the changes that happen, especially for clandestine organizations including multiple and conflicting identities.

Of course, if the organization represents itself as one identity in part to satisfy interests of organizational leaders and various constituents (members, stockholders, community members, etc.) it simultaneously precludes holding other identities, often creating tensions and contraventions (tensions arising from flow dynamics—see Chapter 9) for members and others affiliated with the organization. For example, when Anheuser-Busch's Bud Light brand provided transgender social-media influencer Dylan Mulvaney a promotional swag bag to help celebrate the one-year anniversary of her coming out as trans, it caused socially conservative individuals to attack the brand, arguing the promotional items indicated the company's identity as a supporter of the transgender community (Wood & Allan, 2024). They called for a boycott of the brand, which caused a dramatic drop in Bud Light sales and stock price within just a few days. Company representatives responded by explaining that they provide these types of swag bags to many individuals to help them celebrate life, which is in line with the socially neutral identity they desired for the company. CEO Michel Doukeris announced that in the future, the company hopes to avoid the spotlight (Allen & Hawkins, 2023). The tension between wanting to help individuals celebrate occasions was linked to how Bud Light wished to position itself as a brand, but that identity became a liability when, in responding to a contravening flow, conservatives sought to reprimand the company for promoting that identity.

With a few exceptions as mentioned earlier, identity can be considered either fairly stable or contested, and the communicative constitution of the organization represents a critical process of creating both legal and social accomplishments. Closely related to the organization as an identifiable entity is its existence within a social system context.

8.5 Social System Actant

Presuming their constitution as social entities with identities, organizations also directly interact with other organizations. These interactions create an immediate environment for organizations in which they operate. As we have previously described: "A second aspect of institutional positioning is environmental exploration, the process of gathering information about potential connections and competitors, opportunities and constraints" (McPhee & Iverson, 2009, p. 82). The enactment of these connections emphasizes the positioning of the institution through direct agentively executed actions, spanning their boundaries and developing their direct system of interaction. For example, a supply chain relationship between organizations creates a direct operating environment such as a brewery needing a supply of equipment, grains, and water. Not only are organizational needs met in these relationships, but values and discourses can be shared, such as sustainability efforts across the supply chain (Allen et al., 2012). Within these interactive arenas, organizations also tend to influence one another through their expectations, mimetic choices, and other forms of isomorphism (DiMaggio & Powell, 1983).

For example, Kelley et al. (2005) describe the change in a San Francisco-based needle exchange organization, Prevention Point. In the early days, the organization was "underground," engaging in needle exchanges as an illegal activity, while its members lobbied for the laws to change. The organization operated at some levels of secrecy, made decisions by consensus, and had limited, but collective formal structure. The organization operated from baby buggies in parks to distribute clean needles to intravenous drug users (IDUs):

> In time, the mobile baby buggy became a routine part of the world of IDUs, recognized by both users and the police. Instead of hiding their actions, the undercover nature of their work provided police and health officials with the opportunity to quietly observe them in the community while maintaining plausible deniability. (p. 368)

The direct interaction with local health organizations and the (lack of) interaction with law enforcement positioned Prevention Point within its environment and created space for them to operate despite the law.

Once they successfully changed the law, expectations from other existing nonprofit organizations and potential partners, along with the prospect of outside funding, led the organization into developing a board of directors, some paid staff positions, a volunteer coordinator, and other isomorphic changes. While these changes are structural (Flow 2), they are also a clear example of institutional positioning, where the organization changed due to its need to work with other direct organizations within their immediate environment. These changes constitute the organization in very different ways, including positioning within the immediate environment. Operating within that local environment can be in relation to a national parent organization (Witmer, 1997) as well as the local operating environment. In each case, the interactions position the organization in an ongoing, communicative process.

8.6 Organization to Individuals

On an individual to organizational level, people inside and outside interact with an organization. Institutional positioning is constituted as meaning for those *within* the organization as various types of membership—for example, personnel policy handbooks (Flow 1), as well as constituting the organization for those external to it. Internally, institutional positioning functions relative to membership negotiation with an answer to the question, "Membership in what?" The institutional positioning flow focuses on the constitution of the "what." The relationship could be as an employer or an organization with other forms of membership, including volunteering (Iverson & McPhee, 2008). Professional organizations such as the American Medical Association or National Communication Association, religious or other affiliative organizations that are labeled voluntary associations (Anderson, 1971) have various types of membership. Institutional positioning creates meaning and a venue for those who wish to join with others to participate as members.

People interact on behalf of organizations. Working for an organization, buying a product, acting as a negotiator, etcetera, constitute an individual interacting for the organization as an entity communicatively constituted across a range of actions, including as a boundary spanner. However, this interaction that constitutes representatives also positions the organization they represent. In many cases of institutional positioning, agents acting individually or in concert with others are, in a sense, acting as a part of the organization, drawing upon the rules and resources available to them to act for the institution. For example, organizational members need to secure resources by engaging in partnerships for a supply chain. Boundary spanning allows members of the organization to, in a sense (as described earlier), "speak for" the organization.

But this organization-to-individuals path runs both ways. Externally, nonmembers interacting with the organization can also have the power to constitute it institutionally. For example, purchasing food from a restaurant or store results in sustaining the organization in the food-shopping institutional milieu. In addition, fans of a sports team or customers for Apple products may line up to be the first ones to buy tickets or a new product. Their loyalty or resistance to the organization constitutes and position the organization. As another example, Carhartt is one of many organizations facing boycotts. After Carhartt clothing company announced its policy requiring vaccination for all employees (an incident of institutional positioning on many levels), customers, celebrities, and other individuals began to boycott the organization, burn their clothes, and work to "cancel" Carhartt (Hirsch, 2022).

The concepts of insider and outsider in membership can be permeable and variable (see Flow 1). For example, a membership at a shopping club such as Costco is needed to engage in a meaningful consumer relationship with the organization. Yet, members/customers are still experiencing Costco from an outsider perspective. When customers say, "I returned that to Costco" and when employees say they work *for* Costco and are paid *by* Costco, they see the organization as separate from themselves. The statements serve two functions. First, the use of a prepositional phrase distinguishes between the person and the organization. Second, the preposition places the organization in a relationship with the individuals in a permeable manner. Both enact institutional positioning. Further examples can be found in Woo et al.' (2023) analysis of remote workers and the challenges they face becoming part of the organization during the COVID pandemic and remote socialization. They found remotely socialized newcomers reported lower levels of organizational assimilation. By maintaining a remote-only relationship, the organization risks alienation and uncertainty of its employees. Site visits (when possible) and other connections can change the relationship between the organization and the members.

8.7 Organization to Organizations in the Institutional System[s]

Interacting with other organizations also positions them within the broader institutional social system. Collaborative agreements, price-gouging, establishing guidelines, creating a supply chain are all institutionalized vehicles of organizational relating at differing levels and across a variety of contexts, in ways that constitute, and reflexively are constituted in, society writ large. A range of interorganizational relationships can exist, from organizations in sets that operate in the same system as competitors, partners, and customers, to cooperative organizations that may work together on a specific task or project, to collaborators that may maintain independence within a formal structure governing them in an interorganizational manner (Heath & Isbell, 2017). This is another reason the term "institutional" is preferred to "organizational" positioning.

Collaboration positions organizations as working together, sometimes forming larger organizations. For example, the United Way serves as an umbrella organization to organize fund raising for a set of community organizations that agree to participate in their process. Each member organization of United Way agrees to the rules of resource allocation that United Way offers through community need assessment. Many for-profit organizations agree to fundraise for United Way, in part to simplify their community giving. Nonmember organizations do not have to face restrictions on fundraising, but they do not receive United Way funds. The overall ecology of the community is negotiated, and each organization positions itself within that landscape through representation, exploration, and negotiation.

As a second example, the National Interagency Fire Center (NIFC) is an interagency organization designed to respond to wildfires:

> The National Interagency Fire Center (NIFC), located in Boise, Idaho, is the nation's support center for wildland firefighting. Eight different agencies and organizations are part of NIFC. Decisions are made using the interagency cooperation concept because NIFC has no single director or manager (https://www.nifc.gov/about-us/what-is-nifc).

While NIFC does not dictate policy for each agency within the federal government, through coordination and decision-making, each member organization is positioned within and through NIFC. Collaborations are active processes in which each organization has representation but maintains its own distinct organizational identity. As Koschmann and Sanders (2020) state, "Collaborations don't merely exist and then we communicate within them or about them; collaboration exists in and through certain communication practices that create and sustain these organizational forms" (p. 80). Institutional positioning within collaborations for organizations is communicatively constituted through the actions of collaborating. Those actions also constitute the collaboration.

Institutional theory (especially as developed by Lammers and his colleagues) takes a more macro-theoretical position by placing organizations within very general contexts that serve a meaningful function and create structures that extend beyond single organizations. This work is at its heart institutional positioning, but recognizes that some actions are beyond the scope of any one organization to change. That said, those broad meanings, rules, norms, and structures reproduced through actions by collections of agents over time. In this way, institutional positioning strongly resembles self-structuring, recognizing that building an environment necessarily builds structures.

Isomorphism is a good exemplification of this work. Organizations mimic one another through adoption of practices, standards, as well as creating expectations for organizations within sectors, learning from each other as they do. Sanders and McClellan (2014) expound on the general discourse that nonprofit organizations face to be more business-like. Although many business practices do not make sense for mission-driven organizations, those discourses bleed into expectations to have a financial bottom line. Such expectations may conflict with the mission of the organization, creating tensions and conflict that must be navigated.

Overall, the four facets of institutional positioning represent a glimpse into the expanse of organizations as they operate in the social landscape. The constitutive nature of institutional positioning can be found by more closely examining transtructions as elaborated in Chapter 3.

8.8 Transtructions

Organizational constitution through institutional positioning can be understood from a transtruction perspective through the modalities of meaning, norms, and power, as the organization's institutional positioning is constituted. Each of the four facets of institutional positioning involves complexes of meaning, constitution, norms, and power. As an example, when an organization takes an action, such as the World Health Organization (WHO) declared COVID-19 a pandemic:

> WHO has been assessing this outbreak around the clock and we are deeply concerned both by the alarming levels of spread and severity, and by the alarming levels of inaction.
>
> We have therefore made the assessment that COVID-19 can be characterized as a pandemic.
>
> Pandemic is not a word to use lightly or carelessly. It is a word that, if misused, can cause unreasonable fear, or unjustified acceptance that the fight is over, leading to unnecessary suffering and death (World Health Organization, 2020).

These opening remarks by the Director-General of WHO on March 11, 2020, signal not only a communicative action, but also an institutional positioning to be understood through transtruction. The *meaning* of this statement is clearly laid out in the explanation of not only the declaration, but the gravity of the use of pandemic as a term. The meaning of the statement is connected to the practice of a media briefing being led by the Director-General of WHO. The position within WHO as well as the official nature of the media briefing create a legitimacy of the statement as being a WHO organizational statement. The power is evident in the fact that WHO asserts its authority to be the one to declare and officially use the term pandemic. Finally, through his meaningful statement, his legitimacy to make such a declaration, and the power that is associated with his role, the statement becomes *constitutive* in a consequential, decisive way. This example illustrates how the four elements are entangled in the one statement—the meaning and legitimacy of WHO constitutes it not only as an organization, but also as positioned within the world as *the* organization to make such a declaration. The action reproduces the WHO as an organization with the power to make such a declaration.

The WHO declaration of a pandemic further illustrates the Four Flows position on organizations and agency. By reporting that "WHO declares a pandemic," the capacity to act otherwise seems like an organizational action. After all, WHO could not have made the declaration that day, or ever. However, ascribing agency to the organization masques the individuals with the capacity to act otherwise within the organization. It is no accident that the Director General, Dr. Tedros Adhanom Ghebreyesus, makes the declaration. Had a lower-level member used the term pandemic, others within WHO could counter by stating that the person was not speaking for WHO, and maintain that WHO has not declared COVID-19 a pandemic as of yet. Such an action would reinforce the institutional positioning of WHO in contrast to an individual within. Institutional positioning encourages scholars to distinguish between utterances that position the institution by a representative and those that do not formally represent the organization but are nonetheless positioning the institution.

Transtructions illustrate how each of the four facets of institutional positioning we have articulated constitute the organization. The meaning is communicatively enacted, which creates a *what* for organizations. The norms of the larger system as well as those within an organization, are present as either being supported or distinguished from the organization's practices. Finally, the power dynamics of leveraging assets, attempting to establish a position within a field of organizations, recruiting the best members, and many other activities open the possibility for understanding power as constitutive of the organization. Within the field of organizational communication, the list of theories and areas of research is nearly limitless. However, two subfields, or topoi, of corporate social responsibility and crisis communication provide excellent examples to demonstrate the interconnected depth of institutional positioning across the four facets of institutional positioning and transtructions.

8.9 Corporate Social Responsibility

One useful focus for analyzing the four facets of institutional positioning is corporate social responsibility (CSR). Although the definitions of CSR vary, Christensen et al. (2022) include "a collections of standards, norms, policies and practices that guide how organizations relate to their stakeholders and wider common good" (p. 354). For instance, Patagonia is widely considered a strong environmental activist organization that has built loyalty through fair trade suppliers instead of sweatshops as well as controversial statements such as, "The President Stole Your Land" as Patagonia's social media campaign in response to President Trump's decision to shrink the Bears Ears National Monument and Grand Staircase-Escalante National Park (Dawson & Brunner, 2020). Organizations such as Patagonia position themselves as both distinct from other less-expensive brands and relative to the values and beliefs of their customers through their practices. CSR initiatives are directed at external audiences, creating interest from public relations scholars that emphasizes external communication that in part establishes the organization's identity. However, CSR illustrates the complexities of institutional positioning by organizations because in order to establish identity, they must interact with others outside the organization and "acknowledge[s] the influence of multiple stakeholders on what communication can accomplish over time" (Christensen et al., p. 355).

CSR is not simply about establishing organizational identity, so it provides a useful example of how a concept crosses into social system context, internal as well as external organizations, and happens within the panoply of organizations. However, as May and Roper (2014) discuss, CSR also includes internal communication to direct operations and guide decision-making. May and Roper call for scholarship to explore "understanding the organizational processes of integrating internal and external communication to produce a seemingly coherent organizational identity" (p. 782). The attempt at coherent identity for the organization through positioning can be internal as well as external. We will revisit those facets of CSR in the next section.

Beyond coherence of image and identity, CSR can also generate interest and activity in the social landscape through tensions and paradox. Dawson and Brunner (2020) explain that the public sphere of today is not a coherent public space for rational discourse as Habermas (1989/1962) envisioned. Rather, it is a wild public network (WPN) where "myriad unique users are interacting in real time across vast distances" using mostly affective appeals (p. 61). Positioning within this landscape involves energizing responses, creating movement, and spurring action. While Patagonia has dozens of professional social media curators and develops documentary films relating to the environment, Patagonia engages in controversial communication such as "The President Stole Your Land" initiative. Patagonia placed a large black and white image on their web page and on social media with the simple message that "The President stole your land" in reference to the reduction of the area for Bears Ears National Monument by President Trump in 2017. This campaign created significant controversy, negative and positive reactions from individual users, organizations, and mass media. Dawson and Brunner note:

> Patagonia, relying on a strong mission and sense of identity, utilizes the paradox of being lauded as both a CSR hero and a money-making corporation to launch an issue into the greater public discourse. (p. 59).

Patagonia's launch generated numerous user comments that Dawson and Brunner label "CSR-based wild public provocations" and categorize as posts in support/opposition, posts addressing the land, posts espousing political views, and posts condemning political activism. These divisive actions position Patagonia as a non-neutral organization and communicate its position. While Patagonia did not respond to individual posts, it did make declarations that promoted a variety of responses and elevated its visibility across platforms while communicating a clear identity through a "productive paradox." The implications for institutional positioning lend itself to explore the transtructive processes in CCO. CSR provides a clear example of transtructions and institutional positioning, highlighting the decentered nature of constitution. For transtructions, *meaning* is generated, changed, and enacted across those within and outside the organization. Patagonia's statements and the varied reactions enact a fairly consistent identity of Patagonia, though it creates division and creates an adversarial position for some responses. *Norms* are both used and violated in the advertisement, spurring of responses about public lands and all position Patagonia as a clear advocate for public lands. In addition, *power* is present in the ability of Patagonia as well as media and congressional representatives' reactions to Patagonia. Generally, CSR provides a means for organizations to interact with the world and use those interactions as a basis to directly communicate the meanings of those actions.

8.10 Crisis Communication

A crisis represents "a specific, unexpected, non-routine event or series of events that creates high levels of uncertainty and a significant or perceived threat to high priority goals" (Sellnow & Seeger, 2013, p. 7). In a moment of crisis, organizations face significant threats that must be handled. Whether it is financial harm, such as the 2008 economic crisis for Goldman Sachs and automobile manufacturers, reputational risks such as Volkswagen losing credibility when caught cheating on emission tests in Deiselgate (Zhang et al., 2021), or security issues like Target faced with a breach of their records, crises happen and organizations must deal with the shift in their institutional positioning. It would be natural for conflicting flow currents, as well as contraventions, to appear as these crises play out—even to be essential features in ongoing discourse.

The threatening nature of a crisis makes the organization and institutional positioning salient. The organization typically receives significant media attention and the overall character of the organization is brought into question. Additionally, the organization must respond and react to the crisis. In some cases, the response of individuals within the organization becomes a focal point, but in others, press releases, statements, and actions are attributed to the organization itself.

As one example, in 2017, United Airlines forcibly removed passenger David Dao from a plane in order to seat a flight crew member on the plane before offering the maximum compensation to get a volunteer. A video recording of the incident went viral, leading to public outrage over the incident and CEO Oscar Munoz's attempt to downplay the incident by blaming Dao for his resistance to being removed from the flight, apologizing to the other passengers, and standing by the United employees. The incident and statements by Munoz contributed to the outrage, reputational harm, and financial losses in stock value of over $1.4 billion. The public responded through memes, such as "United: If we need the seating, you will get a savage beating," a letter from senators on the Senate Commerce Committee, and protests (Ulmer et al., 2018). United reacted to this response with a "do-over" by Munoz that fully apologized and agreed with the public reaction of disgust (Benoit, 2018).

From an institutional positioning perspective, the United actions and responses repositioned the organization through a very different image. This incident highlights the institutional positioning that began with the actions of the United employees on flight 3411. Every interaction between the employees and their customers positions the organization and (re)produces the meaning of the organization. The employees choosing not to raise the offer of compensation, but instead select a passenger to be removed positioned United as an organization that cared about flying employees more than customers. When Dao resisted removal, the United response drew on the procedures and resources of the organization as part of the airline industry to have airport security remove him from the plane. The passengers pleading and demanding that security stop, the recording of the incident, and the social and mass media spread of the incident all position United.

In this way, institutional positioning is not just actions and words from the organization to the public, but instead represents the collective, social practices of positioning.

The initial response from Munoz was a public attempt at responding and taking corrective action to the impact on the organization. The response increased the problems for United and required a further, more complete apology. "United's CEO apparently realized he was piloting his company into a hurricane; he radically changed the course of his defense. Munoz declared, 'It's never too late to do the right thing'" (Benoit, 2018, p. 19). Munoz enacted mortification (regret) on behalf of United on television and issued a long letter. The organization released changes in policy and a letter to customers expressing regret and pledging to be better (Ulmer et al., 2018). The communicative constitution of United in each instance exemplifies how organizations are constituted and positioned in dynamic and ongoing ways.

The research field of crisis and risk communication analyzes important moments of institutional positioning. NASA, for example, faced crises for the organization with the Challenger and Columbia shuttle disasters. The loss of lives and equipment as well as the disruption to the notion that shuttle flights were "routine" caused NASA and the US federal government to respond. The oil spill in the Gulf of Mexico for BP created a major crisis, leading to the resignation of the CEO, significant environmental damage, and the loss of life. The consequences of each crisis lead to various outcomes ranging from destruction of the organization (Enron, e.g.), significant loss (NASA), but also the opportunity for renewal. For example, the Tylenol crisis in the 1980s created a significant disruption for Johnson & Johnson resulting in the complete recall of Tylenol products. The organization responded with tamper-resistant packaging and engaging in rebuilding public trust in the organization.

As a field of study, crisis communication falls under institutional positioning, along with related theories beginning with precrisis organizational actions such as monitoring, risk analysis, and prevention like high reliability organizing (Roberts, 1990). Additionally, such theories cover the responses during the crisis such as avoidance, apologia, image repair (Benoit, 2018), situational crisis communication theory (Coombs, 2004), and stakeholder engagement, all of which detail the various choices made during a crisis for organizational communication. After a crisis, organizations face the crisis of legitimacy and may cease to exist or engage in organizational change made possible by the disruption from the crisis through renewal (Ulmer et al., 2018).

Crises create moments where organizational existence and meaning become much more salient. As a result, crisis communication and theories (Sellnow & Seeger, 2013) in this subdiscipline offer unique opportunities to understand constitution. *Meaning*, such as reputational harm and later, image repair in the United Airlines case demonstrate the focus on the positioning of United Airlines as, for example, the worst of the airlines by comparison through memes, jokes, lost revenue from decreased flying, and even stock price. All of these actions happen within the *norms* of the airline industry, the organization itself, and public expectations. By initially praising the United employees for removing a disrupted customer, the expectations to follow policy are clear. Later, the shift to focus on the customer and apologize shows enacting the expectations of the public. The *power* of those inside and outside the organizations, such as the FAA, demonstrates not only the power of customers and those outside the organization, but also those within to make policy, change policies, and engage in other communication. Although each of these events might be perceived as making the organization seem less competent and disorganized, each constitutes United Airlines as it exists today.

8.11 Conclusion

Institutional positioning has significant confluences with the other flows. Given the encompassing nature of organizational communication connecting to institutional positioning by definition as organizational, the confluences are ubiquitous. However, for purposes of analysis and emphasis, some specific examples provide some illustration. Membership negotiations ranging from recruiting potential members to acting for the institution are negotiating membership while positioning their institution. For example, volunteers for the American Red Cross responding to a disaster are positioning the institution as well as engaging in experiences that change the meaning of their membership (Iverson, 2013). Agreeing to collaboration through a memorandum of understanding coordinates activities as well as structures the organization as well.

9

Confluence of the Four Flows

In the four preceding chapters, we described each of the four flows and how they work to constitute the transtruction process. As we noted earlier, the very metaphor *flow* is itself a representation of communication that offers more breadth and flexibility than older descriptors such as *information transmission* or *transaction*, and, we argue, provides unique insights compared to newer ones like *incarnation* (Cooren, 2020) or *transmission that relates sociomateriality*. (See Chapter 10.) Thinking about any one of our flows brings us into the complexity of what transpires to constitute organizations. But, of course, all of the flows not only influence, but are impossible without each other. It is tempting to think that the flows are distinct in some way: that each instance of communication belongs to just one flow, or that any occurrence in a flow depends only on prior occurrences in that flow, so that the flow can be separated out. We have from the beginning been intent to deny both of those claims. Browning et al. (2009) were among the early researchers to recognize this, but their article must be read, not as a critique of our position (McPhee & Iverson, 2009), but as an elaboration and confirmation of it. As we noted earlier, the idea of the flows leads us to insights about how they are intertwined and a maze of cross currents, as well as the depth of stagnant social tendencies such as the unjust distribution of wealth and structural racism and sexism—what we call *deep structures/currents*. In this chapter, we discuss the confluences of the flows—the relationships between the flows and their interdependences at the micro, meso, and macro levels. We conclude this chapter by discussing deep structures and their persistent role in maintaining the qualities of the flows with enduring effects.

The Communicative Constitution of Organizations: The Four Flows Model, First Edition.
Robert D. McPhee, Karen K. Myers, and Joel O. Iverson.

9.1 The Confluence of the Flows

We begin by once again reflecting on the useful metaphor of a river to illuminate how individual conversations, collective organizational discourse, formal communications reflecting an array of issues and related actions constitute organizations with implications beyond. Similarly, the various currents or flows that make up a river do not travel or affect their surroundings independently of each other. The flow that was enhanced by a tributary, combines with the larger body; the unseen warm thermal spring that bubbles from the bottom is rapidly mixed with the cooler flows that originated from the mountain snow melt; and the swirling flow formed from an eddy on the river's surface might impede movement to at least temporarily slow the river's overall forward advancement. Together, they form the character of the river, distinguishing one river from another, making some rivers strong, raging rivers that continuously reshape their banks and trajectories, and other gentle streams that seem to have little effect on their surroundings. Here, we discuss and provide examples of the intermingling of the discursive flows, their influence on each other, and their constitutive effect on organizations.

As described in Chapter 5, we begin with membership negotiation. Membership negotiation involves the interactions between members to assume a role in an organization with all the associated rights and responsibilities of that role (Ashforth, 2001), and position themselves within the organization (Davies & Harre, 1990). Through this flow individuals learn about and enact what it means to be a member (Scott & Myers, 2010)—they constitute what it means to be a member of the organization. The membership negotiation flow shares a mutually influential relationship with self-structuring because structures define many elements of membership, and the knowledge and skills carried among members. Members also shape structures—formal and informal rules and organizational culture—through their communication and actions associated with their membership. Of course, new members must be absorbed into membership in ways that are formally stipulated through policies and established practices, barring an emergency ad-hoc addition of helpers. For example, new firefighters receive orientation and training based on organizational and professional standards toward developing their knowledge and skills to fight fires, and enhancing their ability to coordinate their activities with others in their organization. These interactions to negotiate membership are not limited to newcomers, but they are ongoing throughout their membership, regardless of the hierarchical level (Jablin, 2001).

Drawing on firefighters to demonstrate these points, even if probationary firefighters don't agree with all the firefighting rules, they understand that newcomers are expected to conform and their colleagues *need* their general conformity, in order to be able to trust the new members when contingencies arise (Myers & McPhee, 2006)—and as their experience grows, so does their understanding of the importance of trust and thus, at times, conformity. As wildland firefighters are assigned their first duties, their behaviors are guided (controlled) by structures that define the scope of their responsibilities on the front line. They know, for example, that the Ten Standard Firefighting Orders require that they actively identify a safety zone (previously burned area or open meadow with little to burn) and an escape route (National Wildfire Coordinating Group, 2018). When firefighters do so, they reinforce those rules and guidelines, and the rules become further solidified in the firefighting role (the force of the flow becomes stronger), so that changing elements of the role in the future can be more difficult. Thus, in some ways the culture of the organization (even firefighting in general) had dictated that roles are performed as described in the Ten Standard Rules—potentially making training easier—and members are less likely to engage in unsafe practices.

However, at times, firefighters respond to their current situations and draw on their own agency. Firefighters might be told about a safety zone from a helicopter above them, but on the ground, they might judge that safety zone to be too difficult to access because of steep terrain or heavy brush (Jahn, 2019a, 2019b). Instead of relying on the safety zone, they choose an alternative escape route. *In situ*, crews make choices about where to go and how to get there, which can deviate from policy. This example demonstrates that while firefighters understand the rules, in some situations, they may interpret the rule differently or feel sufficiently empowered to break the rule by doing what they believe is more reasonable or convenient at the time. Individual firefighters and the overall crew understand that their roles direct them to follow the rule, but instead, they enact their roles differently and coordinate their crew's activities to break the rule. Pushing back a strong current—a flow that is deeply entrenched—can be difficult and with serious consequences. Firefighters' communication and actions—making a choice to follow the rules or break the rules and the consequences of those choices—advance discourses among firefighters, firefighting organizations, supporting agencies, and the general public. On a daily basis and over time, they position firefighters (and firefighting organizations) not as rule breakers versus followers, but rule adapters. The seasoned professionals become agents who make smart choices, and are no longer undisciplined renegades.

While theorists can be critical of organizational powers of control, organizational leaders and long-term firefighters may genuinely believe in the rationale behind the rule. They may previously have seen how the rule has protected them and their crew. If new members are enabled or allowed to push back and alter rules and policies, these and other structures (e.g., legitimacy of training) can potentially lose their power over time, even ones that could save their lives. Regardless, most rule-breaking events invite close scrutiny and evaluation to determine whether and how rules should be revised and how members should be directed to coordinate their activities.

As this firefighting example demonstrates, communication and behaviors enact multiple flows as part of major events and daily life. It is nearly impossible to think of an organization-focused conversation that does not directly entangle at least two of the four flows A conversation between a fire chief and a training officer about how a new safety procedure that he would like incorporated into the training schedule necessarily includes elements of activity coordination. In having the conversation, the two are enacting self-structuring that specifies the hierarchical nature of their relationship, and how the training officer responds to the conversation, potentially taking charge of the assignment or questioning elements of the plan, which involves membership negotiation. What might be less apparent is how this and related conversations position the organization. Introducing the new safety procedure positions the organization in comparison to other firefighting agencies, especially compared to those that do not as readily adopt new safety procedures. It also positions the organization with potential funding agencies who might perceive it as forward-thinking, and with new firefighters who might be impressed with how the agency adopts the procedure and trains firefighting crews. How the chief and training officer interact and follow through with enactment demonstrates the meaning, power, and legitimacy of their relationship, which all position the organization for the two interactants, their colleagues, communities that are served, families of firefighters, and beyond.

9.2 Flows as Foundational Theoretic Constructs for Organizational Communication and CCO Analysis

We advocate the use of the 4F conceptual array as an alternative to a very large history of schemata of organizational features, functions, or even processes. Some specifically communication-relevant lists include an early foundational set of lists from Fayol (1949), and another array given by Mintzberg (1979, 1989), or a list of necessary features presented in passing in Haslett (2013), or another by Weigand et al., (2003). We argue that the 4F array is distinctive for several reasons. First, for each of these authors, no sooner do they present a list of categories than they proceed to detail how the list fails, needs supplement, or disintegrates into a vaguer but more basic list. This sublation occurs for an explicit, commonly recognized reason that the authors spell out: communication, or conjoint action by human agents, is so flexible and creative that it goes beyond empirically constructed schemes or corrodes the logical principle underlying scheme distinctions. Mintzberg (1989) was especially thoroughgoing in his self-critique: after detailing seven organization types based on (communicative) coordination mechanisms, he constructed an inverted second-order analysis about how his types combine, subvert, supplement, evolve, and otherwise complicate one another. Taking a similarly critical attitude toward schematic logics, 4F theory emphatically recognizes that communication in a flow is not an unalloyed process serving organizational goals or powerful interests; instead, flows include both communication that, for example, moves toward a settled understanding of a member's role, plus, equally, processes that undermine or revanche against the member's positioned powers. Each flow brings about some likelihood that the routines, arrangements (assemblages), and practices central to it can also evolve to undermine, or redirect, their organizational efficacy.

Second, and complementing the first, the 4F model emphasizes the dissipative force of communication. In each of its flows, messages, conversation chains, and dispersed currents can disrupt the fabric of meanings, norms, and settled powers; they can create new organizing and cooperation principles to replace or reframe the old; they can sell, revamp, or rearrange the material resources of organizations, as much as the authoritative; they can alter the character, placement, and intentional porosity of boundaries. Just like communication of all sorts, the flows essentially tend to contravene themselves. While in the same breath, the 4F model affirms the crucial importance of the enduring constitution of trustworthy, stable foundations and structural resources to ground innovative transformation, and presents the flows as sites of supportive stability emerge and are maintained in the interweave of communication.

Third, confluence *per se* is a signal direction of insight into organizational constitution. As we have demonstrated, each flow has important constitutive significance. But equally constitutive is the fact that any communication process, by moving along one flow direction, thereby also moves along others. An organizational culture can do self-structuring work to encourage coordinated activity, but the fact that such aspects are common and typical in organizations is itself constitutive of it as an organization *per se*.

9.3 Strains and Contradictions, or Contraventions, Among/Within Flows

The peaceful images of a smoothly flowing stream, or a babbling brook, are appealing but are belied by reality. Flow may suggest unidirectional consanguinity, or the univocal elaboration of meaning to maintain collective accord and achievement. In the vocabulary of our model, communication manifesting each of our flows would ideally enable and maintain activity and resources of the other flows as well as its own; transtructions of one structural modality in a flow would metamorphose seamlessly, one to another. But—as just noted, and in accord with some specific concepts and examples in the earlier chapters—the four flows model may have special value in its suggestion of the omnipresence and importance of communicative discord, including notions such as contradiction and paradox, covered by a term we will advocate, *contravention*.

To remind readers, *contravention* seems, by origins, to mean come against, and carries meanings like obstruct; transgress, violate; and meet in the way of opposition, (https://www.wordnik.com/words/contravene). In that original sense, a claim or argument is immersed dialectically in a communicative flow that leads it to an opposing, or merely discrepant stand. For instance, judges are admonished to "use their trained expertise, but be objective." Setting aside the many well-known contortions in the meaning of *objective* itself, engaging in a decision process based on experience and its range of embedded biases neither begins nor ends in objectivity. The expectations of the judiciary are based on contravention.

We concur with Putnam et al. (2016) in advancing a notion that is expressly cast in the domain of communication, that practically every statement includes tensions (i.e., contraventions).

We approach this expanse of ideas by noting that all of the major forms of discursive tension can have a skeletal statement in static terms. For instance, a logical Contradiction is "X and not-X" (both stated in or by a single source)—a manager who orders subordinates, "cooperate!" and, in the same breath, "compete!" (do the opposite of cooperating). Or Paradox: "X" is, or means. "not-X"—for example, a manager saying "competition is cooperation, and you must do that." Considered in statements like that, the implications are clear—contradictions are logically false, and evidently justify any behavior at all; paradoxes deconstruct the terms they connect, and evidently lead to paralysis of analysis.

But scholars of Organization and Communication are broadly united in holding that concepts like these are much more valuably treated processually and discursively (Smith & Lewis, 2011; Putnam et al., 2016). We join them in recognizing "three key dimensions of [their] constitutive view:

> developmental actions, namely, how tensions evolve over time in the change process; how multiple levels and tensions enter into this process; and praxis, how actors' awareness or consciousness of contradictions becomes a factor in responding to them" (Putnam et al., 2016, p. 34).

We also agree that these phenomena have constitutive potency for organizing; that as they evolve, spread, and are reacted to, they can have results that contribute to the advancement of organizational (and subgroup and agent) goals; that they can in particular lead to variety and creativity across an organization; and that, from a researcher's viewpoint, they have novel value in developing theory and sensitizing research (Van de Ven & Poole, 1995). We can hardly deny the last since, as noted before, core concepts of ST can easily be viewed as paradoxical: the duality of structuration, enablement/constraint, the mutual dependence/individuality of the transtructive dimensions. In looking over the literature in this area, several facts presented themselves: there are many terms that are intended, by various authors, to cover the whole domain: tension, contradiction, paradox. Some of these are looser than others; researchers have argued that some evolve into or are logically dependent on others. Finally, it is hard to shake the static notions of, for example, contradiction or paradox mentioned earlier.

We do think it is valuable to retain a basic distinction between contraventions arising from the flow versus contravention from a single idea (phrase). For one thing, instances of contravention manifested in the flow itself: contradictions or paradoxes might, upon close scrutiny, exist as developing, flowing contrarieties of meaning—stating an idea, then, distanciated from the first idea, articulating its opposite in a way that disrupts the first statement (Putnam et al., 2016). On the other hand, a unit (of varied length) of communication can be *self*-discordant with varied dispersed consequences. These might be analyzed as starting points for flows, and might include overt paradoxes—colorless green, obedient maverick—or contradictions in a static document. But some other examples are starting-points for localized or broad and lasting turbulences of communication. For instance, using a slur word, or even a word like *capitalist*, can have a deep potential to interfere with any ongoing discussion or consequential flow. Using such words to put down another person might itself be disgraceful (be a "put down") of the speaker, or lead to indignation—by the person scorned, and by others (e.g., managers) in the flow of communication resistant to the comment. Those reverberations might include the secondary, tertiary, etc. contradictions found by Canary (2010a, 2010b), mentioned earlier.

The idea that the flows carry contradictions, though, can be understood relative to the nature of the flows themselves. A variety of researchers have suggested typologies of paradoxes/contraventions (Jarzabkowski et al., 2013) Analogously, we think it is valuable to argue that every one of our four flows embodies a primary contradiction (at least one) that is a potential source of organizational or communicative problems. This is obviously one dimension of the structuration *concept dialectic of control* (as are all four of these flow-primary contradictions). Thus, membership negotiation intrinsically involves the strain of member positioning versus individual agency. Moreover, the primary contradictions are confluent with other flows constituting the organization. An individual's expressed, agentive capacity of being a member (position-enacting or producing/reproducing the organization) contradicts the member's agentive freedom to notice and respond to factors that depart from the organizational goals. For example, they can think about bending the rules to secure a promotion, or pushing coordination practices to serve one's own power-resources, or serving the lures of outside jobs or positional success over perceived organizational goals.

Self-structuring overtly implies the strain of clear, meaningful, practical stable self-structuring versus the power of agents to subvert or surpass the bounds of the organization's rules and goals, values and norms, or network integrity—again, a dimension of the dialectic of control. For instance, a supervisor can grant additional, irregular leniency to a worker who needs additional time off.

Activity coordination quickly yields a strain between adaptation to the situation—the task, one's colleagues, or specific possibilities—versus sticking to standard, organizationally sanctioned coordination patterns. For instance, scientists working on a drug may feel a common need, or a need articulated by some but more or less accepted by others, to push for quicker release of the drug for public use even though they break the scientifically proper research-coordination timeline.

Institutional positioning, of course, opens members, practices, and communication to contravention by entities and pressures expressly outside the organization. Thus, members are drawn to goals departing from the organization's practices, or to resource supplies that open the organization to invasion, disintegration, or subjugation of its communication and identity. For example, professional associations often specify practices and standards that might conflict with organizational demands.

However, we want to emphasize that confluences of the flows seem especially prone to make members feel the need to deal with contraventions. Thus, self-structuring such as formal pronouncements or a strong culture of an organization might make it harder, not just to attract members to meet dire staffing needs, but to negotiate an identity—to constitutively connect and include them. A manager who solves problems (expands control) by issuing rules or installing clunky surveillance technology creates ripples that may vitiate collaborative (Flow 3) creativity that thrived and was profitable before the rules or surveillance. We emphasize that research should look for, not just friction or conflict, but instead ways that the constitutive dynamic of one flow collides with another's constitution. As flows are considered, rather than seeing them as categorical, they are interactive and dynamic in ways that open up opportunities for scholars to analyze tensions, explore power, and further test theories within a theoretical framework that is built through the communicative constitution of organizations.

9.4 Confluence of the Flows at Micro, Meso, and Macro Levels

The flows are always present and at work maintaining and transforming the organization at various levels of the organization and of society in different ways. A good means of examining the wide range of effects is to imagine the flows and their confluences at the micro, meso, and macro levels. Although definitions vary across the literature, we mostly rely on Hage's (1980) definitions, sometimes adjusted. Accordingly, the *micro level* focuses on constitutive flows that occur in dyads, interactions among group members, and between groups. At the *meso level*, the analysis focuses on organization-level flows. For example, meso-level discussions are mid-range and include communication between departments or executives' enclaves within an organization. They are meso level because of the dissemination of effects normal for these interactions, which go beyond those internal to an official or regularized group. *Macro levels* are the largest and broadest level of analyses. They include constitutive flows among organizations, within industries, between industries and communities, and even across sociocultural formations like markets or climate-change-alleviation efforts. Thus, they necessarily correlate with Flow 4. Interactions between representatives of universities or university systems and their constitutive relationships to higher education are examples of this flow level. These levels are valuable heuristics which narrow or broaden, but focus, in either case, the scope of analysis, but of course, all of the levels are messages or factors experienced or constructed by individual agents, and maintenance or changes at any level affected by one or several flows can affect the others. For instance, when enough individuals or workgroups request more flexible work policies (micro level), effects of various sorts can emerge or be shaped to influence the meso-level structures in larger organizational departments or organizations. Based on a flow that increases demand for flexibility, the department or organization eventually adopts a flexible work policy, as many companies did during the COVID-19 pandemic. The flow may continue to gain strength and when enough organizations make similar changes, organizations within an industry or systems feel pressure to conform or at least see benefits from conforming, and change occurs at a macro level. Likewise, changes that occur at a macro- or meso-level flow to and affect individuals within them, often in a more immediate way.

As an example of micro-level communication verging on the meso level, consider firefighting crews. The captain who leads the crew coordinating their activities also negotiates their membership through daily interactions that are steered by structural flows. As crew leader, she knows she must follow the agency's policies, but also must consider when and how she applies and enforces those rules. The choices she makes about how she coordinates their work affect their success in attaining goals, and also how her charges perceive her judgment and ability to lead, and whether they will follow her directives in the future. Similar decision flows and necessitating demands also often face commanders at the top of an organization or semiautonomous subunit—heads of divisions in a multidivisional corporation, or executive branch department heads also operates with the confluence of the flows considering how it will affect operations and the overall reputation of the organization. They may struggle with choices about when to put aside a long-standing rule, or even a more recently enacted rule that they enacted. They may be concerned with how their charges will perceive them and how it will affect their careers, but because they are in leadership roles, they likely know that communication from their level can have a significant effect on how firefighters feel about their membership, interactions with others on the job, and about policies in the future. These concerns are constraints, but the captain's sense of her powers, communicative or otherwise, to evoke acceptance of her decisions, and herself, to thread a path dodging obstacles and opposition or summoning allies—these, the flip side of such constraints, are enablements. These issues are necessarily coupled with the bigger responsibilities they feel in the role of protecting firefighters and community citizens in making the choice.

Sometimes rank-and-file workers, managers, and leaders can go beyond breaking or merely stretching the rules to push back on and redefine structures. Others join them in promoting change, they coordinate their efforts to do so, and the strength of the resistance enhances changes in the flow. In small or big ways, their efforts can have short- or long-term effects—flowing up into meso- or even macro-level processes. Firefighting organizations might become more accepting of situations in which rank-and-file firefighters and leaders can break or alter rules. When they are successful in enacting changes that become a part of the overall flow, their coordinated efforts to offer alternative ideas or plainly resist have the power to alter the course of the organization.

From a more meso perspective, firefighting teams also communicate and function at the confluence of the flows. Interactions at the micro level, as discussed in the previous examples, have implications rearticulated at the crew or higher levels (Cooren & Fairhurst, 2004). Individual members' compliance or resistance to training and rules manifest with implications for the crew. When all crew members follow the same rules, their teammates know what to expect—that they can trust each other (Moreland & Levine, 2001)—and they become more unified in their activities. The crew, and potentially the organization, develop a reputation for following rules and resources facilitating reliable coordinated activity. Other crews' members may, as a collective interpretive framing resource, gather that the crew is reliable (Myers, 2005). Conversely, when individual members haven't learned the rules or they break them, the entire crew can be affected, good or bad. Behaviors enacted by individual firefighters can also be observed and enacted by others. The crew enacts their participation (membership) in the organization in their own distinct way interpreting structures to guide their daily work and coordinating their activities accordingly.

Workgroups also develop identities, that is, cultures, based on member skills/knowledge, track record, personalities, etc., and as described earlier, and those qualities are recognized by other groups, organizational leaders, and by individual workers themselves. Those group identities can affect daily functioning and well-being of the group and members. Newcomers and others may vie for membership in their group. Members also may draw on the group's identity as they attempt to negotiate resources such as additional supplies and new members. They may request that a member vacancy be filled with someone who has a particular skill to complete the team or by someone who fits the workgroup's personality. This can enhance or change how members view their crew and their role within it. When a new member joins the group, others may need to adjust their own identity (e.g., they are no longer "the new guy," "the comedian," or the one with the most expertise in a particular area). A group's culture, manifested in all these ways, can filter out organizationally as outsiders engage with members, gossip about the group, and applaud it as a model—or break the group up.

At a macro level, the confluence of the flows has broader effects. Organizations, operating prototypically through organizational leadership, contribute to their own constitution. Through leaders who have legitimate power to communicate and act on behalf of the organization, the organization defines its mission, goals, and policies. They establish its hierarchy—the structure of roles, reporting relationships, and qualifications for who can fill those roles of the organization. In establishing the organization's goals and defining roles and structures, they simultaneously begin to develop resources for activity coordination involving many subsets of members and also the organization's activities connecting it to other organizations (e.g., suppliers, regulators, and customers). The organization's communication and actions through its leaders and members as representatives are, of course, defined by its mission and goals, how it defines membership, and how it coordinates activities.

Many elements of the flows at the macro level can be more closely examined as well. For example, the organization's self-structuring communication, macro-level phenomena, influence many aspects of the member's micro-level role relations, including attractiveness to potential job candidates (Dean & Wanous, 1984), qualifications for employment in the various roles at various levels (Brewer, 1971), training new members receive (Klein et al., 2015), compensation and benefits, and performance standards. Members' perceptions of these structures can affect their job satisfaction (and often their family's satisfaction), organizational/professional identification, and productivity, among other things (Lammers et al., 2008). Alternately, these perceptions can lead them to take contrary actions—organize a union, for instance, or seek or abandon employment in numbers that affect the stability of a company, or even an industry. Of course, if organizations (through their leadership) perceive that elements of their structures are having a negative effect by, for example, lowering productivity, they may choose to revamp those structures. In this example, the organization's activity coordination flow may have been affected by a structural issue, such as a requirement that all workers have college degrees, making it more difficult to hire for some positions or change a policy so that workers can no longer receive bonuses for extra productivity. An organization's communication and activities are also continuously positioning it within the industry and community in which it operates. Its activities might position it as a fierce competitor or an incompetent manufacturer. Its membership flow might cause workers (also their families and friends) to characterize it as a benevolent employer or as a sweatshop.

Of course, it should be evident that meso- and macro-level flows are channelized, often by design, into flows constituting the other levels. For example, a policy (structural) change communicated at the organizational level to change requirements for employment or employee compensation most assuredly sparks conversations about membership among members that both affect and constitute the policy change (Ford & Ford, 1995). Some of the flows may be supportive, giving the combined flows momentum and the policy is thus reinforced. Organizations (its leadership) could hear about member conversations and be influenced by member feedback, solidifying its strength. Alternatively, a change in practice (activity coordination) instigated by a crew and found to be effective, can circulate to be adopted and advanced by other members and even the organization overall.

Much about how we frame the flows using the metaphor of a river presumes that the flows strengthen, that the river develops and becomes more established. Sometimes, however, the confluence of the river becomes slowed and the river's flows are reduced to a trickle or even stall out. Portions of the river veer in a different direction and become stagnant pools. The river becomes a shadow of its former self or ceases to exist as the kind of flow that is—the River Jordan and the Dead Sea. The same is true for the flows of organizations. For example, the self-structuring flow might include an organizational culture that erodes morale causing members to become less identified as a member, leading them to quit or work less productively. Or culture might lead members into overt cynicism about organizational goals and authority, challenging or disorganizing the reproduced organization. The institutional positioning flow could position the organization and its members as ruthless and dishonest, causing it to lose customers, which can lead to worker layoffs, which can affect the activity coordination flow. In other words, the organizational communication circulates, but in ways that can eventually lead to a smaller organization or one that ceases to exist.

In sum, the discursive flows can be identified and are active at every level of the organization from an entry-level worker to the top-level executives. While the flows are often considered at the micro-level when individual members communicate with peers, supervisors, and leaders, the flows can easily be advanced and linked to the group or department level, even the organizational and industry levels. Thus, the flows permeate and influence structures and practices at more than one level. At each level, through transtructions discourse and action are continuously constitutive maintaining, transforming, and at times slowing and winding down organizations.

9.5 Deep Structures/Currents and the Confluence of the Flows

By observing a river from its banks, one can make judgments about the precipitation and tributaries that feed it, the height and stability of its banks, whether the path is mostly straight or winding, the relative number of obstructions such as trees, rocks, and other debris in its path, and the power of the currents. One might also view rapids and whirlpools that can temporarily affect its flow. This surface-level view can cause onlookers to believe that they know a lot and even understand the river and its flows. Another view awaits those who study the riverbed and the deep channels that were cut long ago. These characteristics—that may be visible only to those who are immersed in it or investigate it—affect life inside the river, including its climate and ability to support biodiversity, and whether the river is sustained over long distances, flows in different channels as deeper currents, or mixed in as turbulence reaches water from the depths and roils it with the surface.

As we described in Chapter 2, behaviors and practices are enabled and constrained through structures (Giddens, 1984). By enacting behaviors that initiate, habituate, and support emergent patterns, we create structure-imbued practices that become embedded in the system and over time. All organizations are constituted in systems and contexts that shape them, contexts rooted in the timing of their founding and operations (compare an organization founded in the nineteenth to one founded in the twenty-first century), their location (compare one founded in Chicago to one in Havana or Nairobi), the industry in which they operate (compare pharmaceuticals to education or firefighting), and the resources of its founders and leaders (compare Jeff Bezos, Elon Musk or Richard Branson to, well, almost anyone), to name a few. Each of these quite clearly influences the flows and constitution of the organization, but what lies deep under the surface may not be so visible—even to those within the flows—and is vital to discuss. Here, we mention only a few: racial bias, gender stereotypes, misperceptions about people who have different levels of physical functioning, and socioeconomic status created by wealth, education, and social connections. Admittedly, the roil created by a founder or great leader might well reach considerably into organizational depths. The influence of, say, Henry Ford—creating automated, minimal-communication assembly lines of semi-skilled workers to fashion complex machines that were formerly the work of skilled craftspeople who built entire vehicles from start to finish—as well as reinforcing racist tendencies in the workforce and social order. As we discussed earlier, the four flows model enables us to analyze the influence and persistence of deep structures and their resistance to change.

Deep structure still falls within the structurational concept of structure—rules/resources drawn on and reproduced in interaction—but with several distinctive characteristics. First, deep structure is hard to observe or grasp, being drawn on in mundane implications, or reproduced with results that seem like commonsense, phrasings that get relabeled as "misunderstandings" or "well-meaning actions," or fleeting, project-irrelevant micro-facial expressions (Ballard et al., 2020), or decision standards that on the surface can seem fair and even-handed. For example, for decades many organizations justified hiring people who are "just like us" so that everyone gets along (Kanter, 2008; Shenoy-Packer & Myers, 2013). Second, it is broad and slow moving. The implication is that more easily adopted and observed changes in organizational practices that are designed to change deep structures rarely erode overtly manifested structural transformations. Changes that occur on the surface are often fleeting and unavailing and fail to reach the deeper currents. Results of wave after wave of feminist discourse and activity through many decades that have resulted in some, but not yet enough change, clearly illustrate this point. Third, deep communication flows are often slowed by combinations and contiguities among the structural resources and constraints that are part of the flow. For example, women often have to cope with constraints like a lack of role models, intersecting identity opposition, and other rule-resource patterns mentioned later in combination leading to departure from educational credential pathways. These factors can also lead to job availability that clashes with, for example, childcare needs, while also limiting access to social networks that carry resources for success. This kind of multiplication of constraining effects is reflected in the relatively deep-rooted patterns of transtruction that Giddens characterized as structural sets, including contraventions at various levels, as discussed briefly in Chapters 3 and 4, or even as structural principles.

Racial biases, gender stereotypes, and misperceptions about abilities are part of the deep structures that do not support or inadequately support individuals from underrepresented groups. The structures, often referred to as institutional bias (Cox, 1994), were created by able-bodied, often upper-class white males and meant to affirm principles of meritocracy (Buzzanell, 1995). Most deep structures still operating in organizations today are so firmly entrenched in our systems that their abilities to disadvantage minorities are invisible at the surface (Orbe, 1996; Shenoy-Packer & Myers, 2013). For example, individuals from disempowered groups quite often have less freedom in negotiating their membership. Others, including members, suppliers, and customers, can attempt to position them personally and in their organizational roles based only on outward appearances, often eroding their power (Allen, 1995; Carvalho-Freitas & Stathi, 2017). Small differences in dress, grooming, or use of standardized English can spark unconscious biases (Carrim, 2019; Deprez-Sims & Morris, 2010). Guidelines for advancement such as touting their achievements or working excessively long hours to demonstrate commitment to the organization are unnatural or impossible for them (Shenoy-Packer & Myers, 2013). To make matters worse, potential mentors or allies may be hesitant to support them. Because of these constraints on their membership negotiation, they aren't thought of as leaders and are passed over for leadership roles in their team, division, or organization. In recent decades, organizations have acknowledged that some policies such as gauges for worker evaluation that privilege white, male modes of communication or dress codes that require conformance to traditional business attire that were previously perceived as benign by many leaders, disadvantage or have a negative effect on many minoritized individuals. While some organizations have revised policies to better accommodate diversity in communication styles and attire, these changes in policy may only offer an image of acceptance, while deep structures restrict real change. Many individuals within organizations are persistently guided by traditional standards with biases that may operate out of their conscious awareness. Thus, even individuals who believe they have altered their perceptions actually have not and they continue to operate with an underlying bias. As a result, changes at the surface do little to disturb the deeper flows.

In Chapter 6, in our discussion of self-structuring, we arrayed concepts like bureaucracy and information technology that are decades old and contribute to deep slogs through much organizational thought and activities. Though leaders argue for new organizational forms or communication practices, deep structures supporting bureaucracy or even earlier traditional authority modes resurface in, and are sedimented by, all four flows and their confluences. Socioeconomic structures of the larger social system also present contraventions, for example, by constraining membership negotiation, limiting imagination, or giving rationales for avoiding change. Kanter (2008) famously notes the seemingly sensible arguments for male bias—managers can communicate better with, and unite, others who are like them, creating deeply structured biases. Individuals who are born into higher socioeconomic strata often have parents who encourage career exploration and preparation. They are privileged with better and more education and have better social connections that have facilitated their entry into higher-caliber positions in prestigious organizations. Then, in the activity coordination flow, broader educations and more diverse exposures give them more process and leadership expertise (an ability to manage different groups of knowledge experts to accomplish tasks). These power bases also advantage their membership negotiation and activity coordination once in the organization because they have more confidence in their powers of linking, influencing, and working with other higher-status members including leaders (Lent et al., 2000; Olson, 2014), all of which loop to accelerate their success, rank advancement, and network primacy (Kanter).

In addition, this illustrates one way that contradictions exist and affect organizational life. Primary contradictions exist at deep levels, although as Canary (2010a, 2010b) illustrates, a deep level for one institutional sector does not need to be as deep as one for a whole social order. But in any case, shallower contradictions can follow from a deeper one. Because even higher-level contradictions can exist at the same deep level as the primary ones, they interrelate. For instance, the deep contradiction identified by Marxist economics is that productive relations (e.g., capitalistic ownership by stockholders who have no human connection or interest in employees) are inconsistent with the productive force of employment-requiring, socially cooperative employees. A quaternary contradiction arises because this economic contradiction conflates with the more cultural contradiction of individualism versus necessary social relatedness.

One interesting way to think about deep structure/flows is presented by Seidl and Whittington's (2014) array of analytic schemes for researching organizational strategy, as tall versus flat. *Flat* schemes enjoin us to recognize only the influences to and from a practitioner deciding on strategy, influences that network out to other specific practitioners (or, nonhuman *actants* like strategy computer programs). *Taller* approaches to analyzing strategy encourage us to look at, for example, general professional practices, on up to disciplinary orders imposing or encouraging specific ways of developing strategies, ways that exert pressure even on strategists who vary, creatively or unknowingly, from the norm. Thus, in society at large as well as in organizations, a flat influence would be one person's bigotry modeling another's; a taller analysis would emphasize practices like rallies and, we regret to say, witch-burnings or lynchings, and how those influence everyday suspicion and anxiety patterns. Even taller conceptualizations would identify the mutually supportive assemblages of overt practices supporting intolerance—looking the other way when one person uses demeaning language, or neglecting to build skills and personal networks that would contravene such behavior.

Despite mandates announced by organizations that attempt to equalize opportunities, deep structural biases foster organizational cultures in which minoritized members suffer from an inability to effectively coordinate their activities (Hebl et al., 2020; Van Lear & Janssens, 2011). Coworkers may be hesitant to trust them, either because of ethnic cultural differences or because of perceptions about their capabilities. Division leaders responsible for forming teams might receive pushback when they assign disempowered individuals to teams. Organizations known to have large numbers of disempowered members based on gender, sexual orientation, race, or physical abilities may find that other organizations engage in discrimination and lack confidence in their ability to successfully collaborate, affecting their institutional positioning (Davidson, et al., 2010)

Deep structures label certain organizational activities as tainted or less reputable, which can also affect institutional positioning and the members within them.

For example, occupations and industries in society are privileged differently, which affects the positioning of the organization within the system and also the social validation and self-esteem of members (Ashforth & Kreiner, 1999; Hughes, 1962). Organizations such as prisons, slaughterhouses, houses of prostitution, or factory farms are viewed as distasteful to many and individuals who work in them as tainted or "dirty" (Ashforth & Kreiner, 1999). While one factory farm might be more favorably compared to another–as far as organizations to own, manage, or be employed by—they likely aren't positioned highly compared to other types of organizations, and do not get promoted to posts with broader purview. Similarly, sex workers might negotiate their roles within their organizations much like workers in other industries, but because of their age, their ability to remain in their role is limited (Blithe & Wolfe, 2017). Of course, some professions, such as airline pilots, have age restrictions, but for other reasons.

Overall, these deep structures inhibit or at least influence some members, "teams," and even industries' contributions to the four flows. These affected flows often are not obvious to nonmembers (observers from the banks of the river), and because deep structures often operate as taken-for-granted assumptions, they often are out of the discursive consciousness of members themselves, even those affected. However, because they restrict micro- and meso-level flows, they also constrain the overall flow and the constitutive possibilities of the organization.

9.6 Conclusion

Among the advantages of the communication flows metaphor are its suggestions that discourse and discursive transactions, eddies in a vast river, have content and implications that stream without any single origin or route or docking point, that can pass at many rates, from quicksilver to coagulated/turgid; that can spread in many directions, most of them unintentional; and that can intermingle with other currents, sometimes in reliable or beneficial, but often in disruptive ways. The dynamic nature of flows offers insights into the dynamic processes of CCO. Further, the interactive confluences of the flows provide rich opportunities for exploring the complexities of organizational theories.

Confluences as contraventions and deep structures shape flows. By exploring confluences of the flows, 4F offers more than a list of ingredients needed for an organization. Instead, the dynamic communicative process of constituting becomes more evident. From a critical theory perspective, the recognition within 4F as a framework exposes not only the deep structures of power, but the way those deeper structures influence and contravene across other flows and levels of the organization. Additionally, understanding levels of flows from micro to meso to macro offers understanding of pan-organizational (see Chapter 8) concepts such as those introduced by Lammers and others (Lammers & Barbour, 2006) as they impact and are impacted by communicative constitutional actions. For example, Street (2003) provides an ecological model of patient–provider interactions that considers the wide variety and levels of influence in an interpersonal interaction that draws in the meso-level impacts of the healthcare organization, and macro considerations such as culture and legal implications. Consider, for example, the impact the insurance industry has on medical organizations and thus individual decisions for a person's care. Combining the ecological model with 4F considerations across flows expands the constitutive understanding of healthcare organizations, for example.

Confluences create future opportunities for scholarship, exploration, and understanding. By exploring the connections, whether they are contraventions, complements, amplifications, or dampening effects, the understanding of the communicative constitution of multiple flows offers a great opportunity for organizational research from a variety of perspectives, including critical as well as other ontological and epistemological positions.

10

Contributions to the Ongoing CCO Debates

CCO is by now a subdomain of organizational communication, as attested by coverage in at least one handbook (Basque et al., 2022). 4F, as arguably the first self-described CCO perspective (though obviously much scholarship deserving that label preceded McPhee & Zaug, 2000), has drawn considerable criticism. Moreover, two clear alternate schools (the Montreal School and the Luhmannian position as distinguished in Schoeneborn et al., 2014) have been articulated and elaborated in voluminous research. Before we directly recount our main claims and contributions, we feel obligated to reply to some critical themes raised about ST, and about our model in particular. Though we focus on correcting misunderstandings and justifying our own views where we differ from others, we also attempt to deal constructively with the stimulating discourse of other schools and point toward ways that different schools and research agendas can complement and supplement one another. We consider this engagement as part of the ongoing collegial discourse within a field that has benefited from robust debate.

One simple but frequent critical theme is the claim of inadequate rigor in the ST and 4F approaches. We have some direct replies to these criticisms responding to specific tenets, first of ST, then of 4F (McPhee et al., 2014). The most well-known and frequently cited ST critique is Archer's (1982, 1988) argument that ST performs a "central conflation" by claiming that agents constantly draw on structural resources of institutional scope in the production of local interaction, while simultaneously holding that those agents reproduce—that is, maintain or transform—those same structural resources, including in ways that contribute to macro-institutional change. She advocates instead a more rigorous analysis separating the currents of action fashioning structural change from the sociality of systemic constraints suffered by people in ordinary routine life. Giddens' reply

The Communicative Constitution of Organizations: The Four Flows Model, First Edition.
Robert D. McPhee, Karen K. Myers, and Joel O. Iverson.

here is telling: "Structure and action cannot form a dualism, save from the point of view of situated actors, because each is constituted by and in a single *realm*—human activity" (1990 p. 299). Especially from a communication perspective, there is no source of large-scale structure—neither institutional capitalism nor an authorial voice—transcending, outside of social interaction.

Another charge against specifically 4F theory, articulated by Sillince (2010) but cited by others (Bisel, 2010; Brummans et al., 2014) is that the four flows are not constitutive in the sense of "distinctive about an organization as compared with any other collective" (p. 132). He demands that, to be constitutive, a process like membership negotiation must be present in (all) collectives that are organizations, but absent from all other collectives—absent from social movements, friendship groups, markets, etc. It must be, not just necessary, not quite part of a full list of sufficient conditions, but rather a demarcative condition. This is a high bar to hurdle, but it is not the one we set for ourselves; instead, we distinguish flows that certainly are necessary but in addition are characteristic in making an organization what it is. Like us and a number of other authors drawing on 4F, he agrees that a distinction among multiple flows of communication, with a partial but not complete role in Constitution, can be a valuable approach to CCO. Without, for example, activity coordination, there is no substance behind the label "organization"—so the third flow is necessary, but beyond that, it is a constitutive factor because of the energy, care, and scope of coordination to be found in stereotypical organizations. And, going even deeper, it exists because organizational agents, often very powerful ones, communicate to seek it, devote resources to secure it, and set up quality controls to ensure that the coordination works. This sort of communication we have termed *necessitating*, and it occurs, we allege, most often because those agents desire and work to bring into being the social form they know to accomplish such coordination: an organization. Such necessitation, in turn, brings activity coordination close to valid place on a list of sufficient conditions—the necessitating agents, to get coordinated activity, do whatever else is necessary (the other three flows), and thereby constitute an organization.

As a side note, we must mention that the four processes Sillince claims are "distinctly organizational" can be found in other types of collectivities. Thus, his first process, "emphasizing context," is surely a feature of all communication; to be fair, he qualifies this label in a complex sentence, which evidently focuses on contexts as differentiated functionally or regionally. But obviously cities, with zoning ordinances and business versus red-light districts, involve contexts with "distinct rhetorics" (p. 134). And we confidently assert that social movements of any size include just such contextual differentiation, as does any friendship group involved in multiple types of activities.

His initial example for the organization/market difference is "the car sales market," which he asserts is a *market*, not an organization, because it "does not involve complex distinctions because the mode of behavior in both new and secondhand markets—transactions based on price and contract—is the same" (p. 134). This is blatantly false, not only because the used car sales market involves individuals using want ads who do not market in trade-ins (thus different transactions), but critically because the car sales market *includes* car sales *companies* that, by his own logic, *do* rhetorically emphasize such contextual distinctions, which thus are indeed a feature of the car sales market *per se*. However, we should hasten to note that an analysis of such rhetoric could surely contribute to the elaboration of 4F theory. Further, while 4F does not create exclusive categories for organizations that no other social system possesses, 4F provides a useful framework to discuss the way social movements, for example, have similarities as well as differences from organizations. The better questions for researchers go beyond simple categorization of *organization or not* to understanding the constitutive processes that are similar, interconnected, and may differ in how they are enacted.

Even Bisel (2010), who read the four flows argument more sensitively, focuses his attention on the concept (that he notes is woefully nomothetic) of necessary and sufficient condition. Rather, we *orient* toward the notion, rife in the decades of scholarly literature we seek to answer, that processes like division of labor might be, in some sense, necessary for organizations. But what we aim to do is to recontextualize and problematize the focal notion of *communication just meeting necessary/sufficient conditions* (or—regularly implied in—a functional system).

Recruiting members may be necessary for an organization, but the real import we see in the word *necessary* is membership negotiation, which is almost certainly a *crux* for *necessitating* communication, as discussed in Chapter 5 and elsewhere. This flow of necessitation can aid (or undermine) organizational survival, most vitally, by communicatively advocating (*necessitating*) the need for member-oriented work. For instance, its processes include some communication drawing resources toward individual members, some attracting members who will be politically valuable for special current members, some repelling potential members who would harm the organization or alienate powerful members, some constituting the organization by reifying it relative to the positioned institutions (e.g., the Equal Employment Opportunity Commission), and some that transform the conditions of membership itself. The functional requirement of getting members is herein problematized and reconceptualized: a much more complex interweaving of processes, notably but not inevitably biased in favor of organizational coherence or continuance for powerful interests, is constitutively relevant—maybe contributory, maybe crucial. (That interweaving is also biased toward making sense, toward being legitimate, and toward being the organization.) The dynamic of these processes is captured in the notion, flow. In a word, the charge of vagueness and presence of some flows outside of some systems is a fundamental misunderstanding of our conceptualization.

10.1 Confluence with Luhmann's Theory

The CCO school developing Luhmann's systems theory provides many striking formulations and insights about interrelations and useful distinctions among social and organizational phenomena (cf. Luhmann, 1995). Its clear goal is to transform the idea of system, to retain its rigor but elaborate it in ways that valuably represent social phenomena including organizations. As noted in our first two chapters, Giddens drew ideas from systems theory into his synthetic ST, but conceptualized power, meaning, and normative legitimation by drawing on the more direct sources of Marxism, hermeneutics, etc. Luhmann states that his goal is to erase this whole debate, substituting ideas that are more rigorous, broadly applicable, and that develop new directions of thought. Ironically, 4F practitioners and Luhmann draw on the ideas of Luhmann's old mentor, Talcott Parsons. Giddens drew critically on functionalists like Parsons, but was part of the generation of the 1970s that gave much more weight to interpretive and critical theories, interestingly reworked by Luhmann. In addition, we should note that Luhmann retained but transformed the idea of functional differentiation necessary to address constitution problems, a notion that influenced, in a quite different way, our 4F model. In this response, we recount the central flow of his argument to identify relationships between Luhmann's social system and organizational views, and 4F theory.

His first step is to negate classical systems theory, which merely allows for connection interchange of information; he even rejects tenets like "society consists of people and relations between people." Instead, he distinguishes, most relevantly, social systems—"reproduced on the basis of communication," from psychic systems—"reproduced on the basis of consciousness" (Seidl, 2004, p. 5), as well as from human-body and various other living systems. Communication thus has a central place in his theory.

Luhmann's characteristic idea is that systems—social, human, and biological—are *operationally closed*, with no outside material being drawn into the logic of the system. Decisions follow purely on other decisions, thoughts on other thoughts, utterance/understanding units of communication purely on other such units. A related aspect of such systems is that they are "self-referential": their elements are oriented to reflexively register and take account of one another in distinction from the environment, as a mode of closure of the system. Communications are communications mainly because they take account of other communications, even if to deny them. This is similar to our tenet that communication is equivalent to changes in context.

Luhmann emphasizes operational closure and self-reference because they are prerequisites, and results, of autopoiesis, widely recognized as a property of social as well as living systems. Autopoiesis is a fundamental constitutive process whereby systems "themselves produce not only their structures but also the elements of which they consist in the network of these same elements. [They are constituted out of operations that] must be carried out in the system as an activity with the aid of the system's own distinctions" (Luhmann, 2012, p. 32, 37). Like bodies, composed of cells that grow out of specifically cellular processes, thoughts and communications are generated only from other thoughts or communications. Luhmannian systems theory thus shifts the locus or fundamental notion of communication away from *connectedness* (prototypically understanding or even mutual understanding, or other exchanges) that is manifest in the flow, to constitutive self-organization inside operationally autonomous systems.

Later, we interrogate this crucial assumption, as do some of his proponents (Cooren & Seidl, 2020), who start from his views but stray from them so far as to use a term he would reject, *heteropoiesis*. However, these authors also show the mutual relevance of 4F to many of the ideas they present throughout their article. Considering the commitments to the two alternate positions by these authors, we might suggest that Luhmann combined with TMS adds up to (part of) 4F!

Luhmann's argument for social and communication theory is that social systems, reproduced on the basis of communication, are distinct in their essence from psychic systems—reproduced on the basis of consciousness" (Seidl, 2004, p. 5). "consciousness is neither the *subject* of communication nor in any other sense a *vehicle* of communication. It contributes no operations of any sort to communication" (Luhmann, 2012, p. 57). Yet, to foreshadow our argument, contrariwise, "All communication is structurally coupled with consciousness. ...Communication is totally dependent (in every operation) on consciousness" (p. 56).

The operative process reproducing social systems is indeed communication, which he casts as closed to psychological processes—for example, a psychic-system element like a manger's notion, part of a for what should happen in a conversation—informing, then steering a discussion with employees. Luhmann's idea is that social-communication systems operate autonomously, generating their own boundaries that provide systemic closure, with each communication operating to an array of elements giving rise to the next. He rejects the structuralist view of language as a system—though we suggest that the structurational revision of virtual connectedness in the sign constitution (see Chapter 3) is more compatible with his views. This conception does capture the essential constitutive force and the ongoing, progressive relevance of system communication (and communication as analyzed in many other perspectives). However, it also *prima facie* carries an impression notion of that system's utter arbitrary autonomy, with no *operational* (i.e., system-constituting and meaning-conferring) guidance or input from individual consciousnesses, or material, contextual, or other systems. As he explicitly notes, that gives crucial importance to amendments, or supplementary ideas that we now discuss.

An organization for Luhmann is a major type of social system, with a narrower operative process: the decision or decision communication, a choice with definite contrasted alternatives. Again, the system of decisions is autopoietic, reflexive, and operationally closed. For instance, a hiring decision is based on an assemblage out of past hiring decisions which have "left behind... structural effect[s]" (Luhmann, 1995, p. 67). The reasons given for hiring, the decisions whereby an applicant pool is identified—each is an autopoietic amalgam of—is reflexively created out of—past reasons, pool-creation operations, and in no way constitutively bound to, say, individual interpretations. Similarly, organizational communication is obviously decisional or decision-related interaction; the decisions it articulates are constitutive and distinctive of the organizational system. Here we would note a difference in 4Fs emphases. Communication in flows could be considered as decisional, developing, for example, decisions about *memberhood that are not essentially formal.* However, 4F emphasizes and analyzes how the currents of member inclusion decisions (or consensus) definitely are confluent with the flow of formal decisions that most closely approximates Luhmann's image of truly organizational communication.

Operational closure raises the question of "how a system…organizes its relationship with the environment if it maintains no contact with this environment" (Luhmann, 2012, p. 54). For us, operational closure is the specific question of whether the organizational social system of communication can be discussed without primary reference to human agents, or contrariwise can relate to "the environment" of agent member communicators. Later, we interrogate this crucial assumption, as do some of his proponents (Cooren & Seidl, 2020), who starts from his views but venture, as mentioned above, to find utility even of *heteropoiesis*—a term that overtly concedes the insufficiency of the Luhmannian emphasis on autonomy. Instead, they clearly show the mutual relevance of 4F to many of the ideas they present throughout their article. Indeed, Luhmann and his adherents had developed an interesting range of supplemental concepts to deal with this avowed closedness/relatedness paradox.

First, Luhmann (2012) argues that, despite operational closure, varying systems can, or even must, have a common matter-energy substrate, a "continuum of materiality" (p. 56) or more generally a common grounding for relations among systems. All of the system variants are matters of patterning, of organization, relying on this substrate. For instance, people have material bodies, just as organizations are material in multiple ways—a similarity that can be useful for both sides, or horrific for the people (Foucault, 1977). Analogously, Luhmann notes that organizations, while not composed of human or psychic systems, need to be able to draw on human beings "bound by instructions," seemingly having similar importance as a substrate for the autopoietic system (2018, p. 31–32). Similarly, "bosses" in the environment as living persons, have organizational relevance, but only as they "utter" decision communications and are designated by prior decisions to themselves have decision-making powers (p. 45).

Second, we group several of Luhmann's important, interrelated supplementary concepts, all of which involve ways autopoietic processes can encompass influences or causes that are not purely system operations. One is the concept of irritant, or perturbation, which is a negative element or problem to which autopoiesis reacts and evolves, by learning, disregarding, or eliminating. However, irritants are internal: "[t]here is…no irritation in the system's environment and [hence] no transfer of irritation from the environment system–…always self-irritation—albeit occasioned by environmental effects [sic]" (2012, p. 66). Avoiding the temptation to anthropomorphize, irritation is communicative, a way people have innovative effects in communicating.

Another concept—actually a pair of them—concerning factors influencing autopoiesis without being system operations themselves, with analogous but clearer importance for the development of Luhmann's stance, is *structure* and *structural coupling.* In themselves, structures (for instance conversation topics or departmental divisions) "narrow the scope for suitable connective operations to such an extent that progression from operation to operation can be achieved" (Luhmann, 2012, p. 264). Their value in enabling operations is great enough that Luhmann's concept seems to approach Giddens'—indeed, Luhmann acknowledges the similarity of this idea to the structurational one (2018, p. 57 n34). Structural *couplings* of one system with another "limit the scope of the possible structures with which [one] system can carry out its autopoiesis" (Luhmann, 2012, p. 55). They are "pointers" for an autopoietic system to resolve its indeterminacies; they "include something by excluding other things. They bundle and intensify certain causalities that affect the coupled system, irritating it and thus stimulating it to self-determination" (pp. 55-6). As we understand a system's autopoietic self-production, we can also recognize an "orthogonal" phenomenon, of the self-production being structural coupling between, for example, psychic and communication systems corresponds roughly to the standard notion that "people do organizational communication," although Luhmann's idea emphasizes the idea that intentions and communicative trajectories can vary immensely.

A particular application of this notion is a traditional idea of hierarchy in an organization as a necessary consequence of their nature as decision communication systems.

> Probably the most important consequence of attributing decisions to decision-makers is that the importance of decision-makers increases with the importance of decisions – and vice-versa. Regardless of all actual influence lines and all "informal organization," the decision-making system tends to develop a hierarchy. The important decisions then have to be made higher up, the most important at the very top. But, in the other direction, too: what comes down from the top has to be considered so important that ignoring it must be disguised (Luhmann, 2018, p. 108).

Luhmann has been criticized for this traditionalist leaning (Mingers, 2003), but he does explicitly allow for, for example, consensual organizations, culture, etc.

Fourth, Luhmann (1995) develops a conception of interpenetration, which "permits a relation between autonomous autopoiesis and structural coupling.... We speak of penetration if a system makes its own complexity...available for constructing another system. ...Accordingly, interpenetration exists when this occurs reciprocally, when both systems enable each other by introducing their own already constituted complexity into each other" (pp. 221, 213). They influence each other's operations, but also their structural formations. According to Luhmann (1995):

> [T]he boundaries of one system can be included in the operational domain of the other. Thus, the boundaries of social systems fall within the consciousnesses of psychic systems. Consciousness intervenes and thus acquires the possibility of drawing boundaries for social systems precisely because these boundaries are not, at the same time, boundaries of consciousness. The same holds conversely: the boundaries

> of psychic systems fall within the communicative domain of psychic systems, communication is forced to use what psychic systems have already assimilated in their consciousnesses and what they have not. This is possible because the boundaries of psychic systems are not also boundaries of communicative possibilities. …Thus, [each] system can actualize its own superiority in complexity, its own modes of description, and its own reductions in relation to the other and thus make its own complexity available to the other (p. 217).

One instance of this is the inclusion, within each psychic system, of remembered communication interchanges—and vice versa; every chain of communication or decisions carries implied versions of the consciousnesses of the parties… so that an observer of a communication sequence could guess (perhaps errantly) what was on the minds of the communicators. So, there are various facets to this notion of interpenetration, especially between psychic and communication/social systems.

This intersection is especially marked for the phenomenon of *meaning*, which "can insert itself into a sequence that is bound to bodily feelings; then it appears as consciousness. However, meaning can insert itself into a sequence that involves others' understanding; then it appears as communication" (Luhmann, 1995, p. 98). But even greater theoretic force is provided by language.

So, fifth, and even further from the simple autopoietic system, language overcomes the systems division between the psychic and social systems. "Whereas before the development of language, living beings lived in structural coupling, and were therefore subject to co-evolution, language also enables operational coupling, which can be monitored by participants. …a special autopoietic system of linguistic communication takes shape that is self-determined in its operations and fully compatible with the deliberate participation of individuals" (Luhmann, 2012, p. 126). There is recognition of the scope for communication-choosing agency compatible with autopoietic, closed systems—such as the decision communication systems of organizations. So, there are various facets to this notion of interpenetration, especially between psychic and communication/social systems. The cross-system penetration, in Luhmann's explicit work, is so striking that perhaps the term *heteropoiesis* (Cooren & Seidl, 2020) is not so far from his explicit thought.

We have gone into such detail about these five aspects of Luhmann's thought because, considered very roughly, one can imagine psychic systems as analogs of ST's agents, though he also defines human organic systems at varied levels (with human beings essentially involving these interpenetrating systems), and persons (which for him boil down to expectation arrays about persons) and personnel being system elements only in so far as they are chosen as system members (and thus involved in communication). Then the psyche-communication interpenetration becomes analogous to ST's ideas of the agency/structure duality and production/reproduction, overcoming Luhmann's antihumanism. Some added interesting analogs occur more specifically between the image of society-inside-consciousness and ST's notions of rationalization, interpretive sphere, and discursive consciousness; and between consciousness-inside-society and ST's sense of action/communication drawing on social resources and constrained agency—though expounding the reflexivity and mustering the potentials of each theory's half of this correspondence is worthy of at least a book. Yet further, Luhmann draws some content or function distinctions, sometimes similar to ours, among the types of decisions constituting an organization; we think it very reasonable to suggest, not one recursive process of decision communication constituting the organization, but four. With a little free play, we think insights from each position can enrich the other. In short, despite Luhmann's avowed antihumanist stance, he is structurally coupled with the current of ST and 4F thought.

On the other hand, Luhmann places as dominant the operationally closed-system/environment distinction, as opposed to the agent/structure distinction fundamental in ST. Then the two schools are engaged in reverse reflected projects: for Luhmann, it is connecting a system with well-defined autopoietic closure with a varied, overall less structured, but (we would say constitutionally) essential environment. For 4F, a major challenge is to find and describe the boundaries that temporarily substantiate and defend closed ongoing processes, while also revealing how those boundaries are, essentially and obtrusively, socially constructed for outsider- as well as insider-motivated reasons, and how *systemness* can have consequences that disperse throughout the flow. In the end, it comes down to a choice of initial perspective: shall we start by assuming a plethora of systems, each primarily understood as self-producing, self-referential, and operationally closed, or by assuming agents with special communicative powers to constitute those systems.

10.2 Confluence with The Montreal School

The other rival school to 4F is a loose, widespread, and well-known collectivity legitimately labeled *The Montreal School (*TMS*)*, to which we have frequently referred in our discussions of agency. Those who draw on TMS have been especially prolific, attracting attention to CCO theorizing in general; we are appreciative of their efforts on that front, to say the least. In addition, their works have caused us to interrogate and clarify our own perspectives. While we find many commonalities in the approaches to CCO between our approaches, and even though they have drawn ideas from ST to help lay the groundwork for their views, explicitly (Taylor et al., 2001) and also perhaps by happenstance. ST and 4F clash, pretty directly, with some crucial tenets each school seems united to defend and elaborate on in their research. The first is that, for TMS, organizations include people but also different types of *agencies* with variable ontologies, which are typically created and mobilized to fulfill the job of organizing and even speak or act in (the organization's) name. The objects that have agency—indeed, are agencies—include organizational subcollectivities; people in a special role *speaking for*, not the other people, but the collectivity itself; plus organizational charts, orders, contracts (which fall neatly into our Self-Structuring flow), but also machines and buildings, CEOs and supervisees, public relations and operations, involving varied ontologies indeed—some definitely defensible as agents, others as activities, others as resources. We are happy to accept that more emphasis should be placed, in communication theories, on entities other than individual humans—though a good deal of unrecognized emphasis has already, since at least the time of early systems theory, been there. We certainly agree that even the most static object can have *effects*; we merely urge that available terms—cause, or influence, or internally related, or refer (for signs), or resemble, etc., are perfectly good, and often more precise, for labeling those effects.

If a fundamental distinction between human agency and other types (preferably not called agents at all, but objects or systems or *actants*, Iverson et al., 2018) were agreed on as CCO scholars across schools have sometimes essentially accepted (cf., Schoeneborn et al., 2014), the obvious next step would be research that would add up to a categorization of types of agency/causation, or ways they contribute to organizing. Such research could be valuable for all schools. Or 4F theory might even contribute to TMS, albeit by suggesting relations of human agents with other factors such as resources, contexts, and conditions that *might appear to have agency*, but in fact, do not.

But a second, more troubling tenet of TMS is that collective entities (such as organizations) are "put together into an orderly, functional, structured whole… which contribute to the emergence or enactment of the organized form…[whose] identity can be understood through all these entities that can act and speak in its name" (Cooren, 2013, p. 83). It is symptomatic that Cooren's early lists of entities, as we have noted repeatedly, reflect the view that a collective entity is an "orderly functional whole"—which can seem true for stockholders, even while the entity's strike-breakers are assaulting its workers, and thus must always be a biased and typically a sovereign-favoring view.

But beyond that, TMS trades on an analogic argument of its own, comparing people who commonsensically do things with nonhuman, material *agencies* that can have causal impact or carry meanings—speak, meanings specifically inscribed by language-enabled humans. For instance, in a TMS-influenced study, Caronia and Colla (2021) recount a case of mother (M) and young child (B) collaborating on homework using a book (textbook) and notebook. At one point, M "moves the Italian book to the side (line 8, fig. 6) uncovering the Italian notebook where B must write the answer. In other words, by manipulating the Italian book, M creates the material conditions for B to perform the verbally required next action (i.e. writing the answer in the notebook, line 7)" (p. 16). Good. But the very next sentence is, "By using the Italian book and notebook to multimodally convey the next relevant action, M 'makes the objects speak,' i.e. she verbally reports the assignments that they index" (p. 16). No, neither book has spoken; worse, it is tempting to conclude that a concern with "the objects speaking" has led the authors to misdescribe "creates the material conditions" as "verbally reports."

An important point is obscured by the notion that the books have the agency to "speak to" the child. Noticing that the notebook has been uncovered creates a deep process of co-orientation (Laing et al., 1966), perhaps routinized in earlier learning between mother and child. The child *infers* from the book movement that writing is appropriate *because* she infers that the movement intends to convey that *because* she infers that the mother intends the child to infer that, and so on ad infinitum. These inferences, grounded in material practices of using book and pencil in teaching, might amount to *nonverbal* communication (not "verbal reporting" by the book), depending on our definition of that term. However, the issue is obscured when we focus on the unwieldy new terminology of objects speaking or the mother making the objects speak. The book does not have the capacity to act otherwise in an agentive manner.

TMS then moves or *scales up* the *nonhuman agency* argument to substantiate higher-level macro-agents, incarnated as organizations with mega-voices through *meta-conversations*. Just as Giddens indicated earlier, analyses using collective concepts like *nation-state* and *structural principle of high modernity* are fine as long as we remember their dependence, for meaningful or practical significance, on humans with powers of understanding and motivated action.

In an illuminating example, the mayor described by Brummans and colleagues (2014), offering a "meta-story enfolding" the grievances of citizens at a public meeting, is able to construct an account, in narrative form, that inevitably formulates the mayoral viewpoint (whereas he *could* allow a random citizen, the union leader or, as often occurs, an outside consultant (Kuhn, 2016) to construct the final account). Construction of this sort of narrative is a transtruction, of formal power into meaning production, legitimated by the norms of *democratic free expression* in a process that has conspicuous constitutive force—the mayor, and the whole process, Constitute the organization by encouraging citizen comments (with their own constitutive force) so as to feed the constitutive narrative from the mayor. Then, the 4F model makes obvious the need to place this document in the flow of self-structuring—of other city documents, *official* statements by the mayor and other formally powerful actors—a flow that includes interpretive reactions by non-city-government members that get registered in the self-structuring process. It also includes the flow *prior to* the town meeting, necessitating it (i.e., fostering the idea that something like this, and specifically this sort of town hall, is needed), setting it up, prepping the mayor and the microphones, etc., to support the meeting. Brummans and colleagues do note how, in a later translation, the communication "Authoring the Organization" can be formalized. They cite an idea from McPhee (2004), of the text being "a relatively permanently inscribed symbolic formulation" (p. 365; Brummans et al., p. 175; the idea certainly also appears in early TMS texts) in a way allowing dissemination, and they do valuably allow, in later translations, for its "degeneration into many voices," and for it being "maintained, and reinforced," but only in "interactions between [organization] representatives and representatives of other macro actors" (p. 181). But in their extreme focus on the mayor as authoring the organization as a reified unity, they derogate the interactive work contextualizing the meeting, resolving discrepancies where noticeable, actually doing the dissemination (newspaper carriers), and thus, sometimes without the peons themselves claiming to be "representatives," reproducing its authority—if it has any, remembering that most official pronouncements have shelf life zero.

4F theory does not assume that, at any special point, member or outsider messages or "experience of…many situated practices" (practices do not experience things) get "mapped into a [univocal] verbal representation that that will furnish a composite image of the whole organization" (Brummans et al., 2014, p. 179). Instead, 4F notes from the very beginning of analysis that any discourse purporting to do such a mapping (perhaps like the formal mission statements studied in Kopaneva and Sias' research cited later) has ideological effects, fulfilling one function of ideology—"mobilizing structures of signification…to legitimate…[through] the representation of sectional interests as universal ones" (Giddens, 1979, pp. 188, 193). It makes clear the necessity of analyzing the status of this sort of announcement relative to the power system of the organizational culture, and its record-generation and information-processing treatment in the organizational network. One broadly recognized reason for rejecting social theories is that the theories themselves reify—they collaborate with powerful agents to represent views, narratives, etc. as *organizational* when the views are really their own (if, we should note), "their own" has a static existence, even analytically, in communication flow. But further, the flow contextualizing the *meta-narrative* as self-structuring has evident confluence (tacitly recognized in their chapter) with the Institutional Positioning flow oriented toward *outsiders*—but an example of confluence less clear is with Membership Negotiation by the mayor and others.

Several other streams of research and theorizing take stands similar to the first one taken by TMS, discussed above. They offer an explanation about the relationship of the material-symbolic, which they reject as idealism. In their 2009 review, Ashcraft et al., (2009) argue that the material-ideal realm should include both communication and also the immaterial, united as a sociomaterial dialectic and be considered dialectics rather than dualisms, such as the duality of structuration. They use the term *relationality* to describe the dialectic. They describe three significant material elements. First, objects directly influence human behavior (Bechky, 2003), but the symbolism associated with object also is implicated (Orlikowski 1992, 1996, 2000) and therefore are foundational in organizing. The authors surmise that due to these simultaneous human–object relations, objects act and hold agency. Second, sites, including culture, politics, locales including physical properties of the building and workspaces offer, the same way agents do, meanings and power that contribute to materiality (Barad, 2007; Orlikowski & Scott, 2008). They describe the effect as conditioning agency because sites include "the constant (re)negotiation of possibilities, such that material and human agencies keep shaping one another" (p. 31). Third, the presence and symbolism of the body also have constitutive effects. Ashcraft and colleagues discuss how the physical body—gender, cultural diversity, attraction, physical (dis)abilities, age, etc.—is symbolic with meanings that beseech members to manage or discipline their physical presence (Trethewey, 1999).

We find considerable value in these insights, though we note how oriented this perspective actually is toward humans with agency interacting ultimately with nonhuman actants. The clearest illustration here is actually provided by Cooren (in, e.g., Schoeneborn et al., 2014, quoted earlier), who posits that objects and people ventriloquize each other, but then immediately (and rigorously) discusses how different processes in the two directions are.

Elsewhere, we (McPhee & Iverson, 2011) explicate our views on materiality that examine ontological significance based on ST highlighting four key concepts. First, *people* often draw on or involve material objects/texts occurring in time and space in a particular context that instead constitute structures, through recursive practice that creates and recreates organizations are structured rather than a material-deal dialectic. The second concept is *resources* which is paired with rules to create structures by which social systems draw upon and reproduce. Resources include allocative resources which include "generating command over objects, goods or material phenomena" (Giddens, 1984, p. 33), and authoritative resources, which provide the ability to organize social time and space, humans for mutual engagement, and also "constitution of chances of self-development and self-expression" (Giddens, 1984, p. 258). Thus, resources may be allocated and also organized. Third, in addition to agency which enables practice, Giddens (1984) also included the other side of the duality, *constraint*, which includes three types: (a) material constraint (limits of physical environment, human body, etc.) but each material constraint can also enable such as an hour-long meeting constrains the number of topics to be discussed, but also guide participants in the amount of time for discussion of the topics; (b) sanctions, that do not necessarily imply punishments, instead, sanctions include positive as well as negative and include religion, law, and ethics that monitor and guide practice; (c) structural constraints are the limits of possibilities available to an actor. The fourth is *conditions*, which is much more than context. Condition includes the conditions created by society and individual actions such as context of social activity (Giddens, 1984), trust in society and its routines, and other societal presumptions that create conditions. These four concepts make some distinctions that, we think, cut cleaner and deeper than the ones offered by sociomateriality scholars that comprise materiality.

So, ST offers its own version of sociomateriality, but involves *human agency* not tacitly but rather explicitly in the world in all the ways we analyze as students of organizational communication. We recommend, in particular, Giddens, 1991, p. 227, as a guide about sociomaterial conditions urgently requiring research—some of which sociomaterialists have valuably explored.

We hope that this contribution sufficiently emphasizes the insight and theoretic worth of the other positions with which we have contrasted our position. We are mindful of the respect they have shown in discussing our perspective and hope we have explicitly demonstrated that respect here, both insofar as we have recounted their views in line with their intent and by reacting to their critiques in accurate, constructive ways. As a field, the productive conversation regarding CCO constructs should continue to include these comparisons and distinctions in order to challenge our collective thinking in a collegial manner.

11

Conclusion

In this conclusion, we first briefly frame the range of arguments made in the book. A fuller notion of the direct content of the book might be obtained by reading Chapter 4, which displays our ideas as organized around *flow*. Then, we discuss some of the need for future theorizing and research, as well as the clearest possibilities for the use of the model in practice.

11.1 Summary of Key Insights

There are a number of central claims we have articulated and elaborated in this book. Here we briefly summarize each and their contributions to theorizing about the nature of organizations and their constitution through human agency and communication. First, we have argued that ST has significant advantages for the study of organizational communication, and specifically CCO. Second, we have reconceived communication, qua ST, as the ongoing, often contravened and contravening; transtruction of the meaning, power, normative; and constitutional dimensions enacted in direct encounters as well as technologically mediated interaction. Thus, every communication accomplishes—nay, is equivalent to, a *change of* both *local* and, to some extent, *global context*, typically along several of these dimensions. Third, while ST would hold that organizations (especially complex organizations) are very important power storage sites affecting modern and contemporary society, we aim to emphasize and explicate their confluent contingent constitution additionally as meaning assemblages, norm/sanction foci, and constitutive interaction processes *per se*. Fourth, we have explained how organizations are constituted, in ways distinct from the constitution of agents which, to

The Communicative Constitution of Organizations: The Four Flows Model, First Edition.
Robert D. McPhee, Karen K. Myers, and Joel O. Iverson.

avoid reification, we define as human beings with definite agentive powers while also displaying that they are not mere names or dramatizations to an outside audience. This perspective differs from traditional conceptions of organizations as nearly life-like entities with boundaries and communication occurring within them. It also draws distinctions from other perspectives by focusing on organizations as human endeavors that essentially intertwine many material and other actants from the world. Instead, we identify how meanings, norms, and power from members, nonmembers, and society reflect and affect communication and behaviors, which accomplish such intertwining while forming the essence of the organization. Fifth, we argue that a worthy metaphor or model for dynamic, disseminated (organizational) communication is *flow*, articulating its implications. Flows (comprised of both messages and text) are dimensions of distanciation: each flow expresses relations among different loci, agents, material practices, meanings, and conditions via constitutive interaction. However, the idea of constitutive flow also thus allows and even urges that there can be *multiple* constitutive flows accomplishing organizational *C*onstitution in distinct ways. Thus, this first set of contributions offers our structuration-based insights about the essence of organizations as communication.

But additionally, our perspective develops and argues for a set of worthwhile theoretic implications resting on the ideas listed earlier, and provides some conceptual tools that should be useful for future theorizing about organizations, differentiating the flows metaphor and how to reconsider the purpose/utility of organizations. So, Sixth, we elaborate a distinct conception of organizational communication as *variegated* transtructive flow, by distinguishing four analytically separate currents of flow: membership negotiation, self-structuring, activity coordination, and institutional positioning. Each of these is analytically well-defined in the abstract; they concurrently draw on, implicate, and spark tension in one another. But as we note, there are similarities among prototypical examples of any flow, which turn out to be multiform and complex, and to be confluent in other flows.

Seventh, these processes go beyond a mere checklist of necessary or sufficient conditions. The flows provide distinctions that can be useful for future theorizing about organizations including the flows metaphor and how to reconsider the purpose/utility of organizations. 4F gives us some guidance in recognizing whether a collective entity has succeeded in coalescing organization-Constituting processes (see Chapter 3) or not—that is, has the mutually supportive powers of an organization or not. If one of the flows is not found, we can speculate that the collectivity is not an organization, and then, if not an organization, what is it? A social movement? Network? Group? Are there logical alternatives by asking what collective form would exist if one of the 4 flows were missing? Each can be argued, but 4F, by arguing that all four flows are necessary, and in addition necessitated by human agents using communication to populate, structure, coordinate activity, and link as system [of agents] to environment, allows a clear set of guiding principles to examine how each is (not) organization-like.

Eighth, use of the 4F and transtruction concepts lets us directly illuminate the nature of immense, highly powerful, but unstable systems we refer to as "complex organizations." The 4F model can be the foundation for explaining how such systems exist and colonize social life today, while still being vulnerable to contraventions and other disorganizing communication and material phenomena. This set of contributions explains the constitution process that occurs through communication and behaviors through human agents. We propose that transtructions produced through the interconnection of meaning, power, norms, and constitution are the building blocks of organizations.

Ninth, while it is tempting to view organizational communication as mainly a useful activity supporting the organizations' purposes, we follow ST in rejecting that functionalist idea; we emphasize the contrary ideas that organizations are ongoing socially constituted entities having no inherent purposes (or other human–agent powers) despite communication that endows certain articulated goals with organizing and productive effects; rather, *they are power constructs* favoring some subgroup interests while exploiting, selectively empowering, and generally challenging the agency of other members as well as outsiders. Organizations are otherwise riven by contraventions, manifest as conflicts, but also warped meanings and misguided processes. Despite all this organizations often cope with these vulnerabilities, and so endure and even thrive as social entities.

11.2 Resources for Practical Appropriation of CCO Thought

Confirming the second set of claims above, a number of researchers have found that a virtue of the 4F model is its accessibility to people outside the rarified circles of CCO theorists (cf., Koschmann & Campbell, 2017). 4F shares with the other CCO schools a basic understanding that communication has constitutive force, and that we need to elucidate the ways *organization* and *organizations* are resultants of communication phenomena. But a potentially useful phenomenon is noted by van Vuuren and Knoers (2022, p. 444): 4F theory has *more direct resonance* with the worldviews, or *natural appeal* due to practitioners' ability to recognize its constructs as relevant to their practices, in contrast with most CCO writings' impenetrable language, perhaps due to the quality of rigor and precision achieved by academics. We hope this book reveals more of the rigor of 4F ideas, but 4F might also help mediate the growth of practical understanding and utility of all CCO as coalescences among the schools are found in the sort of research suggested above. The 4F model enables organizational management to consider the communicative flows that are involved in any concerning organizational issue. For example, if a volunteer organization is having difficulty with its annual fundraising event, management could examine the issue relative to each of the four flows. How do the volunteers perceive their membership relative to the fundraising event? Do they see their roles closely linked to the activities and to the event's success (Flow 1)? Or do they see the responsibilities of organizational role being outside that area of responsibility (Flow 2)? Have activities associated with the event been clearly communicated to them and between participating members (Flow 3)? Has the organization effectively communicated about the mission of the organization and how the fundraiser is a part of that mission to members and nonmembers (Flow 4)? One important instance is the general issue of organizational—and environmental—change.

The 4F perspective enables practitioners to see how the way we talk about experiences and issues has genuine implications for the future. If firefighters talk about national oversight by government as a burden, overlooking and avoiding it, through transtructions, they may constitute the oversight as a troublesome part of how the firefighters perform their role. Change is a tremendous challenge in organizations. It causes organizational members to rethink rules, policies, practices, and often elements of the organizational culture. Because the four flows imply process, implications of the model could enable leaders and managers to consider how organizational change might be approached. The 4F perspective enables management to consider how changes can take place through the four communicative flows. For example, how might a change in remote work policy (Flow 2) affect members' negotiated relationship with others in the organization and the organizational entity (Flow 1)? How would it reposition the company as a desirable place to work (Flow 4)? How is work coordinated when work moves from a centralized location to remote locations (Flow 3)?

When, and how do contraventions develop in the change process?4F more easily offers an opportunity to compare how/why some organizations thrive and others do not. Data collected (quantitative/qualitative) might be able to pinpoint flows that did not support the organizational mission and other reflexive self-structuring, did not support members and their coordination of activities, and/or the organization's institutional positioning. As previously noted, 4F gives us some guidance in recognizing whether a collective entity is an organization. At a practical level, if we identify an alternative social form rather than an organization, what are the implications? Would the collectivity be or do better if it were an organization, or had a (better) organization at its kernel? If so, can they be guided through assessment of the flows toward advancement to an organization? Would some organizations be better off if they were transformed into something else? Are there transcendent goals that are better fulfilled through networks or social movements? These are important theoretical, and certainly practical issues that individuals should consider relative to attaining defined goals.

The 4F model is definitely an alternative vision of the communicative constitution of organizations. While our discussions of many concepts explicitly demand elaboration, we hope, and believe, this book as a whole gives a reasoned and systematic articulation of that vision.

References

Allen, B. J. (1995). "Diversity" and organizational communication. *Journal of Applied Communication Research, 23*, 143–155. https://doi.org/10.1080/00909889509365420

Allen, B. J. (1996). Feminist standpoint theory: A black woman's (re) view of organizational socialization. *Communication Studies, 47*(4), 257–271. https://doi.org/10.1080/10510979609368482

Allen, M. & Hawkins, E. (2023, April 18). How Bud Light became a microcosm of America in 2023. https://www.axios.com/2023/04/18/bud-light-microcosm-america-2023.

Allen, M. W., Walker, K. L., & Brady, R. (2012). Sustainability discourse within a supply chain relationship: Mapping convergence and divergence. *The Journal of Business Communication, 49*(3), 210–236. https://doi.org/10.1177/0021943612446732

Allison, G. T. (1971). *The essence of decision.* Little, Brown.

Allyn, B. (2020). Your boss is watching you: work-from-home boom leads to more surveillance. May 13, 20205:00 AM ET. Heard on All Things Considered. https://www.npr.org/2020/05/13/854014403/your-boss-is-watching-you-work-from-home-boom-leads-to-more-surveillance.

Anderson, R. T. (1971). Voluntary associations in history. *American Anthropologist, 73*(1), 209–222. https://doi.org/10.1525/aa.1971.73.1.02a00150

Archer, M. S. (1982). Morphogenesis versus structuration: on combining structure and action. *The British Journal of Sociology, 33*(4), 455–483. https://doi.org/10.2307/589357

Archer, M. S. (1988). *Culture and agency: The place of culture in social theory.* Cambridge University Press.

Ashcraft, K. L., & Kuhn, T. R. (2018). Agential encounters: Performativity and affect meet communication in the bathroom. In B. H. J. M. Brummans (Ed.), *The agency of organizing: Perspectives and case studies* (pp. 170–193). Routledge.

Ashcraft, K. L., Kuhn, T. R., & Cooren, F. (2009). Constitutional amendments: "Materializing" organizational communication. *Academy of Management Annals, 3*(1), 1–64.

Ashforth, B. (2001). *Role transitions in organizational life: An identity-based perspective.* Routledge.

Ashforth, B. E., & Kreiner, G. (1999). "How can you do it?" Dirty work and the challenge of constructing a positive identity. *Academy of Management Review, 24*, 413–434.

The Communicative Constitution of Organizations: The Four Flows Model, First Edition.
Robert D. McPhee, Karen K. Myers, and Joel O. Iverson.

Ashforth, B. E., Sluss, D. M., & Saks, A. M. (2007). Socialization tactics, proactive behavior, and newcomer learning: Integrating socialization models. *Journal of Vocational Behavior, 70*(3), 447–462. https://doi.org/10.1016/j.jvb.2007.02.001

Ault, M. K. (2018). "Being refined into a better form": The structuration process of missionary identification. *Journal of Communication and Religion, 41*(2), 43–57.

Austin, J. L. (1975). In J. O. Urmson & M. Sbisa (Eds.), *How to do things with words* (2nd ed.). Oxford University Press.

Babajide, R. (2021). Why women don't like to ask for more money: How to get the salary you deserve. *Medium.* https://aninjusticemag.com/why-women-dont-like-to-ask-for-more-money-b5ab44591c30

Babcock, L., & Laschever, S. (2009). *Women don't ask.* Princeton University Press.

Bakhtin, M. M. (1976). The art of the word and the culture of folk humor (Rabelais and Gogol'). *Soviet Studies in Literature, 12*(2), 27–39. https://doi.org/10.2753/RSL1061-1975120227

Ballard, D., Allen, B., Ashcraft, K., Ganesh, S., McLeod, P., & Zoller, H. (2020). When words do not matter: Identifying actions to effect diversity, equity, and inclusion in the academy. *Management Communication Quarterly, 34*(4), 590–616. https://doi.org/10.1177/0893318920951643

Ballard, D. I., & Gossett, L. M. (2007). Alternative times: The temporal perceptions, processes, and practices defining the non-standard work arrangement. In C. Beck (Ed.), *Communication yearbook* (Vol. 31, pp. 269–316). Lawrence Erlbaum Associates.

Barad, K. (2003). Posthumanist performativity: Toward an understanding of how matter comes to matter. *Signs: Journal of Women in Culture and Society, 28*(3), 801–831.

Barad, K. (2007). *Meeting the universe halfway.* Duke University Press.

Barley, S. R. (1986). Technology as an occasion for structuring: Evidence from observations of CT scanners and the social order of radiology departments. *Administrative Science Quarterly, 31*, 78–108. https://doi.org/10.2307/2392767

Barnard, C. I. (1938). *The functions of the executive.* Harvard University Press.

Basque, J., Bencherki, N., & Kuhn, T. (2022). *Routledge handbook of the communicative constitution of organizations.* Routledge.

Bastien, D. T., McPhee, R. D., & Bolton, K. A. (1995). A study and extended theory of the structuration of climate. *Communication Monographs, 62*(2), 87–109. https://doi.org/10.1080/03637759509376351

Bauer, T. N., & Erdogan, B. (2011). Organizational socialization: The effective onboarding of new employees. In S. Zedeck (Ed.), *APA handbook of industrial and organizational psychology, Vol. 3. Maintaining, expanding, and contracting the organization* (pp. 51–64). American Psychological Association.

Bazerman, C., & Bonini, A. (2009). *Genre in a changing world.* Parlor Press LLC.

Bean, H., & Buikema, R. J. (2015). Deconstituting al-Qa'ida: CCO theory and the decline and dissolution of hidden organizations. *Management Communication Quarterly, 29*(4), 512–538. https://doi.org/10.1177/0893318915597300

Bechky, B. A. (2003). Object lessons: Workplace artifacts as representations of occupational jurisdiction. *American Journal of Sociology, 109*(3), 720–752. https://doi.org/10.1086/379527

Beniger, J. (1986). *The control revolution: Technological and economic origins of the information society.* Harvard University Press.

Benoit, W. L. (2018). Crisis and image repair at United Airlines: Fly the unfriendly skies. *Journal of International Crisis and Risk Communication Research, 1*(1), 2. https://doi.org/10.30658//jicrcr.1.1.2

Berger, P. L., & Luckmann, T. (1967). *The social construction of reality: A treatise in the sociology of knowledge.* Anchor.

Berlo, D. K. (1960). *The process of communication: An introduction to theory and practice.* Holt.

Bhaskar, R. (2015). *The possibility of naturalism* (4th ed.). Routledge.

Bierly, P. E., III, & Spender, J. C. (1995). Culture and high reliability organizations: The case of the nuclear submarine. *Journal of Management, 21*(4), 639–656. https://doi.org/10.1016/0149-2063(95)90003-9

Bisel, R. S. (2010). A communicative ontology of organization? A description, history, and critique of CCO theories for organization science. *Management Communication Quarterly, 24*(1), 124–131.

Black, M. (1962). *Models and metaphors: Studies in language and philosophy.* Cornell University Press.

Bleich, D. (2013). *The materiality of language: Gender, politics, and the university.* Indiana University Press.

Bleicher (1980). *Contemporary hermeneutics.* Routledge & Kegan Paul.

Blithe, S. J., & Wolfe, A. W. (2017). Work–life management in legal prostitution: Stigma and lockdown in Nevada's brothels. *Human Relations, 70*, 725–750. https://doi.org/10.1177/0018726716674262

Boden, D. (1994). *The business of talk: Organizations in action.* Polity Press.

Bourdieu, P. (1977). *Outline of a theory of practice.* Cambridge University Press.

Braithwaite, A. (2023). From brand to genre: The Hallmark Movie. *Television and New Media, 24*, 488–498. https://doi.org/10.1177/15274764231171070

Brewer, J. (1971). Flow of communications, expert qualifications and organizational authority structures. *American Sociological Review, 36*, 475–484. https://doi.org/10.2307/2093087

Browning, L. D., Greene, R. W., Sitkin, S. B., Sutcliffe, K. M., & Obstfeld, D. (2009). Constitutive complexity: Military entrepreneurs and the synthetic character of communication flows. In A. Nicotera & L. Putnam (Eds.), *Building theories of organization: The constitutive role of communication: Centering organizational communication* (pp. 89–116). Routledge Taylor & Francis Group. https://doi.org/10.4324/9780203891025

Brummans, B. H. J. M. (2018). *The agency of organizing: Perspectives and case studies.* Routledge.

Brummans, B. H. J. M., Cooren, F., Robichaud, D., & Taylor, J. R. (2014). Approaches to the communicative constitution of organizations. In L. L. Putnam & D. K. Mumby (Eds.), *The SAGE handbook of organizational communication: Advances in theory, research, and methods* (3rd ed., pp. 173–194). SAGE.

Burrell, G., & Morgan, G. (1979). *Sociological paradigms and organizational analysis.* Heinemann Educational.

Buzzanell, P. M. (1995). Reframing the glass ceiling as a socially constructed process: Implications for understanding and change. *Communication Monographs, 62*, 327–354. https://doi.org/10.1080/03637759509376366

Callon, M. (2007). An essay on the growing contribution of economic markets to the proliferation of the social. *Theory, Culture & Society, 24*(7-8), 139–163.

Canary, H. E., & McPhee, R. D. (2009). *Communication and organizational knowledge.* Routledge.

Canary, H. E. (2010a). Structurating activity theory: An integrative approach to policy knowledge. *Communication Theory, 20*(1), 21–49. https://doi.org/10.1111/j.1468-2885.2009.01354.x

Canary, H. E. (2010b). Constructing policy knowledge: Contradictions, communication, and knowledge frames. *Communication Monographs, 77*, 181–206. https://doi.org/10.1080/03637751003758185

Cantu, J., Gharehyakheh, A., Fritts, S., & Tolk, J. (2021). Assessing the HRO: Tools and techniques to determine the high-reliability state of an organization. *Safety Science, 134*, 105082. https://doi.org/10.1016/j.ssci.2020.105082

Caronia, L., & Colla, V. (2021). Objects that matter: The hybrid and distributed agency in parent-assisted homework interactions. *Language and Dialogue, 11*(1), 8–34. https://doi.org/10.1075/ld.00082.car

Carrim, N. M. (2019). Minority employees' ethnic identity in the workplace. In *Oxford research encyclopedia of business and management.* Oxford University Press. https://doi.org/10.1093/acrefore/9780190224851.013.196

Carton, A. M., Murphy, C., & Clark, J. R. (2014). A (blurry) vision of the future: How leader rhetoric about ultimate goals influences performance. *Academy of Management Journal, 57*(6), 1544–1570. https://doi.org/10.5465/amj.2012.0101

Carvalho-Freitas, M. N. D., & Stathi, S. (2017). Reducing workplace bias toward people with disabilities with the use of imagined contact. *Journal of Applied Social Psychology, 47*(5), 256–266. https://doi.org/10.1111/jasp.12435

Cascio, W. F., & Montealegre, R. (2016). How technology is changing work and organizations. *Annual Review of Organizational Psychology and Organizational Behavior, 3*, 349–375. https://doi.org/10.1146/annurev-orgpsych-041015-062352

Castells, M. (2011). *The rise of the network society* (Vol. 12). John Wiley & Sons.

Cheney, G. (1983a). On the various and changing meanings of organizational membership: A field study of organizational identification. *Communication Monographs, 50*(4), 342–362. https://doi.org/10.1080/03637758309390174

Cheney, G. (1983b). The rhetoric of identification and the study of organizational communication. *The Quarterly Journal of Speech, 69*(2), 143–158. https://doi.org/10.1080/00335638309383643

Cheney, G., & Christensen, L. T. (2001). Organizational identity: Linkages between internal and external communication. In F. M. Jablin & L. L. Putnam (Eds.), *The new handbook of organizational communication: Advances in theory, research, and methods* (pp. 231–269). SAGE.

Cheney, G., Christensen, L. T., & Dailey, S. L. (2014). Communicating identity and identification in and around organizations. In L. L. Putnam & D. K. Mumby (Eds.), *The SAGE handbook of organizational communication: Advances in theory, research, and methods* (3rd ed., pp. 695–716). SAGE.

Choi, C. W., & Berhó, D. (2016). Ethnic identity maintenance within the Latino-American church: A structuration perspective. *Journal of Intercultural Communication Research, 45*(2), 91–107. https://doi.org/10.1080/17475759.2015.1086811

Chou, R., & Feagin, J. (2008). *The myth of the model minority: Asian-Americans facing Fascism.* Paradigm.

Christensen, L. T., Penttilä, V., & Štumberger, N. (2022). The communicative constitution of corporate social responsibility. In *The Routledge handbook of the communicative constitution of organization* (pp. 354–367). Routledge.

Clair, R. P. (1996). The political nature of the colloquialism, "a real job": Implications for organizational socialization. *Communication Monographs, 63*(3), 249–267. https://doi.org/10.1080/03637759609376392

Clarke, A. E. (2021). Straussian negotiated order theory c. 1960–present. In *The Routledge international handbook of interactionism* (pp. 47–58). Routledge.

Clelland, I. J., & Zarankin, T. G. (2012). Towards a dynamic model of interpersonal trust: The role of communicative action in workflow negotiation. *International Journal of Strategic Communication, 6*, 109–125. https://doi.org/10.1080/1553118X.2011.634865

Coase, R. H. (1937). The nature of the firm. *Economica, 4*(16), 386–405.

Cohen, I. J. (1989). *Structuration theory: Anthony Giddens and the constitution of social life.* Macmillan.

Congdon, C., Flynn, D., & Redman, M. (2014). Balancing "we" and "me": The best collaborative spaces also support solitude. *Harvard Business Review, 92*(10), 50–57.

Conrad, C., & Cheney, G. (2018). Organizational communication and organizational rhetoric II: The theme of division. In O. Ihlen & R. L. Heath (Eds.), *The handbook of organizational rhetoric and communication* (pp. 33–49). Wiley.

Conroy, S., Henle, C. A., Shore, L., & Stelman, S. (2017). Where there is light, there is dark: A review of the detrimental outcomes of high organizational identification. *Journal of Organizational Behavior, 38*(2), 184–203. https://doi.org/10.1002/job.2164

Contractor, N. S., & Seibold, D. R. (1993). Theoretical frameworks for the study of structuring processes in group decision support systems: Adaptive structuration theory and self-organizing systems theory. *Human Communication Research, 19*(4), 528–563. https://doi.org/10.1111/j.1468-2958.1993.tb00312.x

Coombs, W. T. (2004). Impact of past crises on current crisis communication: Insights from situational crisis communication theory. *The Journal of Business Communication, 41*(3), 265–289. https://doi.org/10.1177/0021943604265607

Cooren, F. (2013). The organizational world as a plenum of agencies. In F. Cooren, J. R. Taylor, & E. J. Van Every (Eds.), *Communication as organizing* (pp. 81–100). Routledge.

Cooren, F. (2018). Acting for, with and through: A relational perspective on agency in MSF's Organizing. In B. H. J. M. Brummans (Ed.), *The agency of organizing* (pp. 142–169). Routledge.

Cooren, F. (2020). Beyond entanglement: (Socio-) materiality and organization studies. *Organization Theory, 1*(3), 2631787720954444. https://doi.org/10.1177/2631787720954444

Cooren, F., & Fairhurst, G. T. (2004). Speech timing and spacing: The phenomenon of organizational closure. *Organization, 11*(6), 793–824. https://doi.org/10.1177/1350508404047252

Cooren, F., & Seidl, D. (2020). Niklas Luhmann's radical communication approach and its implications for research on organizational communication. *Academy of Management Review, 45*(2), 479–497. Zurich Open Repository and Archive, University of Zurich, ZORA https://doi.org/10.5167/uzh-174709. Original DOI: https://doi.org/10.5465/amr.2018.0176

Corman, S. R. (1997). The reticulation of quasi-agents in systems of organizational communication. *Organization Communication—Emerging Perspectives, 5*, 65–82.

Cox, T. (1994). *Cultural diversity in organizations: Theory, research and practice*. Berrett-Koehler Publishers.

Dagnino, G. B. (2009). Coopetition strategy: a new kind of interfirm dynamics for value creation. In *Coopetition strategy* (pp. 45–63). Routledge.

Davidson, M. J., Fielden, S. L., & Omar, A. (2010). Black, Asian and minority ethnic female business owners: discrimination and social support. *International Journal of Entrepreneurial Behavior & Research, 16*(1), 58–80. https://doi.org/10.1108/13552551011020072

Davies, B., & Harre, R. (1990). Positioning: The discursive production of selves. *Journal for the Theory of Social Behaviour, 20*, 43–63. https://d1wqtxts1xzle7.cloudfront.net/8651928/davids-harrc3a9-positioning-theory1-libre.pdf?1391773141=&response-content-disposition=inline%3B+filename%3DPositioning_The_discursive_production_of.pdf&Expires=1711561163&Signature=fspZ4p7ZjRz-tTzEIc8ysMD7JfUumGgD0os7r1-KHWZ30rFr7aUMK7xFpvxEHTPY-0fEwgVus3GHjdJyixjiW8VrmBn87Fe~RAqKupIsGFP0U9TqG098oIBwvfMAsp9fLjWxdJ4WvH-zme8isRJFg~Osd8ATTpogeyatH-UYl~ZLl4A0NcqAldZXw6QzLNdXZSzs0sqprcgW2EU7d2h92YnSZI7wDlG3P9spqZX2JgJl1K2LIhFyqdjW9JHox2F9qzOuJGRD0pqfPcgPeV8d~Z5LN7aECVRbaNt1UMVC6Bd~GvtfQ~~byXoCtyr3EGZEv7yilNVWP3JAxxkEMDyE~Q__&Key-Pair-Id=APKAJLOHF5GGSLRBV4ZA

Davis, C. W., & Myers, K. K. (2019). Past work experience and organizational assimilation in nonprofit organizations. *Nonprofit Management & Leadership*, 1–20. https://doi.org/10.1002/nml.21348

Dawson, V. R., & Brunner, E. (2020). Corporate social responsibility on wild public networks: Communicating to disparate and multivocal stakeholders. *Management Communication Quarterly, 34*(1), 58–84. https://doi.org/10.1177/0893318919884920

de Saussure, F. (2011). *Course in general linguistics*. Columbia University Press.

Dean, R. A., & Wanous, J. P. (1984). Effects of realistic job previews on hiring bank tellers. *Journal of Applied Psychology, 69*(1), 61–68. https://doi.org/10.1037/0021-9010.69.1.61

Deetz, S. (1992). *Democracy in an age of corporate colonization: Developments in communication and the politics of everyday life*. SUNY Press.

Deleuze, G., & Guattari, F. (1987). *A thousand plateaus: Capitalism and schizophrenia*. University of Minnesota Press.

Deprez-Sims, A. S., & Morris, S. B. (2010). Accents in the workplace: Their effects during a job interview. *International Journal of Psychology, 45*(6), 417–426. https://doi.org/10.1080/00207594.2010.499950

Derrida, J. (1976). *Of grammatology*. The Johns Hopkins University Press.

DeSanctis, G., & Poole, M. S. (1994). Capturing the complexity in advanced technology use: Adaptive structuration theory. *Organization Science, 5*(2), 121–147. https://doi.org/10.1287/orsc.5.2.121

DiMaggio, P. J., & Powell, W. W. (1983). The iron cage revisited: Institutional isomorphism and collective rationality in organizational fields. *American Sociological Review, 48*(2), 147–160. https://doi.org/10.2307/2095101

Dobusch, L., & Schoeneborn, D. (2015). Fluidity, identity, and organizationality: The communicative constitution of Anonymous. *Journal of Management Studies, 52*(8), 1005–1035. https://doi.org/10.1111/joms.12139

Drucker, P. (1973). *Management: Tasks, responsibilities, practices*. Harper & Row.

Duffy, M. (2016). *The Agency of Meetings as Systemic Process in the Constitution of Organizations* [Doctoral dissertation, Ph. D.], Dublin Institute of Technology, Dublin, Ireland. http://arrow. dit.ie/cgi/viewcontent.cgi.

Edmunds, A., & Morris, A. (2000). The problem of information overload in business organisations: A review of the literature. *International Journal of Information Management, 20*(1), 17–28. https://doi.org/10.1016/S0268-4012(99)00051-1

El Karhili, N., Hendry, J., Kackowski, W., El Damanhoury, K., Dicker, A., & Winkler, C. (2021). Islamic/state: Daesh's visual negotiation of institutional positioning. *Journal of Media and Religion, 20*(2), 79–104. https://doi.org/10.1080/15348423.2021.1930813

Emirbayer, M., & Mische, A. (1998). What is agency? *American Journal of Sociology, 103*(4), 962–1023. https://doi.org/10.1086/231294

Endacott, C. G., & Myers, K. K. (2019). Extending the membership negotiation model: Previous work experience and the reproduction and transformation of structures. *Management Communication Quarterly, 33*, 455–483. https://doi.org/10.1177/0893318919861555

Engeström, Y. (1999). *Activity theory and individual and social transformation. Perspectives on activity theory*. Cambridge University Press.

Eventbrite.Com. (2023). *Bringing the world together through live experiences*. https://www.eventbrite.ca/about/.

Fayard, A. L., & Weeks, J. (2011, July–August). Who moved my cube? *Harvard Business Review, 89*(7/8), 103–110.

Fayol, H. (1949). *General and industrial management*. Sir Isaac Pitman & Sons.

Feldman, M. S. (2000). Organizational routines as a source of continuous change. *Organization Science, 11*(6), 611–629. https://doi.org/10.1287/orsc.11.6.611.12529

Folger, J. P., Poole, M. S., & Stutman, R. K. (2021). *Working through conflict: Strategies for relationships, groups, and organizations*. Routledge.

Foot, K., & Groleau, C. (2011). Contradictions, transitions, and materiality in organizing processes: An activity theory perspective. *First Monday, 16*(6), 6. https://firstmonday.org/ojs/index.php/fm/article/download/3479/2983

Ford, J. D., & Ford, L. W. (1995). The role of conversations in producing intentional change in organizations. *Academy of Management Review, 20*(3), 541–570. https://doi.org/10.5465/amr.1995.9508080330

Ford, J. L. (2018). Revisiting high-reliability organizing: Obstacles to safety and resilience. *Corporate Communications: An International Journal, 23*(2), 197–211. https://doi.org/10.1108/CCIJ-04-2017-0034

Foucault, M. (1977). *Discipline and punish: The birth of the prison.* Translated by A. Sheridan. Allen Lane.

Frumkin, P. (2002). *On being nonprofit: A conceptual and policy primer. Harvard University Press.*

Gadamer, H. G. (1975). *Truth and method* (2nd ed.). Sheed & Ward.

Galbraith, J. (1973). *Designing complex organizations.* Addison Wesley Publishing Company.

Garner, J. T. (2006). Masters of the universe? Resource dependency and interorganizational power relationships at NASA. *Journal of Applied Communication Research, 34*, 368–385. https://doi.org/10.1080/00909880600911249

Gelles, D. (2019, January 31). Julia Hartz Founded Eventbrite With Her Fiancé. Then She Took His Job. Interview of Julia Hartz by Erik Tanner *New York Times.* A version of this article appears in print on Feb. 3, 2019, Section BU, Page 4 of the New York edition with the headline: She Went From 'Candy Land' to 'Tron'.

Gersick, C. J. (1988). Time and transition in work teams: Toward a new model of group development. *Academy of Management Journal, 31*(1), 9–41. https://doi.org/10.5465/256496

Ghobadi, S., & D'Ambra, J. (2012). Knowledge sharing in cross-functional teams: A competitive model. *Journal of Knowledge Management, 16*(2), 285–301. https://doi.org/10.1108/13673271211218889

Gibson, J. J. (1966). *The senses considered as perceptual systems.* Houghton Mifflin.

Gibson, M. K., & Papa, M. J. (2000). The mud, the blood, and the beer guys: Organizational osmosis in blue-collar work groups. *Journal of Applied Communication Research, 28*, 68–88. https://doi.org/10.1080/00909880009365554

Giddens, A. (1976a). Classical social theory and the origins of modern sociology. *American Journal of Sociology, 81*(4), 703–729. https://doi.org/10.1086/226140

Giddens, A. (1976b). *New rules of sociological method.* Basic Books.

Giddens, A. (1979). *Central problems in social theory: Action, structure, and contradiction in social analysis* (Vol. 241). University of California Press.

Giddens, A. (1981). *A contemporary critique of historical materialism (Vol. I): Power property and the state.* University of California Press.

Giddens, A. (1984). *The constitution of society: Outline of the theory of structuration.* University of California Press.

Giddens, A. (1985). Time, space and regionalisation. In D. Gregory & J. Urry (Eds.), *Social relations and spatial structures* (pp. 265–295). St. Martin's Press.

Giddens, A. (1990). *The consequences of modernity.* Stanford University Press.

Giddens, A. (1991). *Modernity and self-identity.* Stanford University Press.

Giddens, A. (1993). *New rules of sociological method: A positive critique of interpretative sociologies* (2nd ed.). Stanford University Press.

Giles, M. & Myers, K. K. (2020, November). Counterflows: Explaining police and firefighter actions and consequences for the communicative constitution of organizations following policy changes. Presented to the Organizational Communication Division of the National Communication Association conference. Indianapolis, IN.

Goffman, E. (1961). *Encounters: Two studies in the sociology of interaction.* Ravenio Books.

Goldstein, B., & Oldham, J. (1979). *Children and work: A study of socialization.* Transaction Books.

Graen, G. B., & Uhl-Bien, M. (1995). Relationship-based approach to leadership: Development of leader-member exchange (LMX) theory of leadership over 25 years: Applying a multi-level multi-domain perspective. *The Leadership Quarterly, 6*(2), 219–247. https://doi.org/10.1016/1048-9843(95)90036-5

Gross, N., & Kluge, A. (2012). "Why should I share what I know?" Antecedents for enhancing knowledge-sharing behavior and its impact on shared mental models in steel production. *Proceedings from the Human Factors and Ergonomics Society 56th Annual Meeting*, pp. 403–407.

Guowei, J. (2007). Unpacking unintended consequences in planned organizational change: A process model. *Management Communication Quarterly, 21*, 5–28. https://doi.org/10.1177/0893318907301986

Haas, J. E., & Drabeck, T. E. (1973). *Complex organizations: A sociological perspective.* Macmillan.

Habermas, J. (1989/1962)). *The structural transformation of the public sphere.* MIT Press.

Habermas, J. (2015). *Knowledge and human interests.* John Wiley & Sons.

Hage, J. (1974). *Communication and organizational control: cybernetics in health and welfare settings.* Wiley.

Hage, J. (1980). *Theories of organizations: form, process, and transformation.* Wiley.

Hand, M., & Gorea, M. (2018). Digital traces in context| digital traces and personal analytics: iTime, self-tracking, and the temporalities of practice. *International Journal of Communication, 12*, 666–682.

Hansen, K. D., & Canary, H. E. (2015). Constructing specialized knowledge through activity coordination during organizational change. *Journal of Organizational Knowledge Communication, 2*(1), 6–40. https://doi.org/10.7146/jookc.v2i1.20958

Harré, R., & Van Langenhove, L. (1991). Varieties of positioning. *Journal for the Theory of Social Behavior, 21*, 393–407. https://doi.org/10.1111/j.1468-5914.1991.tb00203.x

Harvey Wingfield, A., & Myles, R. L. (2014). Still a man's world? Revisiting men who do women's work. *Sociology Compass, 8*(10), 1206–1215. https://doi.org/10.1111/soc4.12206

Haslett, B. (2013). *Communicating and organizing in context: The theory of structurational interaction.* Routledge.

Haueter, J. A., Macan, T. H., & Winter, J. (2003). Measurement of newcomer socialization: Construct validation of a multidimensional scale. *Journal of Vocational Behavior, 63*(1), 20–39. https://doi.org/10.1016/S0001-8791(02)00017-9

Hawes, L. C. (1973). Elements of a model for communication processes. *The Quarterly Journal of Speech, 59*(1), 11–21. https://doi.org/10.1080/00335637309383149

Heath, R. G., & Isbell, M. G. (2017). *Interorganizational collaboration: Complexity, ethics, and communication.* Waveland Press.

Hebl, M., Cheng, S. K., & Ng, L. C. (2020). Modern discrimination in organizations. *Annual Review of Organizational Psychology and Organizational Behavior, 7*, 257–282. https://doi.org/10.1146/annurev-orgpsych-012119-044948

Heidegger, M. (1927/1962). *Being and time.* (J. Macquarrie & E. Robinson. Trans.). Harper and Row.

Heidegger, M. (1967). *Being and time.* Blackwell.

Hill, L. A. (1992). *Becoming a manager: Mastery of a new identity.* Harvard Press.

Hirsch, P. B. (2022). Forging a new corporate engagement. *Journal of Business Strategy, 43*(3), 193–196. https://doi.org/10.1108/jbs-02-2022-0026

Hoffman, M. F., & Cowan, R. L. (2010). Be careful what you ask for: Structuration theory and work/life accommodation. *Communication Studies, 61*, 205–223. https://doi.org/10.1080/10510971003604026

Hollingshead, A. B. (1998). Communication, learning, and retrieval in transactive memory systems. *Journal of Experimental Social Psychology, 34*, 423–442.

Hollingshead, A. B., Gupta, N., Yoon, K., & Brandon, D. P. (2011). Transactive memory theory and teams: Past, present, and future. In E. Salas, S. M. Fiore, & N. P. Letsky (Eds.), *Theories of team cognition: Cross-disciplinary perspectives* (pp. 421–455). Routledge.

Honneth, A. (2003). 'Anxiety and Politics': The Strengths and Weaknesses of Franz Neumann's Diagnosis of a Social Pathology. *Constellations, 10*(2), 247–255.

Howard, L. A., & Geist, P. (1995). Ideological positioning in organizational change: The dialectic of control in a merging organization. *Communication Monographs*, *62*, 110–131. https://doi.org/10.1080/03637759509376352

Hughes, E. C. (1962). Good people and dirty work. *Social Problems*, *10*, 3–11. https://doi.org/10.2307/799402

Ilies, R., Nahrgang, J. D., & Morgeson, F. P. (2007). Leader-member exchange and citizenship behaviors: A meta-analysis. *Journal of Applied Psychology*, *92*(1), 269–277. https://doi.org/10.1037/0021-9010.92.1.269

Im, H. G., Yates, J., & Orlikowski, W. (2005). Temporal coordination through communication: Using genres in a virtual start-up organization. *Information Technology & People*, *18*(2), 89–119. https://doi.org/10.1108/09593840510601496

Irshad, M., & Bashir, S. (2020). The dark side of organizational identification: a multi-study investigation of negative outcomes. *Frontiers in Psychology*, *11*, 572478. https://doi.org/10.3389/fpsyg.2020.572478

Iverson, J. O., McPhee, R. D., & Spaulding, C. W. (2018). Being able to act otherwise: The role of agency in the four flows at 2-1-1 and beyond. In B. H. J. M. Brummans (Ed.), *The agency of organizing: Perspectives and case studies* (pp. 43–65). Routledge.

Iverson, J. O., Myers, K. K., & McPhee, R. D. (2022). Theorizing communication and constitution of organizations from a four flows (structurational) perspective. In J. Basque, N. Bencherki, & T. Kuhn (Eds.), *Routledge handbook of the communicative constitution of organization* (pp. 74–87). Routledge.

Iverson, J. O. (2010a, November). *Theorizing organizational mission and mission statements in a structuration framework*. Presented in the Organizational Communication Division of the National Communication convention. San Francisco, CA.

Iverson, J. O. (2010b). Knowledge, belonging, and communities of practice. In H. Canary & R. D. McPhee (Eds.), *Communication and organizational knowledge* (pp. 57–74). Routledge.

Iverson, J. O. (2013). Communicating belonging: Building communities of expert volunteers. In M. Kramer, L. Gossett, & L. Lewis (Eds.), *Communication and the volunteer experience: Exploring the organizational dynamics of volunteering in multiple Contexts*. Peter Lang Publishers.

Iverson, J. O., & McPhee, R. D. (2002). Knowledge management in communities of practice: Being true to the communicative character of knowledge. *Management Communication Quarterly*, *16*(2), 259–266. https://doi.org/10.1177/089331802237239

Iverson, J. O., & McPhee, R. D. (2008). Communicating knowing through communities of practice: Exploring internal communicative processes and differences among CoPs. *Journal of Applied Communication Research*, *36*, 176–199. https://doi.org/10.1080/00909880801923738

Jablin, F. M. (1979). Superior–subordinate communication: The state of the art. *Psychological Bulletin*, *86*(6), 1201.

Jablin, F. M. (2001). Organizational entry, assimilation, and disengagement/exit. In F. M. Jablin & L. L. Putnam (Eds.), *The new handbook of organizational communication: Advances in theory, research, and methods* (pp. 732–818). SAGE.

Jahn, J. L. (2019a). Voice enactment: Linking voice with experience in high reliability organizing. *Journal of Applied Communication Research*, *47*, 283–302.

Jahn, J. L. (2019b). Shifting the safety rules paradigm: Introducing doctrine to US wildland firefighting operations. *Safety Science*, *115*, 237–246. https://doi.org/10.1016/j.ssci.2019.02.002

Jarzabkowski, P., Lê, J. K., & Van de Ven, A. H. (2013). Responding to competing strategic demands: How organizing, belonging, and performing paradoxes coevolve. *Strategic Organization*, *11*(3), 245–280. https://doi.org/10.1177/1476127013481016

Jiang, W., An, Y., Wang, L., & Zheng, C. (2021). Newcomers' reaction to the abusive supervision toward peers during organizational socialization. *Journal of Vocational Behavior, 128*, 103586. https://doi.org/10.1016/j.jvb.2021.103586

Johnson, J. R. (2023). What's new about quiet quitting (and what's not). *The Transdisciplinary Journal of Management.* https://tjm.scholasticahq.com/article/72079-what-s-new-about-quiet-quitting-and-what-s-not

Kahn, E., Antognoli, E., & Arbuckle, P. (2022). The LCA commons—How an open-source repository for US Federal life cycle assessment (LCA) data products advances inter-agency coordination. *Applied Sciences, 12*(2), 865. https://doi.org/10.3390/app12020865

Kanter, R. M. (2008). *Men and women of the corporation: New edition.* Basic Books.

Kaufman, H. (1971). *The limits of organizational change.* Routledge.

Kelley, M. S., Lune, H., & Murphy, S. (2005). Doing syringe exchange: Organizational transformation and volunteer commitment. *Nonprofit and Voluntary Sector Quarterly, 34*(3), 362–386. https://doi.org/10.1177/0899764005275568

Kellogg, K. C., Orlikowski, W. J., & Yates, J. (2006). Life in the trading zone: Structuring coordination across boundaries in postbureaucratic organizations. *Organization Science, 17*(1), 22–44. https://doi.org/10.1287/orsc.1050.0157

Kirby, E., & Krone, K. (2002). "The policy exists but you can't really use it": Communication and the structuration of work-family policies. *Journal of Applied Communication Research, 30*(1), 50–77. https://doi.org/10.1080/00909880216577

Klein, H. J., Polin, B., & Leigh Sutton, K. (2015). Specific onboarding practices for the socialization of new employees. *International Journal of Selection and Assessment, 23*(3), 263–283. https://doi.org/10.1111/ijsa.12113

Knight, C., & Haslam, S. A. (2010). Your place or mine? Organizational identification and comfort as mediators of relationships between the managerial control of workspace and employees' satisfaction and well-being. *British Journal of Management, 21*(3), 717–735. https://doi.org/10.1111/j.1467-8551.2009.00683.x

Koschmann, M. & Campbell, T. (2017, November). *Taking stock of taken up: The legacy and relevance of CCO in non-scholarly outlets.* Paper presented at the annual convention of the National Communication Association, Dallas, TX.

Koschmann, M. A., Kuhn, T. R., & Pfarrer, M. D. (2012). A communicative framework of value in cross-sector partnerships. *Academy of Management Review, 37*(3), 332–354. https://doi.org/10.5465/amr.2010.0314

Koschmann, M. A., & Sanders, M. L. (2020). *Understanding nonprofit work: A communication perspective.* John Wiley & Sons.

Kramer, M. W., Hoelscher, C. S., Nguyen, C., Day, E. A., & Cooper, O. D. (2017). Structuration processes in an interagency collaboration: Enabling and constraining participation and efficiency. *Journal of Applied Communication Research, 45*(4), 429–444. https://doi.org/10.1080/00909882.2017.1355558

Kreiner, G. E. (2006). Consequences of work-home segmentation or integration: A person-environment fit perspective. *Journal of Organizational Behavior: The International Journal of Industrial, Occupational and Organizational Psychology and Behavior, 27*(4), 485–507. https://doi.org/10.1002/job.386

Kuhn, T. R. (2008). A communicative theory of the firm: Developing an alternative perspective on intra-organizational power and stakeholder relationships. *Organization Studies, 29*(8–9), 1227–1254. https://doi.org/10.1177/0170840608094778

Kuhn, T. R. (2016). Communicatively constituting organizational unfolding through counter-narrative. In S. Frandsen, T. Kuhn, & M. W. Lundholt (Eds.), *Counter-narratives and organization* (pp. 17–42). Routledge.

Kuhn, T. R. (2014). Knowledge and knowing in organizational communication. In L. L. Putnam & D. K. Mumby (Eds.), *The SAGE handbook of organizational communication: Advances in theory, research, and methods* (pp. 481–502). SAGE.

Laing, R. D., Phillipson, H., & Lee, A. R. (1966). *Interpersonal perception: A theory and method of research*. Springer Publishing.

Lammers, J. C., & Barbour, J. B. (2006). An institutional theory of organizational communication. *Communication Theory, 16*(3), 356–377. https://doi.org/10.1111/j.1468-2885.2006.00274.x

Lammers, J. C., Garcia, M., & Kim, M. (2008, November). *The professional worker and the organization: Identification, fun, burnout, and effort in a call center*. Presented to the Organizational Division of the National Communication Association, San Diego, CA.

Larson, G. S., & Gill, R. (2017). *Organizations and identity*. John Wiley & Sons.

Larson, G. S., & Pepper, G. L. (2011). Organizational identification and the symbolic shaping of information communication technology. *Qualitative Research Reports in Communication, 12*, 1–9.

Latour, B. (2007). *Reassembling the social: An introduction to actor-network-theory*.

Lave, J., & Wenger, E. (1991). *Situate learning: Legitimate peripheral participation*. Cambridge University Press.

Lee, A. R., Son, S. M., & Kim, K. K. (2016). Information and communication technology overload and social networking service fatigue: A stress perspective. *Computers in Human Behavior, 55*, 51–61. https://doi.org/10.1016/j.chb.2015.08.011

Lee, T. W., & Mitchell, T. R. (1994). An alternative approach: The unfolding model of voluntary employee turnover. *Academy of Management Review, 19*(1), 51–89. https://doi.org/10.5465/amr.1994.9410122008

Lent, R. W., Brown, S. D., & Hackett, G. (2000). Contextual supports and barriers to career choice: A social cognitive analysis. *Journal of Counseling Psychology, 47*, 36–49. Retrieved from http://associationdatabase.com/aws/NCDA/pt/sp/cdquarterly

Li, L., Mazer, J. P., & Ju, R. (2011). Resolving international teaching assistant language inadequacy through dialogue: Challenges and opportunities for clarity and credibility. *Communication Education, 60*(4), 461–478. https://doi.org/10.1080/03634523.2011.565352

Louis, M. R. (1980). Surprise and sense making: What newcomers experience in entering unfamiliar organizational settings. *Administrative Science Quarterly, 226–251*. https://doi.org/10.1300/J111V04N01_08

Lucas, K., & Buzzanell, P. M. (2004). Blue-collar work, career, and success: Occupational narratives of sisu. *Journal of Applied Communication Research, 32*(4), 273–292. https://doi.org/10.1080/0090988042000240167

Luhmann, N. (1995). *Social systems*. Stanford University Press.

Luhmann, N. (2012). *Theory of society* (Vol. 1). Stanford University Press.

Luhmann, N. (2018). *Organization and decision*. Cambridge University Press.

Lyotard, J. F. (1984). *The postmodern condition: A report on knowledge* (Vol. 10). University of Minnesota Press.

Mael, F., & Ashforth, B. E. (1992). Alumni and their alma mater: A partial test of the reformulated model of organizational identification. *Journal of Organizational Behavior, 12*, 103–123. https://doi.org/10.1002/job.4030130202

March, J. G., & Simon, H. A. (1958/1993)). *Organizations* (2nd ed.). Blackwell.

Martin, J., Feldman, M., Hatch, M. J., & Sitkin, S. B. (1983). The uniqueness paradox in organizational stories. *Administrative Science Quarterly, 28*, 438–453. https://doi.org/10.2307/2392251

Martínez-Córcoles, M., & Vogus, T. J. (2020). Mindful organizing for safety. *Safety Science, 124*(1), 1–5. https://doi.org/10.1016/j.ssci.2020.104614

May, S. K., & Roper, J. (2014). Corporate social responsibility and ethics. In L. Putnam & D. Mumby (Eds.), *The SAGE handbook of organizational communication: Advances in theory, research, and methods* (pp. 767–789). SAGE.

Mayo, E. (1933, new ed. 1946). *The human problems of an industrial civilization*. Harvard University Press.

McCall, L. (2005). The complexity of intersectionality. *Signs: Journal of Women in Culture and Society, 30*(3), 1771–1800. https://doi.org/10.1086/436800

McClelland-Cohen, A. (2020, June). "Building the plane while flying it": Negotiating tensions in an emerging hybrid organization. Dissertation, Department of Communication, University of California, Santa Barbara.

McPhee, R. D. (1985). Formal structure and organizational communication. In R. D. McPhee & P. K. Tompkins (Eds.), *Organizational communication: Traditional themes and new directions* (pp. 149–178). SAGE.

McPhee, R. D. (1988). Vertical communication chains: Toward an integrated view. *Management Communication Quarterly, 1*(4), 455–493. https://doi.org/10.1177/0893318988001004002

McPhee, R. D. (1989). Organizational communication: A structurational exemplar. In B. Dervin, L. Grossberg, B. J. O'Keefe, & E. Wartella (Eds.), *Rethinking communication (vol. 2) Paradigm Exemplars* (pp. 199–212). SAGE.

McPhee, R. D. (2004). Text, agency, and organization in the light of structuration theory. *Organization, 11*(3), 355–371.

McPhee, R. D. & Canary, H. E. (2009, November). *Distanciation and organizational communication.* Presented at the Annual Conference of the National Communication Association, Chicago, Illinois.

McPhee, R. D., & Corman, S. R. (1995). An activity-based theory of communication networks in organizations, applied to the case of a local church. *Communication Monographs, 62*(2), 132–151. https://doi.org/10.1080/03637759509376353

McPhee, R. D., Corman, S. R., & Iverson, J. (2006). "We ought to have. . . gumption. . .": A CRA analysis of an excerpt from the videotape corporation: After Mr. Sam. In F. Cooren (Ed.), *Interacting and organizing: Analyses of a management meeting* (pp. 131–162). Taylor and Francis.

McPhee, R. D., & Iverson, J. (2002, November). Discourse systems structure organizations and their discursive resources. *Paper presented at the annual meeting of the National Communication Association*, New Orleans, LA.

McPhee, R. D., & Iverson, J. (2009). Agents of constitution in Communicad: Constitutive processes of communication in organizations. In L. Putnam & A. M. Nicotera (Eds.), *Building theories of organization: The constitutive role of communication* (pp. 49–87). Routledge.

McPhee, R. D., & Iverson, J. O. (2011). Materiality, structuration, and communication. In T. Kuhn (Ed.), *Matters of communication: Political, cultural, and technological challenges to communication theorizing* (pp. 65–80). Hampton.

McPhee, R. D., & Iverson, J. O. (2013). Activity coordination and the Montreal School. In D. Robichaud & F. Cooren (Eds.), *Organizations and organizing: Materiality, agency, and discourse* (pp. 109–124). Taylor & Francis.

McPhee, R. D., & Poole, M. S. (2016). Models of communication. In K. B. Jensen, R. T. Craig, J. Pooley, & E. W. Rothenbuhler (Eds.), *The international encyclopedia of communication theory and philosophy* (pp. 1263–1294). John Wiley & Sons. https://doi.org/10.1002/9781118766804.wbiect274

McPhee, R. D., Poole, M. S., & Iverson, J. (2014). Structuration theory. In L. L. Putnam & D. K. Mumby (Eds.), *The SAGE handbook of organizational communication: Advances in theory, research, and methods* (pp. 75–100). Sage.

McPhee, R. D., & Zaug, P. (2000). The communicative constitution of organizations: A framework for explanation. Electronic. *Journal of Communication, 10*(1/2), www.cios.org/getfile/McPhee_V10n1200

McPhee, R. D., & Zaug, P. (2009). The communicative constitutive of organizations: A framework for explanation. In L. L. Putnam & A. M. Nicotera (Eds.), *Building theories of organization: The constitutive role of communication* (pp. 21–48). Routledge.

Mead, G. H. (1932). *The philosophy of the present*. University of Chicago Press.

Mead, G. H. (1934). *Mind, self, and society from the standpoint of a social behaviorist*. University of Chicago Press.

Meindl, J. R., Ehrlich, S. B., & Dukerich, J. M. (1985). The romance of leadership. *Administrative Science Quarterly, 30*, 78–102. https://doi.org/10.2307/2392813

Mercier, M., & Reid, G. (1990). A global red cross and red crescent identity. *International Review of the Red Cross (1961-1997), 30*(276), 191–200. https://doi.org/10.1017/s0020860400075537

Miller, V. D., & Jablin, F. M. (1991). Information seeking during organizational entry: Influences, tactics, and a model of the process. *Academy of Management Review, 16*(1), 92–120. https://doi.org/10.5465/amr.1991.4278997

Mingers, J. (2003). Observing organizations: An evaluation of Luhmann's organization theory. In T. Bakken & T. Hernes (Eds.), *Autopoietic organization theory drawing on Niklas Luhmann's social systems perspective* (pp. 103–122). Abstract, Liber). Copenhagen Business School Press.

Mintzberg, H. (1979). *The structuring of organizations*. Prentice Hall.

Mintzberg, H. (1989). *Mintzberg on management: Inside our strange world of organizations*. Simon and Schuster.

Mintzberg, H., Raisinghani, D., & Theoret, A. (1976). The structure of "unstructured" decision processes. *Administrative Science Quarterly, 21*(2), 246–275. doi.org/10.2307/2392045

Moreland, R. L., & Levine, J. M. (2001). Socialization in organizations and work groups. In M. E. Turner (Ed.), *Groups at work: Theories and research* (pp. 69–112). Lawrence Erlbaum.

Morrison, E. W. (1993). Newcomer information seeking: Exploring types, modes, sources, and outcomes. *Academy of Management Journal, 36*(3), 557–589. https://doi.org/10.5465/256592

Morrison, E. W. (2002). Newcomers' relationships: The role of social network ties during socialization. *Academy of Management Journal, 45*(6), 1149–1160. https://doi.org/10.5465/3069430

Mumby, D. K. (1987). The political function of narrative in organizations. *Communication Monographs, 54*(2), 113–127. https://doi.org/10.1080/03637758709390221

Mumby, D. K. (1988). *Communication in power in organizations: Discourse, ideology and domination*. Ablex.

Mumby, D. K. (2019). Work: What is it good for? (Absolutely nothing)—a critical theorist's perspective. *Industrial and Organizational Psychology, 12*(4), 429–443.

Murray, A., Rhymer, J. E. N., & Sirmon, D. G. (2021). Humans and technology: Forms of conjoined agency in organizations. *Academy of Management Review, 46*(3), 552–571. https://doi.org/10.5465/amr.2019.0186

Myers, K. K. (2005). A burning desire: Assimilation into a fire department. *Management Communication Quarterly, 18*, 344–384. https://doi.org/10.1177/0893318904270742

Myers, K. K., Jahn, J. L. S., Gailliard, B., & Stoltzfus, K. (2011). Vocational anticipatory socialization (VAS) related to science and math: A model of academic and career interests. *Management Communication Quarterly, 25*, 87–120. https://doi.org/10.1177/0893318910377068

Myers, K. K., & McClelland-Cohen, A. (2024). Coordination. In V. D. Miller & M. S. Poole (Eds.), *Handbook of organizational communication theory and research*. DeGruyter.

Myers, K. K., & McPhee, R. D. (2006). Influences on member assimilation in workgroups in high reliability organizations: A multilevel analysis. *Human Communication Research, 32*, 440–468.

National Wildfire Coordinating Group. (2018). *Incident Response Pocket Guide*. https://www.nwcg.gov/publications/461

Neff, G., & Stark, D. (2004). Permanently beta. *Society online: The Internet in context*. ISEPR Working Paper. file:///C:/Users/User/Downloads/2002_05.pdf

Negandhi, A. R. (1973). *Modern organizational theory*. Kent State University Press.

Nicotera, A. M., & Clinkscales, M. J. (2010). Nurses at the nexus: A case study in structurational divergence. *Health Communication, 25*(1), 32–49. https://doi.org/10.1080/10410230903473516

Nicotera, A. M., & Mahon, M. M. (2013). Between rocks and hard places: Exploring the impact of structurational divergence in the nursing workplace. *Management Communication Quarterly, 27*(1), 90–120. https://doi.org/10.1177/0893318912458214

Nicotera, A. M., Zhao, X., Mahon, M. M., Peterson, E. B., Kim, W., & Conway-Morana, P. (2015). Structurational divergence theory as explanation for troublesome outcomes in nursing communication. *Health Communication, 30*(4), 371–384. https://doi.org/10.1080/10410236.2013.863139

Nordbäck, E., Myers, K. K., & McPhee, R. D. (2017). Workplace flexibility and communication flows: A structurational view. *Journal of Applied Communication Research, 45*, 397–412. https://doi.org/10.1080/00909882.2017.1355560

Oliver, M. (2005). The problem with affordance. *E-learning and Digital Media, 2*(4), 402–413. https://doi.org/10.2304/elea.2005.2.4.402

Olson, J. S. (2014). Opportunities, obstacles, and options: First-generation college graduates and social cognitive career theory. *Journal of Career Development, 41*(3), 199–217. https://doi.org/10.1177/0894845313486352

Orbe, M. P. (1996). Laying the foundation for co-cultural communication theory: An inductive approach to studying "non-dominant" communication strategies and the factors that influence them. *Communication Studies, 47*, 157–176. https://doi.org/10.1080/10510979609368473

Orlikowski, W. J. (1992). The duality of technology: Rethinking the concept of technology in organizations. *Organization Science, 3*(3), 398–427. https://doi.org/10.1287/orsc.3.3.398

Orlikowski, W. J. (1996). Improvising organizational transformation over time: A situated change perspective. *Information Systems Research, 7*(1), 63–92.

Orlikowski, W. J. (2000). Using technology and constituting structures: A practice lens for studying technology in organizations. *Organization Science, 11*(4), 404–428.

Orlikowski, W. J., & Yates, J. A. (1994). Genre repertoire: Norms and forms for work and interaction. *Administrative Science Quarterly, 39*, 541–574. https://doi.org/10.2307/2393771

Orlikowski, W. J., & Scott, S. V. (2008). Sociomateriality: Challenging the separation of technology, work and organization. *Academy of Management Annals, 2*(1), 433–474.

Pacanowsky, M. (1988). Communication in the empowering organization. *Annals of the International Communication Association, 11*(1), 356–379. https://doi.org/10.1080/23808985.1988.11678696

Palmer, R. E. (1969). *Hermeneutics: Interpretation theory in Schleiermacher, Dilthey, Heidegger, and Gadamer*. Northwestern University Press.

Parchoma, G. (2014). The contested ontology of affordances: Implications for researching technological affordances for collaborative knowledge production. *Computers in Human Behavior, 37*, 360–368. https://doi.org/10.1016/j.chb.2012.05.028

Parsons, T., & Smelser, N. J. (1965). *Economy and society*. Free Press.

Peirce, C. S. (1955). *Philosophical writings of Peirce*. Dover.

Pentland, A. (2012). the new science of building great teams. *Harvard Business Review, 90*(4), 60–69.

Perrow, C. (1961). The analysis of goals in complex organizations. *American Sociological Review, 26*, 854–866. Available at: https://www.taylorfrancis.com/chapters/edit/10.4324/9780429422553-25/analysis-goals-complex-organizations-charles-perrow

Perrow, C. (1970). *Organizational analysis: A sociological view*. Brooks/Cole.

Perrow, C. (1984). *Normal accidents: Living with high-risk technologies*. Basic Books.

Polanyi, M. (1966). *The tacit dimension*. Routledge & Kegan Paul.

Poole, M. S., & DeSanctis, G. (1992). Microlevel structuration in computer-supported group decision-making. *Human Communication Research, 19*, 5–49. https://doi.org/10.1111/j.1468-2958.1992.tb00294.x

Poole, M. S., & McPhee, R. D. (1983). A structurational theory of organizational climate. In L. Putnam & M. Pacanowsky (Eds.), *Communication and organizations: An interpretive approach* (pp. 195–219). SAGE.

Popper, K. R. (1962). *The open society and its enemies* (2nd ed.). Routledge.

Putnam, L. L. (2013). Primary and secondary contradictions: A literature review and future directions. *Management Communication Quarterly*, *27*(4), 623–630. https://doi.org/10.1177/0893318913504139

Putnam, L. L. (2022). Forward: The emerging paradigm of communication constitutes organization (CCO). In J. Basque, N. Bencherki, & T. Kuhn (Eds.), *Routledge handbook of the communicative constitutions of organizations* (pp. xxvi–xliv). Routledge.

Putnam, L. L., Fairhurst, G., & Banghart, S. (2016). Contradictions, dialectics, and paradoxes in organizations: A constitutive approach. *The Academy of Management Annals*, *10*(1), 65–171. https://doi.org/10.1080/19416520.2016.1162421

Putnam, L. L., Phillips, N., & Chapman, P. (1996). Metaphors of communication and organization. In S. R. Clegg, C. Hardy, & W. Nord (Eds.), *Handbook of organizational studies* (pp. 375–408). SAGE.

Reckwitz, A. (2002). Toward a theory of social practices: A development in culturalist theorizing. *European Journal of Social Theory*, *5*(2), 243–263. https://doi.org/10.1177/13684310222225432

Reichers, A. E. (1987). An interactionist perspective on newcomer socialization rates. *Academy of Management Review*, *12*(2), 278–287. https://doi.org/10.5465/amr.1987.4307838

Rice, R. E., Zackrison, E. J., & Seibold, D. R. (2017). Coordination. In C. R. Scott & L. Lewis (Eds.), *The international encyclopedia of organizational communication (online)*. John Wiley & Sons.

Ricoeur, P. (1981a). The hermeneutical function of distanciation. In J. B. Thompson (Ed.), *Hermeneutics and the human sciences: Essays on language, action and interpretation* (pp. 131–144). University of Cambridge Press.

Ricoeur, P. (1981b). What is a text? Explanation and understanding. In J. B. Thompson (Ed.), *Hermeneutics and the human sciences: Essays on language, action and interpretation* (pp. 145–164). University of Cambridge Press.

Roberts, K. H. (1990). Managing high reliability organizations. *California Management Review*, *32*(4), 101–113. https://doi.org/10.2307/41166631

Roberts, K. H., Rousseau, D. M., & La Porte, T. R. (1994). The culture of high reliability: Quantitative and qualitative assessment aboard nuclear powered aircraft carriers. *Journal of High Technology Management Research*, *5*, 141–161. https://doi.org/10.1016/1047-8310(94)90018-3

Rodó-de-Zárate, M., & Jorba, M. (2012). Commentary the complexity of intersectionality. Humana. *Mente Journal of Philosophical Studies*, *22*, 189–197. https://philarchive.org/archive/RODCTC

Roe, A. (1956). *The psychology of occupations*. John Wiley & Sons.

Roethlisberger, F. J., & Dickson, W. J. (1939). *Management and the worker*. Harvard University Press.

Roggio, B. (2014, June 29).). ISIS announces formation of Caliphate, rebrands as 'Islamic State.' *The Long War Journal*. http://www.longwarjournal.org/archives/2014/06/isis_announces_formation_of_ca.php

Rubenstein, A. L., Kammeyer-Mueller, J. D., & Thundiyil, T. G. (2020). The comparative effects of supervisor helping motives on newcomer adjustment and socialization outcomes. *Journal of Applied Psychology*, *105*(12), 1466–1489. https://doi.org/10.1037/apl0000492

Sacks, H., Schegloff, E. A., & Jefferson, G. (1978). A simplest systematics for the organization of turn taking for conversation. In *Studies in the organization of conversational interaction* (pp. 7–55). Academic Press. https://doi.org/10.1016/B978-0-12-623550-0.50008-2

Saldanha, F. P., Pozzebon, M., & Delgado, N. A. (2022). Dislocating peripheries to the center: A tecnologia social reinventing repertoires and territories. *Organization*. https://doi.org/10.1177/13505084221124192

Sanders, M. L., & McClellan, J. G. (2014). Being business-like while pursuing a social mission: Acknowledging the inherent tensions in US nonprofit organizing. *Organization, 21*(1), 68–89. https://doi.org/10.1177/1350508412464894

Santistevan, D. (2022). Boundary-spanning coordination: Insights into lateral collaboration and lateral alignment in multinational enterprises. *Journal of World Business, 57*(3), 101291. https://doi.org/10.1016/j.jwb.2021.101291

Schein, E. H. (1990). Organizational culture. *American Psychologist, 45*(2), 109–119. https://doi.org/10.1037/0003-066X.45.2.109

Schein, E. H. (1992). *Organizational culture and leadership* (2nd ed.). Jossey-Bass.

Schneider, B. (1987). The people make the place. *Personnel Psychology, 40*(3), 437–453. https://doi.org/10.1111/j.1744-6570.1987.tb00609.x

Schoeneborn, D., Blaschke, S., Cooren, F., McPhee, R., Seidl, D., & Taylor, J. (2014). The three schools of CCO thinking: interactive dialogue and systematic comparison. *Management Communication Quarterly, 28*(2), 285–316. https://doi.org/10.1177/0893318914527000

Schrodt, P., Baxter, L. A., McBride, M. C., Braithwaite, D. O., & Fine, M. A. (2006). The divorce decree, communication, and the structuration of coparenting relationships in stepfamilies. *Journal of Social and Personal Relationships, 23*(5), 741–759. https://doi.org/10.1177/0265407506068261

Scott, C. R., Corman, S. R., & Cheney, G. (1998). Development of a structurational model of identification in the organization. *Communication Theory, 8*(3), 298–336. https://doi.org/10.1111/j.1468-2885.1998.tb00223.x

Scott, C. W., & Myers, K. K. (2010). Toward an integrative theoretical perspective of membership negotiations: Socialization, assimilation, and the duality of structure. *Communication Theory, 20*, 79–105. https://doi.org/10.1111/j.1468-2885.2009.01355.x

Scott, C. W., & Trethewey, A. (2008). Organizational discourse and the appraisal of occupational hazards: Interpretive repertoires, heedful interrelating, and identity at work. *Journal of Applied Communication Research, 36*(3), 298–317. https://doi.org/10.1080/00909880802172137

Searle, J. (1969). *Speech acts: An essay in the philosophy of language*. Cambridge University Press.

Searle, J. (1975). A taxonomy of illocutionary acts. In K. Gunderson (Ed.), *Language, mind and knowledge* (pp. 344–369). University of Minnesota Press.

Seibt, J. (2009). Forms of emergent interaction in general process theory. *Synthese, 166*(3), 479–512.

Seidl, D. (2004). Luhmann's theory of autopoietic social systems. *Munich Business Research, 2*, 1–28.

Seidl, D., & Whittington, R. (2014). Enlarging the strategy-as-practice research agenda: Towards taller and flatter ontologies. *Organization Studies, 35*(10), 1407–1421. https://doi.org/10.1177/0170840614541886

Sellnow, T. L., & Seeger, M. W. (2013). *Theorizing crisis communication*. John Wiley & Sons.

Shannon, C., & Weaver, W. (1949). *The mathematical theory of communication*. University of Illinois Press.

Shenoy-Packer, S., & Myers, K. K. (2013). Challenges to organizational assimilation. *The International Journal of Organizational Diversity, 12*, 1–15. http://d12.cgpublisher.com/proposals/350/index_html

Shontell, A. (2012, February 14). How to marry your cofounder and not kill your 200-million startup or each other in the process. https://www.businessinsider.com/how-to-marry-your-cofounder-and-not-kill-your-200-million-startup-or-each-other-in-the-process-2012-2

Sillince, J. A. (2010). Can CCO theory tell us how organizing is distinct from markets, networking, belonging to a community, or supporting a social movement? *Management Communication Quarterly*, *24*(1), 132–138. https://doi.org/10.1177/0893318909352022

Simon, H. (1945). *Administrative behavior*. Macmillan.

Sivunen, A., & Myers, K. K. (2022). Visibility in open workspaces: Implications for organizational identification. *International Journal of Communication*, *16*. http://ijoc.org

Smircich, L. (1983). Concepts of culture and organizational analysis. *Administrative Science Quarterly*, *28*, 339–358. https://doi.org/10.2307/2392246

Smith, R. C. (1993, May). *Images of organizational communication: Root-metaphors of the organization communication relation*. Paper presented at the meeting of the International Communication Association Annual Conference, Washington, DC.

Smith, R. C., & Turner, P. K. (1995). A social constructionist reconfiguration of metaphor analysis: An application of "SCMA" to organizational socialization theorizing. *Communication Monographs*, *62*(2), 152–181. https://doi.org/10.1080/03637759509376354

Smith, W. K., & Lewis, M. W. (2011). Toward a theory of paradox: A dynamic equilibrium model of organizing. *The Academy of Management Review*, *36*(2), 381–403. https://doi.org/10.5465/amr.2009.0223

Star, S. L., & Griesemer, J. R. (1989). Institutional ecology, translations' and boundary objects: Amateurs and professionals in Berkeley's Museum of Vertebrate Zoology, 1907-39. *Social Studies of Science*, *19*(3), 387–420.

Stephens, K. K. (2018). *Negotiating control: Organizations and mobile communication*. Oxford University Press.

Stephens, K. K., & Dailey, S. L. (2012). Situated organizational identification in newcomers: Impacts of preentry organizational exposure. *Management Communication Quarterly*, *26*(3), 404–422. https://doi.org/10.1177/0893318912440179

Stohl, C. (1986). The role of memorable messages in the process of organizational socialization. *Communication Quarterly*, *34*(3), 231–249. https://doi.org/10.1080/01463378609369638

Strauss, A., Schatzman, L., Ehrlich, D., Bucher, R., & Sabshin, M. (1963). The hospital and its negotiated order. In E. Freidsen (Ed.), *The hospital in modern society* (pp. 147–169). Free Press.

Street, R. L., Jr. (2003). Communication in medical encounters: An ecological perspective. In *The Routledge handbook of health communication* (pp. 77–104). Routledge.

Stryker, J. B., Santoro, M. D., & Farris, G. F. (2012). Creating collaboration opportunity: Designing the physical workplace to promote high-tech team communication. *IEEE Transactions on Engineering Management*, *59*(4), 609–620. https://doi.org/10.1109/TEM.2011.2170995

Taylor, J. R., Groleau, C., Heaton, L., & Van Every, E. (2001). *The computerization of work: A communication perspective*. SAGE.

Taylor, J. R., & Van Every, E. J. (2000). *The emergent organization: Communication as its site and surface*. Lawrence Erlbaum.

Taylor, J. R., & Van Every, E. J. (2014). *When organization fails: Why authority matters*. Routledge.

Thackaberry, J. A. (2004). "Discursive opening" and closing in organisational self-study: Culture as trap and tool in wildland firefighting safety. *Management Communication Quarterly*, *17*(3), 319–359. https://doi.org/10.1177/0893318903259402

Thompson, J. D. (1967). *Organizations in action: Social science bases of administrative theory*. McGraw-Hill.

Trace, C. B. (2011, January). Documenting work and working documents: Perspectives from workplace studies, CSCW, and genre studies. In *2011 44th Hawaii international conference on system sciences*. IEEE. pp. 1–10. http://dx.doi.org/10.1109/HICSS.2011.170

Treem, J. W., & Leonardi, P. M. (2012). Social media use in organizations: Exploring the affordances of visibility, editability, persistence, and association. *Communication Yearbook, 36*, 143–189.

Trethewey, A. (1999). Disciplined bodies: Women's embodied identities at work. *Organization Studies, 20*(3), 423–450.

Trier, M., & Richter, A. (2015). The deep structure of organizational online networking–an actor-oriented case study. *Information Systems Journal, 25*(5), 465–488.

Tyler, T. R., & Blader, S. L. (2003). The group engagement model: Procedural justice, social identity, and cooperative behavior. *Personality and Social Psychology Review, 7*, 349–361. https://doi.org/10.1207/S15327957PSPR0704_07

Ulmer, R. R., Sellnow, T. L., & Seeger, M. W. (2018). *Effective crisis communication: Moving from crisis to opportunity*. SAGE.

Urry, J. (2007). *Mobilities*. Polity.

USFS. (2005). *Fire suppression: Foundational doctrine*. USDA Forest Service.

Van de Ven, A. H., Delbecq, A. L., & Koenigh, R., Jr. (1976). Determinants of coordination modes within organizations. *American Sociological Review, 41*, 322–338. https://doi.org/10.2307/2094477

Van de Ven, A. H., & Poole, M. S. (1995). Explaining development and change in organizations. *The Academy of Management Review, 20*(3), 510–540. https://doi.org/10.5465/amr.1995.950808032

Van Laer, K., & Janssens, M. (2011). Ethnic minority professionals' experiences with subtle discrimination in the workplace. *Human Relations, 64*(9), 1203–1227. https://doi.org/10.1177/0018726711409263

Van Maanen, J., & Schein, E. (1979). Toward a theory of organizational socialization. *Research in Organizational Behavior, 1*, 209–264.

Van Vuuren, M., & Knoers, P. (2022). CCO and the academic-professional gap: Combining rigor and relevance in organizational communication. In J. Basque, N. Bencherki, & T. Kuhn (Eds.), *The Routledge handbook of the communicative constitution of organization* (pp. 437–452). Routledge.

Van Zoonen, W., & Sivunen, A. E. (2022). The impact of remote work and mediated communication frequency on isolation and psychological distress. *European Journal of Work and Organizational Psychology, 31*(4), 610–621. https://doi.org/10.1080/1359432X.2021.2002299

Vangelisti, A. L. (1988). Adolescent socialization into the workplace: A synthesis and critique of current literature. *Youth & Society, 19*, 460–484. https://doi.org/10.1177/0044118X88019004007

Vantaggiato, F. P., Kassim, H., & Connolly, S. (2021). Breaking out of silos: Explaining cross-departmental interactions in two European bureaucracies. *Journal of European Public Policy, 28*(9), 1432–1452. https://doi.org/10.1080/13501763.2020.1784253

Weber, M. (1946). *Essays in sociology*. Oxford University Press.

Weber, M. (1968, orig. 1922). *Economy and society*. (G. Roth, Trans.). Claus Wittich, Bedminster Press.

Weick, K. (1979). *The social psychology of organizing* (2nd ed.). Addison-Wesley.

Weick, K. E., & Roberts, K. H. (1993). Collective mind in organizations: Heedful interrelating on flight decks. *Administrative Science Quarterly*, 357–381. https://doi.org/10.2307/2393372

Weick, K. E., Sutcliffe, K. M., & Obstfeld, D. (2005). Organizing and the process of sensemaking. *Organization Science, 16*(4), 409–421. https://doi.org/10.1287/orsc.1050.0133

Weigand, H., van der Poll, F., & de Moor, A. (2003). Coordination through communication. In H. Weigand, G. Goldkuhl, & A. de Moor (Eds.), *Proceedings of the 8th International Working Conference on the Language-Action Perspective on Communication Modeling (LAP 2003)* (pp. 115–134). Tilburg University Press.

Whitehead, A. (1929 [1985]),). *Process and Reality*, (Gifford Lectures 1927–28),. Macmillan. Corrected edition, D. R. Griffin & D. W. Sherburne (eds.), New York: The Free Press

Wickersham, A., Johnson, K., Kamath, A., & Kaboli, P. J. (2018). Novel use of communication technology to improve nurse-physician communication, teamwork, and care coordination during bedside rounds. *Journal of Communication, 11*, 56–61.

Wieland, S. M. (2010). Ideal selves as resources for the situated practice of identity. *Management Communication Quarterly, 24*(4), 503–528. https://doi.org/10.1177/0893318910374938

Willis, P. (1977). *Learning to labour*. Saxon House.

Witmer, D. F. (1997). Communication and recovery: Structuration as an ontological approach to organizational culture. *Communication Monographs, 64*, 324–349. https://doi.org/10.1080/03637759709376427

Wittgenstein, L. (1953). *Philosophical investigations*. (G. E. M. Anscombe, Trans.). Blackwell.

Woo, D. (2019). Reconceptualizing interorganizational collaborations as tensile structures: Implications of conveners' proactive tension management. *Communication Monographs, 86*(2), 158–183. https://doi.org/10.1080/03637751.2018.1526389

Woo, D. J., Endacott, C. G., & Myers, K. K. (2023). Navigating water cooler talks without the water cooler: Uncertainty and information seeking during remote socialization. *Management Communication Quarterly, 37*(2), 251–280. https://doi.org/10.1177/08933189221105916

Woo, D. J., & Myers, K. K. (2020). Organizational membership negotiation of boundary spanners: Becoming competent 'jack of all trades' and master of interactional expertise. *Management Communication Quarterly, 34*(1), 85–120. https://doi.org/10.1177/0893318919887371

Wood, N. T., & Allan, D. B. (2024). *This bud light's for you—him/her/them*. SAGE Publications: SAGE Business Cases Originals. SAGE.

Woodrow, C., & Guest, D. E. (2020). Pathways through organizational socialization: A longitudinal qualitative study based on the psychological contract. *Journal of Occupational and Organizational Psychology, 93*(1), 110–133. https://doi.org/10.1111/joop.12285

World Health Organization. (2020). *WHO Director-General's opening remarks at the media briefing on COVID-19 - 11 March 2020*. World Health Organization. https://www.who.int/director-general/speeches/detail/who-director-general-s-opening-remarks-at-the-media-briefing-on-covid-19—11-march-2020.

Yang, I. (2014). What makes an effective team: The role of trust (dis)confirmation in team development. *European Management Journal, 32*, 858–869. https://doi.org/10.1016/j.emj.2014.04

Yates, J. A. (1989). The emergence of the memo as a managerial genre. *Management Communication Quarterly, 2*, 485–510. https://doi.org/10.1177/0893318989002004003

Yates, J. A., & Orlikowski, W. J. (1992). Genres of organizational communication: A structurational approach to studying communication and media. *Academy of Management Review, 17*(2), 299–326. https://doi.org/10.5465/amr.1992.4279545

Yi, V., & Museus, S. D. (2015). Model minority myth. *The Wiley Blackwell Encyclopedia of Race, Ethnicity, and Nationalism, 1–2*. https://doi.org/10.1002/9781118663202.wberen528

Yoon, K., & Zhu, Y. (2022). Social media affordances and transactive memory systems in virtual teams. *Management Communication Quarterly, 36*(2), 235–260. https://doi-org.proxy.library.ucsb.edu/10.1177/08933189211032639

Zackrison, E., Seibold, D. R., & Rice, R. (2015). Organizational coordination and communication: A critical review and integrative model. In E. Cohen (Ed.), *Communication yearbook 39* (pp. 195–233). SAGE.

Zhang, M., Atwal, G., & Kaiser, M. (2021). Corporate social irresponsibility and stakeholder ecosystems: The case of Volkswagen Dieselgate scandal. *Strategic Change, 30*(1), 79–85. https://doi.org/10.1002/jsc.2391

Zuboff, S. (1988). *In the age of the smart machine: The future of work and power*. Basic Books, Inc.

Zuboff, S. (2019). *The age of surveillance capitalism*. Public Affairs.

Zweig, D., & Scott, K. (2007). When unfairness matters most: Supervisory violations of electronic monitoring practices. *Human Resource Management Journal, 17*(3), 227–247. https://doi.org/10.1111/j.1748-8583.2007.00040.x

Index

Note: *Italic* page references indicate figures.

The Communicative Constitution of Organizations: The Four Flows Model, First Edition.
Robert D. McPhee, Karen K. Myers, and Joel O. Iverson.

Printed and bound by CPI Group (UK) Ltd, Croydon, CR0 4YY

02/07/2026

14912644-0001